WHEN FORESTS BURN

ALSO BY ALBERT MARRIN

Black Gold: The Story of Oil in Our Lives

FDR and the American Crisis

Flesh & Blood So Cheap: The Triangle Fire and Its Legacy
A National Book Award Finalist

A Light in the Darkness: Janusz Korczak, His Orphans, and the Holocaust
A YALSA Award for Excellence in Nonfiction Finalist

Thomas Paine: Crusader for Liberty

A Time of Fear: America in the Era of Red Scares and Cold War

Uprooted: The Japanese American Experience During World War II
A Sibert Honor Book

Very, Very, Very Dreadful: The Influenza Pandemic of 1918

A Volcano Beneath the Snow: John Brown's War Against Slavery

WHEN FORESTS BURN

The Story of Wildfires in America

ALBERT MARRIN

Alfred A. Knopf • New York

THIS IS A BORZOI BOOK PUBLISHED BY ALFRED A. KNOPF

Text copyright © 2023 by Albert Marrin
Jacket photograph (forest fire) used under license from Getty Images
All other jacket photographs (firefighters, embers, paper) used under license from Shutterstock.com

All rights reserved. Published in the United States by Alfred A. Knopf, an imprint of Random House Children's Books, a division of Penguin Random House LLC, New York.

Knopf, Borzoi Books, and the colophon are registered trademarks of Penguin Random House LLC.

For picture credits, please see page 226.

Visit us on the Web! rhcbooks.com

Educators and librarians, for a variety of teaching tools, visit us at
RHTeachersLibrarians.com

Library of Congress Cataloging-in-Publication Data is available upon request.
ISBN 978-0-593-12173-3 (trade) — ISBN 978-0-593-12174-0 (lib. bdg.) — ISBN 978-0-593-12175-7 (ebook)

The text of this book is set in 11.7-point Charlotte Std. Book.
Interior design by Cathy Bobak

MANUFACTURED IN CHINA
10 9 8 7 6 5 4 3 2 1

First Edition

In the hour when the Holy One, blessed be He, created the first man,

He took him and let him pass before all the trees in the Garden of Eden,

and said to him:

"See My works, how fine and excellent they are!

Now all that I am going to create for you I have already created.

Think about this and do not corrupt or destroy My world;

for if you destroy it, there is no one to restore it after you."

Ecclesiastes Rabbah 7:28 (Talmud, eighth century CE)

To the heroic men and women who dedicate
their lives to defending our natural heritage

CONTENTS

ICE, FIRE, AND FOREST

From out of the north, it came. Inanimate, inexorable and indifferent: Nothing could withstand its cancerous growth. With the patience of inevitability, it slowly consumed North America. It chewed up the terrain, pulverized granite and left nothing alive in its wake. When it had grown to maximum size, some seven million square miles, it broke the back of the continent. Nothing can withstand . . . The Ice Age!

—Whit Bronaugh, "North American Forests in the Age of Nature," 2012

About sixty years ago, my wife and I rented a small house for the summer in the Catskill Mountains of New York. We are city folk from the Big Apple, and two months in the "country" was what we needed to catch up on reading and just veg out from teaching. The house sat a little way back from a dirt road, with open woods stretching behind. One day, a neighbor, a dairy farmer, came shouting. I, dozing in a hammock, was startled awake. "Fire!" he cried. A wildfire was burning in the woods! Already, neighbors were racing toward it with rakes, shovels, brooms, and fire extinguishers. He ordered me to join them, and I did.

I remember clambering over a low wall, really an old field divider made of smooth rocks. The fire had not climbed into the trees, but its low flames moved across the ground, consuming dead leaves and brush. It was not a windy day, so the fire spread slowly, and we were beating it down with all our might. Still, without our noticing, it crept behind us. That was scary, but after an hour or so we put it out and headed home. On the way back, a local man said it was no big deal; fires broke out nearly every summer and fall. They came with the land. "They've been going on, sonny, since them lines was scratched in that boulder over there, and those fence rocks got worn smooth!" Though I didn't know it then, this book was conceived that day.

ICE

If we could build a time machine and return to the distant past, we would not recognize our world. For the land we live on has not always been as it is today. Earth is a dynamic, restless planet, constantly changing. Nothing, however solid it may feel beneath our feet, stays the same forever. We may not notice the changes, because the individual human's life span is short, scarcely the blink of an eye on Mother Nature's time scale. Earth's geological history is the story of its physical structure, the changes brought on by immense forces scientists are still learning about: earthquakes, volcanoes, and continental drift, the gradual movement of the continents across the planet's surface over the course of millions of years. Geological history also deals with ancient mountain ranges, many times higher than today's Rockies, rising and eventually being worn away by wind and water. Where today there are sandy deserts and rolling prairies, there were once warm seas teeming with the ferocious fifty-foot shark called the megalodon (from the Greek for "big tooth"), which makes today's great white almost seem tame. At the same time, dinosaurs roamed the land, and pterosaurs ("winged lizards"), with wingspans ranging from nine to forty feet, filled the sky, searching for prey.

Our story begins when Earth's climate was colder than it is today. Climate and weather, often confused, are not the same. Weather is localized and short-term. If, say, it rains for a few days where you live, that is weather. But if it rains every few days for centuries, that is climate, which is the average of weather measured over long spans of time. However, climate is far from stable; climate change, an issue of much concern today, seems never-ending. Specialized scientists called climatologists have documented five extremely cold periods, commonly known as ice ages, during the 4.6 billion years since our planet was formed. These periods, they believe, were likely caused by temporary variations in Earth's position relative to the sun, reducing the amount of sunlight, and therefore warmth, reaching the planet's surface.

As the climate grew colder, snow accumulated until the earlier, lower layers became so tightly packed that they solidified into ice, and the ice in turn formed glaciers. A glacier is a gigantic ice mass, weighing billions of tons. Glaciers move because weight creates pressure, and pressure creates heat, causing the ice at the glacier's base to melt. The meltwater acts as a lubricant, enabling the glacier to slide at the rate of a few feet per year. As it advances, snow continues to build up behind it and turn to ice, causing the glacier's continued growth. An iceberg is part of

Snow accumulates and becomes so tightly packed that it solidifies into ice, and then into a glacier. This image is of a glacier in Patagonia, Argentina. (Date unknown)

a glacier that breaks off a landmass and falls into a body of water, usually an ocean. When several glaciers come together, they form a continuous ice sheet, also called a continental glacier. What scientists call "glaciations," or "glacial periods," have lasted tens of thousands of years. Yet glaciations have always been followed by "interglacial periods," during which the climate warms, causing the ice masses to retreat or melt back. Interglacial periods have lasted only a few thousand years; eventually, temperatures fell, the climate cooled again, and the glaciers resumed their advance. Climatologists believe that we are now in an interglacial period and that another ice age is coming, though nobody can say when it will occur or how long it will last. If they are right, and the pattern holds true, vast regions home to hundreds of millions of people will become totally uninhabitable. Where these climate change refugees might go, and how they could survive, would be the gravest challenge humanity has ever faced.

The most recent ice age is known as the Pleistocene Epoch, from the Greek words *pleistos* ("most") and *kainos* ("new" or "recent"). The Pleistocene began about 2.6 million years ago and lasted until around 11,700 years ago, with about twenty periods during which the glaciers advanced, retreated, regrew, and advanced again. Today, the Antarctic ice sheet, covering 5.4 million square miles, is the largest block of ice in existence; it could cover the combined surface area of the United States and Mexico to an estimated depth of almost three miles. The Greenland ice sheet, the second largest, is much smaller, covering "only" 656,000 square miles, an area nearly three times the size of Texas. If these ice sheets melted, the level of the world's oceans would rise disastrously, drowning low-lying islands and flooding coastal lowlands.

The opposite happened at the height of the Pleistocene Epoch. In Europe, nearly all of the western part of the continent, including the British Isles, lay under a blanket of ice. In North America, what scientists call the Laurentide ice sheet (named for a region in Canada) averaged two miles thick. Covering an area of more than five million square miles, it buried nearly all of Greenland, Canada, and the northern third of the United States. On Manhattan Island, which marked its southernmost advance, the ice is thought to have stood twice as high as the Empire State Building. We can only imagine the sounds that filled the air. Though there were no people to hear them, there must have been the continuous howling of the frigid wind and the snapping of trees as the moving ice cliffs slowly crushed entire forests. There was undoubtedly also the dull scraping of giant boulders caught beneath the ice, gouging out valleys and grinding hills into gravel and sand. The Rocky Mountains were buried, save for the tops of the tallest peaks, while the Adirondacks and White Mountains were worn down hundreds of feet.[1]

With so much water trapped as ice, the levels of the world's oceans fell by as much as four hundred feet, causing shallow coastal

At the time, glaciers stood as tall as the Empire State Building, which stands at 1,454 feet.

areas to emerge and become dry land. Islands turned into peninsulas, portions of a mainland jutting out into a body of water. A land bridge arose where the English Channel is

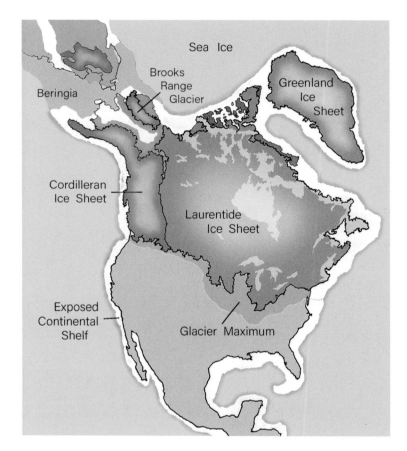

Map of glaciers in North America during the Pleistocene Epoch.

bridges go, this one was extraordinary; actually, it was a landmass roughly the size of the continent of Australia. Dubbed Beringia by scientists, after Vitus Bering, the Danish discoverer of the strait that bears his name, this land bridge likely stretched a thousand miles north to south and three thousand miles west to east, from Siberia to Alaska and the Yukon Territory in northwestern Canada. Evidently, glaciers were unable to form in Beringia because the climate there was too dry.

Some scientists say that about thirty thousand years ago, bands of hunters began to trek eastward from the Asian mainland. Over decades, perhaps centuries, they may have moved from Siberia into western Beringia in pursuit of game. These migrants may have been the first humans to set foot in what European explorers would later call the

today, joining southern England to the European continent at France and Holland. Another land bridge emerged from beneath the Bering Strait, a water passage that now connects the Arctic and Pacific Oceans. As

Americas or the New World. Other scholars, including some geologists and linguists, state that people have been in America since before the Bering Strait was formed. There is also evidence that the first humans to arrive in the Americas came by sea or lived near the ocean. There are Native American scholars who combine this information with Native American oral traditions that point to their ancestors sailing to the new continent much earlier. Either way, Beringia was not an icy desert devoid of life, but a vast plain dotted by oases, or "refuges," areas that supported wildflowers, shrubs, and stands of stunted willow and birch trees. Large grazing animals such as caribou, long-horned bison, antelope, camels, and woolly rhinoceros fattened on the nutritious grasses. The largest of these animals, the woolly mammoth, was the size of a modern African elephant, but had a smaller trunk, ears, and feet, adaptations to reduce the surface area exposed to the cold. It also had a thicker hide covered with long brown hair for insulation. We know this from fossilized remains found in Alaska and "freeze-dried" animals dug out of the permafrost, a layer of soil that remains frozen throughout the year. Preying on the grazers were carnivores like American lions, saber-toothed cats, short-faced bears, and dire wolves, "fearsome

Mural of woolly mammoths near a river. (1916)

wolves" measuring five feet long and weighing 150 pounds; all of these ferocious meat eaters are now extinct.[2]

Early hunters must have traveled light. They may have used the travois, a type of sledge consisting of two joined poles dragged by a person or a prehistoric dog, a creature scientists describe as "a wolf in dog's clothing." They gathered everything they needed to survive from their environment. There were wild berries to pick in season, and animals to kill for meat and for skins to fashion into clothing and shelters. To keep warm and cook meals, they mostly burned bones for fuel. Scientists have found the charred remains of woolly mammoths and other animals in ancient hearths in eastern Siberia, Alaska, and Canada, proof that these hunters relied on one of nature's most marvelous creations: fire.

FIRE

Humans have always sought to explain how we came to possess fire. One story is as good as another, for no proof exists. My favorite is a legend from the Alabama tribe. When the world was young, it says, Fire was owned by Bear. One day, Bear set Fire down at the edge of a forest while he went with his family to raid honeybee hives. It must have gone slowly, for bees protect their precious sweet stuff by swarming thieves and stinging them in sensitive spots such as their snouts. As time passed, Fire began to get hungry; it flickered and sputtered and grew steadily smaller. In desperation, Fire cried out to Bear, "Feed me! Feed me!" But Bear didn't come. Just then, Man walked by. When Fire said it was hungry, Man asked what it ate. "I eat sticks and wood of all kinds," Fire replied. Man brought wood, and Fire revived, rearing up and dancing for joy. Fire warmed Man, and Man was glad. From then on, "Man and Fire were very happy together, and Man fed Fire sticks whenever it got hungry. . . . And now Fire belongs to Man."[3]

Greek mythology tells a different story. A trickster named Prometheus stole fire from the gods, who lived on Mount Olympus, and gave it to humans. Angered by the theft,

Zeus, king of the gods, ordered Prometheus chained to a rock, where heat tormented him by day and cold by night, and a ravenous eagle tore at him with beak and talons, eating his newly regrown liver every day.

At the dawn of science, ancient Greek and Roman philosophers taught that the universe is made up of four elements: earth, air, water, fire. However, fire is not an element in the way modern scientists define an element: a form of matter, a substance that has mass and takes up space. Technically, fire is the visible effect of matter changing form in a chemical reaction called combustion,

Depiction by Theodoor Rombouts of the punishment of Prometheus. (c. 1620)

a.k.a. burning. Three ingredients, dubbed the "fire triangle," need to be present for fire to happen: fuel, heat, and oxygen. Fuel is anything that can burn. A fire also requires heat to raise the fuel to its burning temperature; different kinds of fuel have different temperatures at which they will ignite. Finally, a fire needs oxygen, a gas found in the atmosphere, to continue the burning process. When started, a fire will burn as long as it has the necessary ingredients to "feed" it.

The three components of fire.

Should any one of them be removed, the fire will go out.

Amazingly, fire did not exist for roughly half of our planet's history. This is because two of the fire triangle's three "sides"—oxygen and fuel—were absent. In that long-ago time, there was only heat, from meteor strikes and lightning, a violent discharge of electricity in the atmosphere, and lava ejected in volcanic eruptions, giving off heat as a visible red glow. But heat and light are not fire.

Life gave birth to fire. While scientists do not know precisely when or how life began on Earth, they do believe that it emerged about 3.5 billion years ago, almost as soon as the planet's surface cooled sufficiently to permit it to come into being. Apparently, the first life-forms were single-celled bacteria, microorganisms that lived in a carbon dioxide–based atmosphere. Earth's early atmosphere was largely carbon dioxide, an odorless, colorless gas; oxygen was present only in trace amounts. About 2.3 billion years ago, certain types of microorganisms known as blue-green algae formed thin films on the surfaces of ponds, lakes, and oceans. Over time, these "scums" developed—evolved—a unique feature called photosynthesis, from the Greek *photos* ("light") and *synthesis* ("putting together"). Photosynthesis is the ability to take energy from sunlight and use it to make food out of carbon dioxide and water. This is how all green plants get their food today.[4]

Oxygen is a waste product of photosynthesis. It is also poisonous to carbon dioxide–loving life-forms, which, to survive, must release oxygen into the atmosphere. That need triggered a critical turning point in Earth's history: the "Great Oxidation Event," or the "Great Oxygenation Event." Gradually, over hundreds of millions of years, the accumulation of "waste" oxygen transformed Earth's atmosphere. At the same time, more complex forms of life, the ancestors of all trees, shrubs, grasses, and flowers, began to develop and colonize the land. Thus, starting roughly 400 million years ago, there was

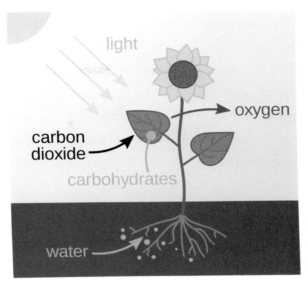

Diagram outlining the process of photosynthesis.

enough oxygen in the air and fuel on the land to make fire when the fuel was heated to its ignition point. Similarly, primitive creatures began to explore the world outside the water. Little by little, they gained the ability to live on land, evolving to breathe air and feed on plants—and on each other.[5]

"We are, uniquely, a fire creature," says fire historian Stephen J. Pyne. "Other animals knock over trees, dig holes, eat plants, and hunt, but only human beings apply and withhold fire." Humans owe a great deal to fire: one is tempted to say almost everything that makes us who we are. Of all creatures, humans alone have mastered fire. Fire was among our earliest tools; anthropologists, who study past and present societies and cultures, have never found a society that lacked fire. Of all creatures known to science, only we can make and use fire to serve our purposes.[6]

Mankind evolved to eat cooked food. Cooking aids digestion, enabling the process of breaking down food substances so they can be more efficiently used by the body. Better digestion, in turn, produces more energy for work and, indeed, for the very act of thinking. For example, the human body gets thirty percent more energy from cooked oats and wheat than from the raw grains. Cooking also fights disease by killing harmful bacteria and parasites such as tapeworms, creatures that attach themselves to the human gut, "sharing" any food that comes their way and sickening their "hosts." Some foods, like potatoes, contain chemicals that make them toxic when eaten raw; that is why potatoes are cooked, baked, boiled, mashed, and made into french fries. As if this were not enough, fire made humans more comfortable and sociable. Campfires lit the night, permitting people to gather, discuss, share, and, yes, fall in love. People used fire to fashion tools and weapons and to wage war. In short, fire played a central role in making us Earth's dominant species—a force of nature in our own right.[7]

OUT OF BERINGIA

Beringia became the hunters' homeland. If some chose to return to Siberia, nothing (as yet) is known of them, because writing did not yet exist anywhere on Earth. But those who remained stayed put: they had no choice. Moving farther east and south of Beringia was out of the question, as the ice sheet barred their way. Ultimately, however, they were forced to leave—or drown.[8]

Around seventeen thousand years ago, the climate started to warm, ushering in another interglacial period. As temperatures rose little by little, the ice sheet halted its advance and began to melt. Relentlessly, ocean levels rose, and the Bering Strait was restored to what it is today, engulfing the land bridge.

The retreat of the ice did not happen uniformly. The speed varied from place to place; indeed, in some places the ice returned, only to retreat later. Nevertheless, over a period of several thousand years, mountain ranges emerged from their frozen tombs. Land that had been depressed by the ice sheet's incredible weight began to rebound, rising a few inches each century. No longer did the sounds of cracking, scraping, and grinding rock fill the air, but those of splitting ice and rushing water. Cataracts that dwarfed today's Niagara Falls tumbled down the faces of ice cliffs. Now-vanished rivers carved valleys and overflowed their banks, flooding thousands of square miles on either side. Immense lakes far greater than the Great Lakes—many with huge icebergs floating in them—dotted the landscape. The Great Lakes themselves were formed as the receding ice sheet gouged the land and then filled the spaces with

As the climate started to warm, giant cataracts, even bigger than Niagara Falls (pictured here), were created. (Date unknown)

An ancient Incan road in Peru. (2018)

meltwater. The modern Great Lakes contain more than twenty percent of the world's surface fresh water.[9]

Melting caused ice-free gaps and corridors to open along the Pacific coast, on the eastern flank of the Rocky Mountains, and in the interior valleys. Around thirteen thousand years ago, the inhabitants of Beringia began to follow these routes southward and eastward. Whether they traveled in large groups or small family units is unknown, as is everything about their social arrangements. But move they did, thus becoming the true discoverers of the New World. Scholars refer to the migrants as "Paleo-Indians," or ancient Indians, the ancestors of those later known simply as American Indians or Native Americans. Over the centuries, these venturesome folks found their way into every corner of their new world. Different groups adapted to different environments. Some learned to live in deserts or mountains, in forests or on the "land of the big sky," the Great Plains. Some remained nomadic hunters; indeed, several scientists think their overhunting caused the extinction of the woolly mammoth and other large grazing animals, and thus of the ferocious predators that fed on them. Other people, having somehow learned to farm, settled in villages and large towns. The Aztecs of Mexico, the Maya of Central America, and the Incas of Peru built vast cities linked by stone highways. Such were the people the early European explorers met when they arrived in the "New World."

FORESTS

As the ice retreated, it left in its wake a weird landscape. The newly exposed ground was raw and barren, scraped down to bare rock. It was a world without vegetation; there were no birds, animals, or insects. Stones of all sizes, some big as school buses, littered the ground, often hundreds of miles from where the ice sheet had picked them up centuries earlier. Many boulders bore ridges, furrows, and gashes made by other stones that, sandpaper-like, had rubbed against them. Some can be seen today, mute, solitary things in parks and fields.

But for the first time in thousands of years, the land saw the sun. And so, little by little, life found its way back. South of the towering ice cliffs, beyond their grasp, trees survived in warmer areas, chiefly along the Gulf of Mexico and on the southern Atlantic coastal plain. They were the same trees that still grow in the United States and Canada: oak, maple, beech, elm, hemlock, walnut, spruce, and pine, to mention only the most common of the thousand-plus species. As the ice retreated, the trees began to advance northward and westward, creating the woodlands the Paleo-Indians would find when they finally arrived. In parts of the Upper Midwestern United States and in Canada there were large blocks of ice that took centuries to melt. These eventually created many of the lakes in the northern United States and Canada.

We use the term "advance" loosely, for individual trees cannot get up and move. Trees have no legs or wings, no fins or flippers; like all plants, they are "planted," rooted in the soil. Those that found themselves in front of an advancing ice cliff were crushed. What *can* move are soil and seeds. In the wake of the ice, the wind blew loose grains of soil from the areas that were still ice-free onto the treeless lands. Over the course of centuries, these grains accumulated, covering the rocky surface and forming a bed able to support the windblown seeds of grasses, shrubs, and trees. The seeds took root and grew into plants, which produced more seeds and plants. In this way, the "dead zone" came back to life. And as it did, the forest "followed" the retreating ice northward at an estimated rate of thirty to fifty miles a century. The restored forest in turn attracted insects, birds, and other animals, all of which played vital roles in its further development.[10]

A forest is more than a collection of trees: it is an ecosystem. Ecology (from the Greek words for "dwelling" and "study") is the branch of science that studies the relationships between living beings and their physical surroundings. Mountains, oceans, coral reefs, rivers, lakes, deserts, plains, jungles, and Arctic regions: all are distinct environments. Each is home to unique life-forms that interact with and depend on their physical surroundings and one another. The great horned owl, for example, is an American forest dweller that cannot exist without rodents to eat, animals that in turn feed on grass, grains, and small twigs. Ultimately, of course, all life in the forest depends on

the trees. They are the "keystone"; destroy enough trees, and the entire ecological system collapses into chaos.

Forests are vital to the health of our planet. Nature has given them many roles to play, chief among them removing carbon dioxide from the air and replacing it with the oxygen all air-breathing life-forms, including us, need to stay alive. According to the U.S. Department of Agriculture, "One acre of for-

The great horned owl is part of a unique ecosystem that supports a wide range of life. (Date unknown)

est absorbs six tons of carbon dioxide and puts out four tons of oxygen. This is enough to meet the annual needs of 18 people." In 2019, Earth had a population of 7.7 billion people, none of whom could survive without the "waste" oxygen given off by trees and green plants. In effect, forests are the "lungs of the world."[11]

But forests do more than give off oxygen. They make soil, which is a mixture of dead branches, twigs, leaves, and pine needles; decayed animal remains; and broken-down rock. At the same time, forests protect the soil by breaking the force of the wind and acting as enormous sponges to regulate the flow of water over the land. This is because tree roots form countless interconnected networks. These networks serve as anchors, holding the trees in place, but also preventing the soil from eroding, being washed away by rain or blown away by wind. When forests are destroyed, especially on hillsides, mudslides and flooding inevitably follow. Worldwide, about 36 billion tons of fertile

soil is lost to erosion each year. It takes an estimated five hundred years for nature to replace one inch of lost topsoil.

Forests also influence local weather conditions. When wind moves through them, trees release stored moisture into the air. Warm, moist air rises, meets cooler air, forms clouds, and falls back to the earth as precipitation—rain, sleet, hail, or snow. The forest canopy, the upper layer of mature treetops, acts as an immense filter, trapping dust and absorbing pollutants from the air. It also reduces wind speeds and provides shade, thereby lowering local temperatures—a kind of natural air-conditioning. Last but not least, forests nurture wildlife with food, nesting places, and protection from enemies.[12]

And forests burn.

WILDFIRE

It has been said that wildfire is "the dominant fact of forest history." Wildfire is a natural phenomenon that all forests, including tropical rain forests, experience from time to time. In its broadest sense, however, wildfire is any fire that occurs in a wilderness or natural environment: forest fire, brush fire, grass fire, prairie fire, swamp fire, hill fire. The term also has a more sinister connotation: a fire that runs "wild," raging out of human control. In everyday speech, when we say that something—a disease, for example—"spreads like wildfire," we mean that it moves rapidly and uncontrollably.[13]

Scientists believe that wildfire is nearly as ancient as the first plants, which arose on land about 400 million years ago. Wildfires in forests actually "write" their history. Each tree records its own story in growth rings; one ring is formed every year of its life, and you can tell a tree's age by counting the rings, which are visible when the trunk is cut crosswise. Growth rings can also give information about past climates and what the atmosphere was like at a given time. When fire breaks out, the rings register the event in burn scars, which are deformed and blackened patches. Paleobotanists, specialists in the study of ancient vegetation, have found burn scars in petrified wood, fallen tree trunks buried in mud and turned to stone by absorbing liquefied minerals. Some of these scars date back 360 million years, to a time when the ancestors of the dinosaurs roamed North America.

The fires that made these scars were likely caused by ash and lava from volcanic eruptions or by dry lightning, which occurs with little or no rain. Thunderstorms happen frequently. Worldwide, there are eighteen hundred of them an hour and three billion lightning strikes a year. A lightning bolt packs a terrific wallop, enough electrical energy "to lift the SS *United States* six feet into the air." Wildfires can also be ignited by branches rubbing together and sparking, by falling stones giving off sparks when striking against each other, or by sparks from deer hooves knocking small stones together. Even prolonged exposure to the sun's rays can set off a wildfire. The ignition point of wood is 572 degrees Fahrenheit, or 300 degrees

Celsius. When wood is heated to this temperature, it releases gases that mix with the oxygen in the air, ignite, and burst into flame. Burnt wood leaves a charcoal residue; fossilized charcoal is further evidence of wildfires in the distant past. In modern times, most wildfires are caused by human carelessness, ignorance, and plain cussedness. Whatever the cause, thousands of wildfires are recorded in North America every year.[14]

Forests need fire; it is natural, and as necessary to their well-being as soil and sunlight, rain and chemical nutrients. Fire is primarily a cleansing agent. While animals bathe, lick, scratch, and pick at themselves to get rid of dirt, dead skin, and parasites, forests rely on fire to ward off disease. Fire kills infections caused by harmful bacteria and insects that prey on trees. Fire removes aged and unhealthy trees and clears the forest floor of fallen branches, leaf litter (fallen leaves), and pine needles. If debris accumulates unchecked, it becomes kindling; the forest will eventually be ravaged by a run-away blaze. Moreover, fire opens the forest canopy to allow sunlight to reach the floor, helping plants that do not like shade and cannot compete with other plants that do. Fire further supports growth by enriching the soil. For when fire turns debris into ash, rain dissolves the captured chemical nutrients, enabling them to filter back into the soil, where tree roots absorb them.[15]

Certain tree species have adapted to fire in specific ways. Over millions of years, they've become "fire tolerant"—that is, they have developed ways to protect themselves from fire, or to recover after being burned. Ponderosa pines, for example, have thick, corklike bark, which acts as natural "plate armor." Not only does the bark not catch fire easily, it also protects the living tissue underneath. Shortleaf pines, on the other hand, burn readily, but they have a widespread root system with buds that sprout only after being stimulated by heat. Several tree species are actually "fire dependent," unable to reproduce without the assistance of fire. Among

Bark of the ponderosa pine.
(Date unknown)

The Grizzly Giant,
the largest sequoia
in the Mariposa
Grove. (2007)

these are California's sequoias and giant redwoods; with life spans of up to thirty-five hundred years, they, along with bristlecone pines, are the oldest living things on Earth. The mature trees are virtually fireproof, protected as they are by bark that can be as thick as two feet. Sequoia seed cones, however, are tightly sealed by hardened resin, a type of natural glue. Only fire can melt the resin, permitting the cone to open and its seeds to fall to the ground, which fire has cleared of debris so they can take root. By contrast, when the trunk of a dwarf pitch pine, native to eastern North America, is damaged by fire, new sprouts grow from the wound.[16]

Forests composed largely of a single species of tree burn according to different time scales, known as *fire regimes.* Take the pine family, which is native to much of the Northern Hemisphere. Wildfires normally occur every five to twenty-five years in the ponderosa pine forests of Washington and Oregon. The jack pine forests of the Great Lakes region, however, experience fire at intervals of

125 to 180 years. Fires in the lodgepole pine forests of Idaho, Montana, and Wyoming have more varied burn cycles, ranging anywhere from 80 to 300 years. The frequency and intensity of fire are largely determined by the *fuel load,* or the amount of fuel available, and the weather pattern. Wildfires are more likely in very hot, dry, and windy conditions than in moister, cooler, calmer periods. Some regions have regular, predictable *fire seasons,* when wildfires occur every year. California, for example, has two fire seasons. During the summer, from June to September, dry, sun-heated vegetation easily ignites; in autumn, the blistering hot, dry Santa Ana winds blow toward the coast of the Golden State at up to seventy miles an hour.[17]

Regardless of their specific causes, effects, and frequency, wildfires spread in three well-defined patterns.

Ground fires attack *ground fuels,* anything that can burn below the surface of the ground: roots, decaying matter, and even coal deposits, the remains of trees that died millions of years ago. Coal fires may burn for centuries; vegetation-fueled ground fires may smolder and smoke quietly for days and weeks until they die out, or wind may fan them into wildfires of the second main type.

Surface or *crawling fires* are fueled by the litter—fallen leaves, twigs, and branches—covering the forest floor. This kind of fire tends to move slowly, though steep slopes and wind can increase its speed. Even before the flames reach a given spot, thermal radiation, the intense heat along the fire front, warms the air, preheating and drying flammable materials in the path of the blaze. Wind can blow flaming embers hundreds of feet ahead of a blaze, igniting *spot fires.* In settled areas, embers are especially dangerous when they fall on roofs made of flammable materials.

Crown or *canopy fires* usually arise from the *ladder effect,* in which the heat of intense ground or surface fires rises to ignite a tree's lower branches; that fire then climbs to the upper layers of foliage. In a dense forest, such a fire in a single tree may easily set off a chain reaction, spreading fire to its neighbors, which spread it to their neighbors, particularly in strong winds.

Though wildfires are inevitable, the most severe ones rarely seem to occur in nature. To begin with, a fire in totally windless conditions is almost never dangerous; it moves slowly and usually burns out on its own when it runs out of fuel or reaches a barrier such as a river. Better yet, small fires make large fires less likely. Small fires work their magic by preventing the buildup of flammable debris on the forest floor, thereby reducing the fuel available for an inferno. A very severe fire, dubbed a *firestorm,* is all-consuming, taking everything in its path until it, too, runs out of fuel or meets an impassable barrier. Until it does, it releases massive amounts of energy, greater, indeed, than the output of "one average-sized atomic bomb every minute."[18]

Yet even these firestorms have a place in nature's scheme. A forest immediately after an intense fire may seem like a hellish landscape of rubble. But looks are deceiving, for this "rubble" is brimful of opportunities for new life. Forest rebirth begins almost as soon as the fire goes out, and it gains momentum with the passing seasons. In the western United States, for example, downed logs and standing dead trees of all sizes, called snags, attract wood-boring beetles. These insects have chemical sensors that enable them to detect burnt-out areas miles away. When they do, the beetles home in, bore into the charred bark, and mate; the females lay their eggs under the bark. After the eggs hatch, the wriggling larvae attract black-backed woodpeckers, which thrive on them; one bird can eat an amazing 13,500 beetle larvae every year. These birds also peck out nesting cavities in the dead trees, in which they lay their eggs and rear their young. Eventually, the young birds fly away, and species such as bluebirds that can't make their own nesting cavities move into them. These birds feed on seeds they gather outside the burnt area, some of which fall

Rebirth in the forest begins immediately in the aftermath of a wildfire. (2018)

to the ground and germinate, producing flowers, shrubs, and new trees. Butterflies, bees, and other insects are attracted; these pollinate the plants, encouraging further growth. In time, mammals such as squirrels, rabbits, bats, deer, and elk arrive, followed by the bears, wolves, and snakes that prey on them. Where there is opportunity, life finds a way.[19]

II

ONCE UPON A TIME IN AMERICA

When questioned by an anthropologist on what the Indians called America before the white man came, an Indian said simply, *"Ours."*

—Vine Deloria Jr., *Custer Died for Your Sins: An Indian Manifesto,* 1988

WHEN DIFFERENT WORLDS MET

If the wind was right, and the ship's sails caught an offshore breeze, the first hint you had of the unseen North American mainland was the fragrance of forests and flowers. In 1524, Italian explorer Giovanni da Verrazzano's ship, *La Dauphine,* was cruising somewhere off the mid-Atlantic coast. The trees, Verrazzano wrote in his account of the voyage, "for a long distance, exhale the sweetest odors." Sixty years later, in July 1584, Sir Walter Raleigh's Virginia-bound colonists, "though they saw no land," noted "so strong a smel, as if we had bene in the midst of some delicate garden abounding in all kinde of odoriferous flowers." And forty-six years after that, in 1630, as the good ship *Arbella* approached the coast with Puritan colonists bound for Massachusetts, their leader, John Winthrop, recalled how all aboard were astonished by "a smell off the shore like the smell of a garden." From time to time, an America-bound vessel might even plow through masses of flowers floating miles off the coast. These, a captain noted in his log, were "sometymes scattered abroad, sometymes joyned in sheets 9 or 10 yards long, which we supposed to be brought from the low meadows by the tide."[1]

Other voyagers, however, had different first im-

Giovanni da Verrazzano. (1767)

pressions. What they saw and smelled depended on where the coast first came into view and the time of year. Obviously, there was a vast forest extending into the interior for God only knew how far. But there was also acrid smoke—lots of it. As David Peterson de Vries, a Dutch merchant sailing along the New Jersey coast, noted in November 1632, "The Indians [set] fire, at this time of year, to the woods and thickets. . . . When the wind blows out of the north-west, and the smoke too is driven to sea, it happens that the land is smelt before it is seen."[2]

Native Americans had long been wise to the ways of forests and fire. Observation and experience taught them how forests work and how to use them to satisfy their needs. Forests fed them: in season, Native Americans gathered berries and nuts, hunted deer and bears and birds, and grew maize (corn), beans, pumpkins, and squash in fields carved from the forest. Some tribes even relished a kind of candy that resulted from burning sugar pine cones. In Virginia, First peoples grew tobacco, bound to become the rage in Europe; not only was it smoked in pipes, but it was also used as medicine to treat diseases ranging from loose bowels to cancer. These farming tribes had no choice but to abandon the nomadic lifestyle. To be able to tend their fields, they settled in villages, families living in wigwams (round, domed huts cov-

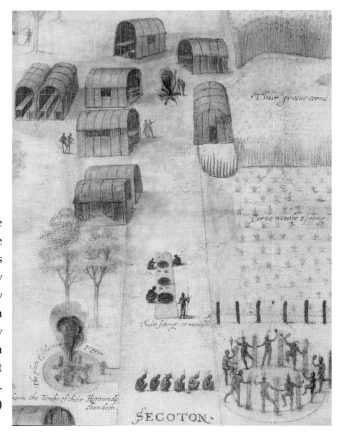

The Native American village of Secoton. This engraving by Theodor de Bry was based on a drawing by John White, an English colonist and artist. (c. 1500s)

ered with bark) or in longhouses (communal dwellings shared by several related families). An Iroquois longhouse sheltered twenty or more families.

Because America's First peoples had no metal of any sort, the forest was essential to nearly every aspect of their lives. In addition to feeding them, it provided wood, their key building material. Villages were often surrounded by defensive palisades, sturdy fences or walls formed of logs embedded upright in the ground and sharpened to a point. Utensils, canoes, and weapons—bows, arrows, spears—were made of wood. For close-in fighting, warriors wielded wooden "swords," heavy sticks edged with rows of flint points or broken seashells rubbed razor-sharp.

Like people everywhere, Native Americans used wood for cooking and warmth. Able-bodied men felled trees by using stone-headed axes or by "girdling" them. An English traveler named Henry Tudor described the girdling process: "This consists of chopping off a circular breadth of bark from the [trunk], at the height of two or three feet from the earth, and leaving it to wither away; since the communicating channel of the bark, by which the sap rises, and nourishment is conveyed through the trunk to the various branches, being thus cut off, the tree dies as a necessary consequence." Once a tree was dead and dried out, it could easily be knocked over or chopped down. Until then, it stood bare and skeleton-like, a testimony to its slow death.[3]

The fires Europeans saw as their ships neared the coast had been set for reasons beyond food preparation and warmth. Native Americans were skilled land managers, able to use fire to alter their environment, making it more productive without seriously spoiling it. Of course, things could go wrong. A sudden gust of wind might blow a fire out of control, burning a large area. But such mishaps were unintended and unpredictable; deliberately setting a massive blaze would have been the same as willfully de-stroying an essential resource and its animal inhabitants. Native people did not hunt for fun or to collect trophies to hang on walls. Needlessly destroying animals went against deeply held spiritual beliefs. As a general rule, after a kill a hunter thanked his prey for graciously sacrificing itself so people could eat. Failing to do so would have been a sign of disrespect, indeed, a grave insult. It was believed that the spirits of living animals would learn of the offense to their kind and would, in the future, stay away.[4]

Early in the spring and fall, when the weather was cool and damp, Native Americans set what today's wildland firefighters call controlled burns. Europeans were struck by the results. Burning opened the forest, making travel easier. In the 1620s, Captain John Smith wrote from Jamestown, Virginia, that "a man may gallop a horse amongst these woods any waie, but where the creeks and Rivers shall hinder." If not for burning, another settler observed, the countryside "would otherwise be so overgrown . . .

[that] people would not be able in anywise to pass . . . out of the beaten track." In 1632, a Massachusetts settler noted that annual burning "means the trees grow here and there, as in our [English] parks, and makes the country very beautiful." In fact, in certain places in New England, the woods were so open that from a hilltop one could see "deer and turkeys a mile away."[5]

First peoples used fire for what we might term ecologically sound reasons. Low-intensity fires not only cleared a desired area but nourished the soil with nutrient-rich ashes. This in turn promoted the growth of plants that do not do well in dense, shady forests: blackberries, raspberries, and strawberries. While such berries were considered luxuries in Europe, fit only for royalty and the superrich, in the 1600s an observer near the Potomac River, in what is today Washington, DC, noted that "your foot can hardly direct itself where it will not be dyed in the blood of large and delicious strawberries." Berries, along with the grassy meadows that grew in fire-cleared areas, attracted deer, rabbits, and other animals, which Native Americans hunted by "fire surround." This involved a large body of hunters setting fires in a circle extending over several miles. As the flames and smoke drove the terrified animals toward the center, hunters finished them off with bows and arrows, spears, and clubs. Some forest tribes used a similar method to collect crickets and grasshoppers, fine sources of protein. In their homes, they lit smoky fires to ward off pesky flies, ticks, fleas, and mosquitoes. Smoke also flushed honeybees from their hives, raccoons out of their dens, and bears out of their caves.[6]

The use of fire as a hunting tool was also favored by western tribes, among them the Lakota and Cheyenne. In the early 1800s, explorers Meriwether Lewis and William Clark noted, "Every spring the plains are set on fire and the buffalo are tempted to cross the [Missouri] river in search of the fresh grass which immediately succeeds the burning."

As they crossed, individual animals often became isolated on ice floes moving downstream, allowing hunters to kill them at their leisure.[7]

THE LEGIONS OF DEATH

The notion that the earliest European arrivals hacked their farms and settlements out of virgin forest is a myth. More often than not, Native Americans of that time period had already done the job for them. Every dozen years or so, when they had nearly exhausted the local wood supply for fuel and their fields were becoming less fertile, some Indigenous peoples abandoned their villages and moved to more favorable locations. During the following decades, the old fields recovered their fertility, so when the whites arrived, they simply took them over. Indeed, it was said, "Wherever we meet an Indian old field or place where they have lived, we are sure of the best ground." Nor is it accidental that several early Massachusetts towns, despite their English names—Boston, Plymouth, Salem, Medford, Watertown—were built on lands of First peoples.[8]

In displacing Native Americans, Europeans had an invisible ally, a veritable angel of death, aiding them. First peoples had benefited from geography in a special way. When it came to health, the immense ice sheets were a blessing. Combined with the Pacific and Atlantic Oceans bordering the coasts, the ice isolated the New World from humanity's deadliest scourges. Not that Native Americans lived in disease-free bliss: their most common afflictions seem to have been tuberculosis, hepatitis, and parasites such as intestinal worms, ribbonlike creatures up to twelve feet long that rob their host of essential nutrients (these they acquired by eating infected animals). They did not, however, suffer from zoonotic diseases. Zoonotic diseases—from the Greek *zoio* ("animal") and *nosos* ("disease")—are those that can spread from animals to humans, and then from person to person, sparking epidemics. Such diseases as smallpox, influenza, chicken pox, measles, typhus, whooping cough, and scarlet fever originated in domesticated animals: cows, sheep, goats, pigs, geese, chickens. While such diseases may not sicken the host animals, they can cause untold human misery. Native Americans had escaped zoonotic infections because the animals that harbored the bacteria and viruses reached the Americas only when Europeans brought them. Europeans had lived close to those animals from time immemorial, often taking them into their homes to keep them from wandering off or being stolen. By doing so, they built up resistance over many generations, which helped them avoid the illnesses the animals carried entirely or at least suffer less severe cases. While it was common, say, for Europeans (even royalty, including England's Queen Elizabeth I) to have deep smallpox scars on their faces, by surviving they gained lifelong immunity to future infection. First peoples, however, had no domestic animals other than the dog. While the bite of an infected dog can trans-mit the rabies virus, only in rare cases does the disease spread between humans, when infected saliva gets into another person's open wound or the mucous membranes that line the mouth.[9]

The size of North America's Native population when the first Europeans arrived is uncertain. Modern scholars estimate their number at between 10 and 12 million—18 million at most. What is clear is that zoonotic diseases accompanied the explorers and colonists. Wherever they went, Europeans carried them in their bodies, breath, snot, spittle, sweat, puke, excrement, and clothes. Frequently, too, they brought pigs and cattle as a walking source of fresh meat—and infection. Once foreign bacteria and viruses had been introduced into the Native population, disease raced ahead of the strangers, carried by those infected during visits to other villages. The results were epidemics that spread, for want of a better word, like wildfire.[10]

Lacking any resistance, let alone immunity, entire communities sickened and died within just a few days. During the 1580s, explorer Thomas Hariot described the aftermath of a visit to Roanoke Island, off the North Carolina coast. An unnamed disease would attack a Native village soon after the English left it. "Within a few dayes after our departure from euerie such towne," Hariot wrote, "the people began to die very fast, and many in short space; in some townes about twentie, in some fourtie, in some sixtie, & in one six score. . . . The disease [was] so strange, that they neither knew what it was, nor how to cure it; the like by report of the oldest men in the countrey never happened before." Such epidemics left survivors—if there were any, and there often weren't—shattered, physically and emotionally. In the blink of an eye, their entire world—families, friends, beliefs, customs, music, dances—had vanished.[11]

Reports like Hariot's appear in the writings of European travelers and colonists with shocking regularity. In 1626, for

Illustration of the *Mayflower* at sail in turbulent seas. (1893)

example, six years after the Pilgrims reached Plymouth aboard the *Mayflower*, the English trader Thomas Morton noted that all through the coastal forest of Massachusetts Native Americans had "died on heapes, as they lay in their houses." To be sure, "the bones and skulls upon the several places of their habitations made such a spectacle" that the woods seemed like "a new-found Golgotha," the "Place of the Skull," where the ancient Romans held executions during their occupation of Jerusalem. (Jesus Christ was crucified there.) Some Europeans realized they were disease carriers, but not exactly how, because they had no idea germs existed. In some cases, they traded blankets used by white smallpox victims to First peoples, hoping they'd come down with the disease. Today, we would call this germ warfare. Relatives customarily gathered at a sufferer's bedside with the village medicine man to lend moral support while the sickness ran its course, thereby spreading the mysterious disease more rapidly. It got so bad that Native Americans said the mere sight of a white person could strike everyone dead. Puritan clergymen often counted these plagues as blessings. God, said one, had lately sent a "wonderful plague" that destroyed First peoples and left their lands free for "civilized occupation." In 1634, John Winthrop wrote an English friend that "For the natives, they . . . are neere all dead of the small Poxe, so as the Lord hathe cleared our title to [the lands] we possess." In the 1670s, the famed Cotton

Mather of Boston credited God with clearing the woods of "those pernicious creatures . . . to make room for a better growth." By definition, settlers, as Christians, were better, worthier people, at least in their own eyes.[12]

Apart from the shattering human tragedy, zoonotic epidemics led to the collapse of Native American fire ecology along the Atlantic seaboard. But then again, Mother Nature does not stand still; she has her own rhythms. Inevitably, in areas where disease had wiped out Native Americans decades before Europeans set eyes on them, the forest returned thicker than ever. Trees grew fast. As Robert Beverley observed in his 1705 *History of Virginia,* "Wood grows at every man's door so fast, that after it has been cut down, it will in seven years time grow up again . . . and in eighteen or twenty years it will come to be very good board timber." Another settler noted that "wherever [lands] have been for a considerable time free from fires, the young trees are now springing up in great numbers, and will soon change these open grounds into forests if left to the course of nature."[13]

In the meantime, change was in the air. Fresh waves of colonists were arriving in the early 1700s, hoping to make a better life in America. As a result, land hunger grew, forcing new arrivals to look to the forest that dominated the continent's interior.

EXPERIENCING THE GREAT FOREST

There was nothing like it in their home countries. When it came to forests, European kings and nobles were of two minds. First, they saw forests as the haunts of "beasts," primarily those of the two-legged kind. During the Middle Ages, forests were lawless places, refuges for vagabonds, rebels, and robbers. In English legend, Robin Hood and his merry band stole from the rich and gave to the poor, eluding the wicked sheriff of Nottingham by hiding in the depths of Sherwood Forest. Yet the Robin Hood legend is just that, a legend. The reality was quite different. If Robin Hood had been real, Sher-

Forests were thought to be a den of thieves and outlaws. Sherwood Forest was the mythical home of fictional outlaw Robin Hood, pictured here with Guy of Gisborne. (1832)

wood Forest might have shared the fate of Selwood Forest, felled in the early 1300s to destroy an outlaw haven. Across the English Channel, in France, kings ordered forests bordering major roads severely cut back in order to increase visibility, alerting travelers to lurking danger.

European rulers also valued forests as exclusive hunting reserves. Owning a forest was a mark of power and prestige. After his invasion of England in 1066, for instance, William "the Bastard" of Normandy, dubbed William the Conqueror, created the New Forest by destroying no fewer than twenty farming villages, depriving the inhabitants of their homes and livelihoods. His Majesty was a keen hunter, and it was said that his affection for the "tall deer" was greater than for his human subjects. Special courts administered royal forest law. Anyone caught taking anything, even fallen branches, from a forest designated "royal" was to be handed over to the public executioner. According to one chronicler, "The death of a hare was a hanging matter; the murder of a plover a capital crime. Death was inflicted on those who spread nets for pigeons; wretches who had drawn a bow upon a stag were to be tied to the animal alive." Lesser infractions were punishable by having the right hand amputated, nostrils slit, an eye put out, or ears cut off. In France, a chronicler reports, three noble children were "straightaway hanged without any manner of trial" for shooting rabbits with bows and arrows.[14]

By the early 1500s, the few remnants of wilderness in Europe were restricted to small tracts of land, islands amid a sea of towns and cities, cultivated fields and road networks. Wood was at once a valuable commodity and a rapidly dwindling resource. Until the 1700s, when a way was found to extract iron from its mineral ore by melting it with coal-fueled fires, the heat to produce a single ton of metal came from burning two acres of trees. Building a frigate, a large warship, required two thousand mature oak trees, which meant felling a minimum of fifty acres of forest. The mainmast for a massive ship of the line, a three-deck vessel mounting scores of cannon, had to be more than three feet wide at its base and at least a hundred feet tall. At the same time, European towns and cities consumed vast amounts of firewood, which was hawked by sellers in the streets.[15]

There were no forest laws or lack of trees in colonial America. Once you left the settled

The USS *Constitution* is a three-masted frigate and the oldest commissioned warship in the U.S. Navy. (2006)

coastal areas and seized Native lands, you entered the Great Forest. Having reclaimed the land after the retreat of the ice sheet thousands of years earlier, the forest thrived, as did the areas that rebounded after the Indians stopped cutting them. Europeans who ventured into the Great Forest reported gigantic trees, their trunks entangled by vines as thick as a man's thigh. "Pressed against each other," a nineteenth-century traveler wrote, "their branches intertwined, the forest trees seem to form only a single whole, an immense and indestructible edifice" that "stretches before you even to the arctic pole and the Pacific ocean." The forest was so thick that, incredibly, it was said a squirrel might leap through the canopy, from branch to branch, for a thousand miles without having to touch the ground![16]

Settlers entered an "impenetrable forest," a place "as dark as a cellar" where "the sun had never shone on the ground since the Creation." This world of shadows stoked feelings of isolation, uneasiness, anxiety— terror. J. D. Schoepf, a surgeon in the British army during the American Revolution, noted, "In the eternal woods it is impossible to keep off a particularly unpleasant, anxious feeling, which is excited irresistibly by the continuing shadow and the confined outlook." In the early 1800s, a pioneer described his sense of isolation in the woods and the need to destroy the trees to keep his sanity. "Trees must fall," he wrote, "because danger lurked in their very shadow and we must have breathing space and sunlight around our house. . . . The trees were an obstruction, an enemy to extirpate, not a thing of beauty or a friend to be cherished. It was woods, woods, everywhere; trackless, savage, terrifying. [The forest] seemed to smother us, and we gasped to drink in the open sky. . . . What wonder that we grew to hate a tree, and clap our hands over his downfall!"[17]

Nighttime felt especially menacing. It was pitch-black, the moon and stars obscured by

The forest was home to a great variety of animals, including wolves, "those sneaking loafers of the forest." (c. 1850)

the leafy canopy. Out of the darkness came the eerie sounds of wind whistling, branches creaking, leaves rustling, and animals calling. The only light was the greenish glow of luminescent fungi and the twinkling of "lightning-flies"—fireflies. "The trees are [so] filled with these little animals," a traveler noted, "one would have said a million sparks [were] leaping in the air." The forest, he continued, was also infested by buzzing, biting, humming, stinging insects. Swarms of gnats, tiny winged bloodsuckers, filled the air. Though a swarm had thousands of individuals, it seemed to have a single mind, twisting and turning in unison. But each gnat's "sting is so strong and sharp that . . . I have never experienced a torment like to what they made me suffer. . . . At night they circled about us by thousands, [so] each part of the body that we left uncovered instantly served as a rendez-vous." Come daylight, every inch of exposed flesh had itchy red welts.[18]

Wildlife was more abundant and varied than in the Old World. Streams of cold, clear water churned with "infinite numbers" of fish; if quick enough, you could catch a fat trout with your bare hands. There were bobcats, bears, moose, elk, and wolves, "those sneaking loafers of the forest" that howled in the darkness. There were symphonies by croaking bullfrogs big as puppies, and plodding snapping turtles that could effortlessly slice off a finger. "Yea there are some Serpents called Rattle-snakes," wrote a Protestant minister, "that have Rattles in their Tailes, that will not flye from a man as others will, but will flye upon him and sting him so mortally, that hee will dye within a quarter of an houre after." There was also a beautiful little black-and-white creature called the skunk. When frightened, it lifted its bushy tail and sprayed a liquid smelling "like the odor of sin."[19]

The forest echoed to the cackling, cooing, cawing, chirping, crowing, hooting, screeching, quacking, and gobbling of birds. Lakes and rivers swarmed with ducks and geese. At night, owls rose silently from the trees in search of prey. A feathered Goliath of the forest, the wild turkey might stand three feet tall and weigh twenty pounds. William Bartram, an early American naturalist, was awed by these birds. "They begin at early dawn, and continue till sun-rise," he wrote. "The high forests ring with the noise . . . the watch-word being caught and repeated from one to another, for hundreds of miles around; insomuch that the whole country is for an hour or more in an universal shout . . . [and] the deep forests seem to tremble with their shrill noise."[20]

But nothing could compare to the passenger pigeon. At sixteen to eighteen inches in length, it was larger and more colorful than the wild pigeons seen in city parks today. Native to the eastern and midwestern United States and Canada, it fed on acorns, chestnuts, and beechnuts. The most numerous bird species in recorded history, likely of all time, passenger pigeons flew in flocks so large as to defy the power of words. Astonishingly, their flocks numbered in the hundreds

Martha, pictured here, is believed to be the last living passenger pigeon. (1912)

of millions, possibly billions—so large, indeed, that observers reported that the birds would "shut out the sunshine" for hours at a time. In 1860, W. Ross King could hardly believe his eyes. "Early in the morning," the Englishman wrote, "I was apprised by my servant that an extraordinary flock of birds was passing over, such as he had never seen be-fore. Hurrying out . . . I was perfectly amazed to behold the air filled, the sun obscured by millions of pigeons, not hovering about but darting onwards in a straight line . . . in a vast mass a mile or more in breadth, and stretch-ing before and behind as far as the eye could reach. . . . The duration of this flight being about fourteen hours, viz. from four a.m. to six p.m., the column . . . could not have been less than three hundred miles in length, with an average breadth, as before stated of one mile." Though King did not try to guess the number—an impossible task—a scientist estimated that this particular flock num-bered 3,717,120,000 pigeons. If so, the total population of passenger pigeons could not have been fewer than 6 billion![21]

In the early 1800s, Alexander Wilson, known as the father of American ornithol-ogy (the study of birds), described "the liv-ing tornado" that passed over his campsite. The noise as a flock came down to nest in the trees was deafening. During a tour of central New York State in 1845, novelist James Fenimore Cooper described a nesting site and what he and some friends heard when adult birds returned with food for their young:

> Every tree was literally covered with nests. . . . The place had the odor of a fowl-house, and squabs just fledged sufficiently to trust themselves in short flights, were fluttering around us in all directions, in tens of thousands. . . . It was not easy to hear each other's voices when we did speak. . . . A noise was heard rising above that of the incessant fluttering which I can only liken to that of the trampling of thousands of horses on a beaten road. This noise at first sounded distant, but it increased rapidly in proximity and power, until it came rolling in upon us, among the tree-tops, like a crash of thunder. The air was suddenly darkened, and the place where we stood as somber as a dusky twilight. . . . In a word, we seemed to be in a world of pigeons.[22]

Known as "pigeon cities," nesting sites might be forty miles long and two miles wide. The largest nesting ever recorded covered 850 square miles, and likely contained hundreds of millions of mature birds and their young. In 1813, artist John James Audubon came upon an immense city along the banks of the Ohio River in Kentucky. Individually, an adult passenger pigeon weighed ten to twelve ounces. But when birds and nests occupied every inch of a tree branch, it might not be strong enough to bear the combined load. "Here and there," Audubon wrote in his classic book *The Birds of America*, "the perches gave way under the weight with a crash, and, falling to the ground, destroyed hundreds of the birds beneath." Elsewhere, Audubon reported, their dung "fell in spots, not unlike melting flakes of snow."[23]

Pigeon flocks recognized no boundary lines drawn on maps. Time and time again, they flew over cities. In the 1620s, a flock "shut out the sunshine" over New Amsterdam, the Dutch settlement at the tip of

Newspaper spread depicting the shooting of passenger pigeons in Louisiana. (c. 1870s)

Manhattan Island. In the mid-1770s, a flock took half a day to fly over Philadelphia, pelting buildings and people with dung. Pigeons overflew Columbus, Ohio, in the spring of 1855. The experience was nerve-racking for the people below. A "growing cloud" blotted out the sun as the flock neared the city, and "a low-pitched hum" was heard. "As the watchers stared," an eyewitness recalled, "the hum increased to a mighty throbbing. Now everyone was out of the houses and stores, looking apprehensively at the growing cloud. . . . Children screamed and ran for home. Women gathered their long skirts and hurried for the shelter of stores. Horses bolted. A few people mumbled frightened words about the approach of the millennium, and several dropped on their knees and prayed. . . . And then the dark cloud was over the city. . . . Day was turned to dusk. The thunder of wings made shouting necessary for human communication." The flock took two hours to pass, leaving the town looking "ghostly in the now-bright sunlight that illuminated a world plated with pigeon ejecta." Few Americans in 1855 could imagine that these "millions of millions" of birds were doomed to extinction at the hand of thoughtless humans.[24]

BELIEFS

Europeans arrived in the New World with deep-rooted beliefs about wild places, especially forests. In the mythologies of ancient Greece and Rome, forests were depicted as the haunt of ghosts, goblins, evil spirits, and centaurs, half-horse, half-human beasts representing lust, chaos, and savagery. Pan, god of the wild, had the hindquarters and horns of a goat; he was able to shout so loudly as to cause overpowering fright—indeed, the word "panic" comes from his name. The medieval folklore of northern Europe was rich in forest-dwelling trolls, grotesque creatures full of spiteful mischief, and ogres with a woman's face, a pig's body, and a horse's legs. Witches were said to fly to the woods at night on broomsticks to worship Satan and cavort with demons. In Germany, villagers living near forests cringed at the thought of stumbling upon the Wild Hunt, ghostly men and their ferocious hounds slaying all who crossed their path. Europeans also imagined forests as the domain of bloodsucking vampires and repulsive dwarfs. Werewolves, literally "man-wolves," were supposedly humans able to turn themselves into wolves, prowling the woods on full-moon nights. If bitten by a werewolf, the victim had no choice but to become a werewolf, too.[25]

The attitudes toward wilderness that European colonists brought to the New World were also shaped by religious teachings, some dating back to the rise of Christianity in Roman times. The fathers of the early church, among its greatest thinkers and writers, drew a sharp line between mankind and the natural world. According to *The City of God,* written in the early fifth century by the theologian Saint Augustine, "There are no common rights between us and the beasts and trees." Similarly, in the thirteenth century, Saint Thomas Aquinas of the University of Paris, revered as a doctor of the church, taught that "the life of animals and plants is preserved not for themselves but for man." Since God created animals for man's use, Aquinas reasoned, cruelty to them was not inherently wrong, and it was to be condemned only if it inspired cruelty toward fellow humans.[26]

Such attitudes were grounded in the Bible. In Genesis 1:28, God commands mankind to "be fruitful, and multiply, and replenish the earth, and subdue it: and have dominion over . . . every living thing that moveth upon the earth." In other words, mankind is special. Having been created in the Almighty's image, humans were viewed not as part of the natural order but as separate from and above it. Accordingly, everything that exists on Earth was put there for just one purpose: to serve humanity's needs. The Creator, it was believed, had given humans the right to subdue and exploit the natural world for His glory and their benefit. It has been said that the Bible is the most influential book that has ever existed. To be sure, for many centuries, if a family, however low its station in life, owned any book at all, it was the Good Book.

Viewing the American wilderness through the lens of scripture, the early settlers, especially New Englanders, saw it as a "cursed" land inhabited by "benighted savages," "heathens" who "knew not the True God." Upon arriving in 1620, William Bradford, who'd led his Pilgrim flock to Plymouth aboard the *Mayflower,* found "a hideous and desolate wilderness, full of wild beasts and wild men. . . . And the whole countrie, full of woods and thickets, represented a wild and savage heiw."

The Indigenous Nations, of course, were sophisticated cultures with rich traditions. At the time, these damaging stereotypes served to justify the land theft. Unfortunately, they continue to be pervasive today.[27]

Preachers and layfolk used military images to depict wilderness as an "enemy" to be "conquered," "subdued," and "vanquished" by a "pioneer army" of the godly. Benjamin Franklin, eighteenth-century America's foremost scientist and a Founding Father, echoed this theme in his writings. "*Scouring our Planet, by clearing America of Woods,*" he declared in 1751, would make "this Side of our Globe reflect a brighter Light to the Eyes of Inhabitants in Mars or Venus." In the opinion of the man who discovered that lightning is electricity, deforesting North America would remove all useless beings— human, animal, vegetable—that stood in the way of progress.[28]

MAKING LAND

Such ideas shaped the pioneer farmer's outlook. Upon entering the Great Forest, he would attend to his family's immediate needs by building a lean-to or small log shelter and shooting a few deer for food. That done, he had to "make land"—that is, open the soil so that he could "put in" a crop. But no seeds could go into the ground until it was cleared of trees. Not surprisingly, the pioneer felt that the only good tree was a dead tree. To him, wilderness was a foe; the Bible said so, the preacher said so, and so did his own self-interest. Those who sped forest destruction were doing the Lord's work, standing on the side of progress. Nothing, if we can believe contemporary accounts, so gladdened the pioneer's heart as felling a tree—and the more the better.

While visiting the new nation in the 1790s, the Irish merchant Isaac Weld Jr. was amazed to find that its citizens seemed to lack any appreciation of natural beauty. Americans, he wrote, "have an unconquerable aversion to trees . . . and cut away all before them without mercy." Trees, Weld continued, "are looked upon as a nuisance, and the man that can cut down the largest number, and have the field about his house most clear of them, is looked upon as the most industrious citizen."[29]

The attitude Weld described had not changed an iota by 1831, when the French diplomat and historian Alexis de Tocqueville toured the Michigan frontier. The pioneer, he noted, was a materialistic person, captivated by the useful and the profitable rather than the beautiful and the spiritual. "Besides, living in the wilds," the Frenchman reported in *Journey to America*, "he only prizes the works of man. He will gladly send you off to see a road, a bridge, a fine village. But that one should appreciate the great trees and the beauties of solitude, that possibility completely passes him by." Four years later, in *Democracy in America*, a classic study of ideas and government in the young nation, Tocqueville declared, "In Europe people talk a great deal of the wilds of America, but the Americans themselves never think about them; they are insensible to the wonders of inanimate nature and they may be said not to perceive the mighty forests that surround them till they fall beneath the hatchet. Their eyes are fixed upon another sight: the American people views [only] its own march across these wilds, draining swamps, turning the course of rivers, peopling solitudes, and subduing nature." To the typical American, then, "taming the wilderness" was the true meaning of "improvement," a catchword at the time. In Europe, improvement meant making things better, but in the United States it meant more people, more houses, more prosperity, more cleared land—more of everything, at the expense of wilderness.[30]

Yet nothing could be planted until the pioneer could clear a field and plant a crop. To do so, he might fell trees in the Native American tradition, by girdling. The results weren't pretty. Another French traveler, the Marquis de Chastellux, explained that "their leaves no longer spring, their branches fall, and their trunk becomes a hideous skeleton." Upon seeing a stand of girdled trees, Basil Hall, a retired British naval officer, was stunned, comparing the "horrid" scene to a group of men standing "with their throats cut."[31]

Though a girdled tree died within a week or two, it took at least two years to decay to the point where it could easily be pushed over or cut down. The quickest way to fell a tree was with the ax. However, this was dangerous work; a slipup could easily cost a foot or a leg. A skilled axman was an artist—cool, keen-eyed, unerring, swift. "Ain't he chain-lightin'?" admiring onlookers would cry. In the 1760s, Benjamin Franklin watched pioneers build a log fort for the British army in the Pennsylvania backcountry. "Seeing the trees fall so fast," he wrote, "I had the curiosity to look at my watch when two men began to cut a pine; in six minutes they had it upon the ground, and I found it of fourteen inches diameter." For the pioneers' sons, felling a tree with an ax was a rite of passage, a key stage in life, symbolizing entry into manhood. One remarked that when he was a boy, his father had given him a hatchet to "hack

Girdling was commonly practiced by Native Americans and later by European settlers. (Date unknown)

down saplings." Yet nothing beat the thrill of cutting down his first tree with a full-sized ax. "I loved it," he recalled years later, "in proportion to the facility with which I could destroy [a tree]."[32]

Ax and fire were essential to making land quickly. Early in the spring, the pioneer would chop down a stand of trees, taking care that they fell inward, toward each other. After the summer, when the fallen trees had dried, he set them on fire. When the fire died out, there remained a jumble of charred trunks. The pioneer, his sons, and his neighbors would then stack these in heaps and set them on fire again, reducing them to ashes. Among the blackened stumps, he would plant a grain crop, usually barley, rye, or corn. Stumps were deep-rooted and almost impossible to extract just after the trees were cut; they could be blown up with gunpowder, but that was expensive. Only after several years, when the roots had sufficiently decayed, could oxen pull the stumps out with chains. Meanwhile, the pioneer built a log cabin, enclosed his fields with split logs placed one on top of another in a zigzag pattern, and sawed whatever he needed into firewood.

Raw as backwoods farms and settlements appeared to outsiders, they filled their occupants with the pride of achievement. Novelist Anthony Trollope, another English visitor,

Woodcut of a log cabin. (1839)

noted that, above all, the pioneer saw himself as independent. While most English farmers did not own their land or homes but were tenants of noble landlords, apt to be evicted on a whim, the American pioneer was beholden to no one, needing no one else's approval. He made his own decisions and lived with the consequences, good or bad. "He is his own master, standing on his own threshold," Trollope noted. "He is dirty and per-

haps squalid. His children are sick and he is without comforts. His wife is pale, and you think you see shortness of life written in the faces of all the family. But over and above it all there is an independence, which sits gracefully on their shoulders. . . . [As one told me], 'I find a kind of comfort when I am at work from daybreak to sundown, *and know that it is all my own.*'" Abraham Lincoln, a son of frontier Kentucky, grew up with this mindset. The future president thought the spirit of independence bred in the woods was an innate human right, the very essence of democracy. Lincoln said it was even the humblest person's "right to rise in life."[33]

THE WOODS AFLAME

Though First peoples planned their woodland fires to avert runaway blazes, they were not always successful; humans make mistakes, and nature does not always act as expected. Pioneers, however, had mixed feelings about burning woodlands. On the one hand, they accepted man-made fires as facts of life, as normal as sunrise and sunset. Whether in the settled areas or on the frontier, farmers set fire to the woods not only to make land but to speed the growth of grass for their livestock, kill snakes, and get rid of pesky insects. Then again, they were often reckless with fire. Busy men might let piles of discarded tree trunks, stumps, branches, and leaves dry on the ground until fall, when they got around to burning them in bonfires— fires that went "wild" if the wind picked up. Worse, people seemed to set forest fires without giving thought to the environmental costs. While researching this book, I was amazed to find that the history of colonial America and the early republic is filled with accounts of massive man-set forest fires.

One memorable incident illustrates this point. On May 19, 1780, George Washington was camped with the Continental Army at Morristown, New Jersey. Late that morning, the general noted in his diary a "heavy & uncommon kind of Clouds—dark & at the same time a bright and reddish kind of light

intermixed with them—brightning & darkning alternately."[34]

While Washington did not know it at the time, he was witnessing the distant effect of what New Englanders would call the Dark Day. At sunrise that morning, from the Canadian border south to Connecticut, the sky darkened, songbirds fell silent, frogs peeped, and crickets chirped "as if night was falling." By noon, when farmers came home for lunch, their wives had to light candles, and, wrote a correspondent for the *Massachusetts Spy,* "those who had good eye sight could scarcely see to read common print." It got worse. By nightfall, "all was a universal black," the darkest night anyone had ever seen, and the moon rose "blood-red."[35]

What was going on? What did it mean? In many traditions, light is a symbol of goodness and purity, darkness symbolic of evil and sin. The Bible warns that a dark day will signal the end of days, when God calls sinful humanity to account. Isaiah 13:10–11 foretells a day when the Lord will command that "the

A FEW LINES COMPOSED ON THE

DARK DAY,

MAY 19, 1780.

LET us adore, and bow before,
　The sovereign Lord of might ;
Who turns away the shining day,
　Into the shades of night.

All nature stands, when he commands,
　Or changes in its course ;
His mighty hand rules sea and land,
　He is the Lord of Host.

Nineteenth of May, a gloomy day,
　When darkness veil'd the sky ;
The sun's decline may be a sign,
　Some great event is nigh.

Let us remark, how black and dark,
　Was the ensuing night ;
And for a time the moon decline,
　And did not give her light.

Can mortal man, their wonder skan ?
　Or tell a second cause ?
Did not our God, then shake his rod,
　And alter nature's laws ?

What great event, next will be sent,
　Upon this guilty land ?
He only knows who can dispose,
　All things at his command.

Our wickedness we must confess,
　Is terrible and great ;
Sin is the thing, that we should shun,
　The thing God's soul doth hate.

Our mighty sins, God's judgment brings,
　But still we harden'd grow ;
Then judgments great may not abate,
　Until our overthrow.

How sin abounds, in all our towns,
　Now in these Gospel days ;
How vice prevails and virtue fails,
　And Godliness decays.

If we reflect, can we expect,
　According to our doing ?
But that we are, as we may fear,
　Just on the brink of ruin.

Awake, awake, your sins forsake,
　And that immediately ;
If we don't turn, his wrath will burn,
　To all eternity.

This is the day, that sinners may,
　Repent, and turn to God !
If they delay and won't obey,
　Then they must feel His rod.

How good and kind, would sinners find
　Their great Redeemer now ;
If they'd awake, their sins forsake,
　And to his Sceptre bow.

The gospel call, is unto all !
　Repent ! why will you die ?
Why will you go to endless woe,
　And pass my mercy by ?

Come unto me ! Jesus doth say !
　All ye that weary are ;
Ye shall find rest ! ye shall be blest !
　For so his words declare !

If after all, this gracious call,
　You utterly refuse ;
And stop your ear, and will not hear,
　But your own ruin choose.

Mercy abuse, and grace refuse,
　Justice then takes the throne ;
And in some hour Almighty Power,
　Will make his vengeance known.

O dreadful state, when 'tis too late,
　For sinners to return ;
When life and breath is lost in death,
　The soul in Hell must burn.

What mortal tongue, what human pen,
　The terror can declare,
That sinners all in Hell who shall
　That dreadful torments bear ?

Eternity ! Eternity !
　Behold there is no end ;
Where sinners lie, and wish to die,
　Who into atoms —

And now let all, who hear this call,
　And saw the day so dark !
Make haste away without delay,
　And get into the Ark !

Then safe shall he, forever be,
　That doth to Jesus come,
He need not fear though death be near,
　Since Heaven is his home.

"A Few Lines Composed on the Dark Day." (1780)

sun shall be darkened in his going forth, and the moon shall not cause her light to shine. And I will punish the world for their evil, and the wicked for their iniquity." Fearing the worst, New Englanders crowded into their churches, begging the Lord's forgiveness. The crowning sin, declared some not-so-keen patriots, was the American Revolution itself—and the chief sinner was George Washington, general of the rebel army. For rebellion violated the "divine right" of kings, the doctrine that challenging the powers that be is immoral because kings get their authority from God and are accountable only to Him, not to the people they rule.[36]

Other New Englanders, however, believed the Dark Day had a natural and not a supernatural cause. They noticed that for several days before the event, newspapers in Massachusetts, Rhode Island, Connecticut, and New Hampshire had carried articles about a strong smell of smoke in the air, "like the burning of the woods." Near Boston, observers noted "a black scum like ashes" on rainwater collected in tubs, while at Harvard College in Cambridge, rain "fell thick and sooty" and tasted like the "black ash of burnt leaves." There were also reports of farmer-set fires raging from Canada to as far south as the woods around Fort Ticonderoga in New York. Clearly, the Dark Day had nothing to do with God's wrath. As one eyewitness, the historian William Gordon, explained, "It is the American custom to make large fires in the woods, for the purpose of clearing the lands in the new settlements." Despite the bitterly fought war, "this was practiced in the spring of the present year [1780] in a much greater degree than usual . . . all round the frontiers."[37]

Americans continued to set woodlands ablaze. In 1781, French soldiers set out from New York to join George Washington's forces. As the troops marched, they saw towering plumes of smoke rising in the distance, often from several fires burning at once. An officer reported that they "caused no excitement at all among the nearby Americans, whose country is full of forests. Sometimes they even congratulated themselves on having a big conflagration, as it saves them the trouble of cutting down the trees to clear the land." The next year, a British immigrant traveling along the Delaware River reported "immense tracts of country lying in ashes. . . . Philadelphia was sometimes covered with smoke, from a vast morass which had taken fire . . . and kept burning . . . for an extent of many miles around."[38]

Fifty years later, nothing had changed; one could scarcely venture east of the Mississippi River without seeing man-set forest fires, some of which raged for days before burning out on their own. Frances Trollope, the English novelist and tireless foe of slavery, traveled to frontier Ohio in the 1820s. What a letdown! "The lurid glare of a burning forest," she wrote, "was almost constantly visible after sunset, and when the wind so willed, the smoke arising from it floated in heavy vapor over our heads. [Nothing] could prevent its heavy horror wearying the spirits."[39]

The burning continued unchecked; indeed, even the most destructive blazes were regarded as merely local events, ignored by the big-city press. In the summer of 1855,

Charles Richard Weld, a popular English writer and historian, visited the New York portion of Lake Champlain, near the Canadian border. "War to extermination against the forest is the settlers' rule," he declared. During an overnight steamboat tour of the lake, Weld saw the woods ablaze. He was appalled by "the awful spectacle which the heavens presented at night, appearing like a mighty furnace. The oppressive heat was sickening, and the smoke so acrid as to cause excessive smarting pain to my eyes. . . . At every station where we stopped, crowds of terrified men and women made anxious inquiries respecting the progress of the conflagration. The march of the fire seemed endless, for when we came to localities where it was almost extinct, a few yards farther, long tongues of flame played among the trees. . . . The whole country was wrapped in flames and smoke—gloom and despair were on every face." Then again, not all forest fires terrified people; some were happily set—for fun. Well into the 1890s, there were reports of how tourists around Mount Rainier in Washington "frequently set fire to the resinous fir trees for the pleasure of seeing their lives go out in sudden flashes of flame."[40]

How lethal these fires were, or if they killed anyone at all, was not recorded. What is certain, however, is that pioneers continued to view forests as nuisances; they could not imagine them as sources of immense wealth. That began to change in the 1850s, with the rise of big-time lumbering as the Industrial Revolution slipped into high gear.

HARVESTING THE NORTHWOODS

Black spruce and Norway pine,
Douglas fir and Red cedar,
Scarlet oak and Shagbark hickory.
We built a hundred cities and a thousand towns—
But at what a cost!
We cut the top off Minnesota and sent it down the river.
We cut the top off Wisconsin and sent it down the river.
We left the mountains and the hills slashed and burned,
And moved on.

—**Pare Lorentz, *The River,* documentary film about the Mississippi River, 1938**

A WOODEN NATION

Once upon a time, the United States was almost entirely a nation of small farms and small towns. Craftspeople worked for themselves with their own hands and their own tools in their own shops. Fathers taught their trade to their sons, who worked beside them. If they needed an extra "hand," they hired a local fellow, who slept in their house, ate at their table, and earned a small wage until he learned enough and saved enough to set up shop on his own. Whatever craftspeople made or repaired—boots, furniture, clocks, nails, tools, guns, cutlery, plows, horseshoes, harnesses, kettles, wagons—was destined for the local market, bought by customers they knew personally as neighbors, friends, and relatives.

That lifestyle began to change around the year 1815. By then, the nation was experiencing the early effects of an economic upheaval that would change the way Americans lived, worked, and thought. Dubbed by historians the Industrial Revolution, this upheaval had begun in England in the mid-1700s. Increasingly, innovative businesspeople used machinery to manufacture whatever goods consumers wanted. "Manufactured," in its original meaning (from the Latin *manus*, "hand"), was simply another term for "handmade." Thus, using machinery to make things replaced making them by hand. At first, the spread of machines powered by flowing water or steam rendered the making by hand of many items obsolete, forcing craftspeople to seek other ways of earning a living. Grouping machines at central points, called factories, enabled the mass production of an ever-increasing variety of products. Mass production in turn spurred the growth of cities,

to which the lure of factory jobs drew both Americans seeking new opportunities and fresh waves of European immigrants. As a result, the U.S. population leaped from 7.2 million in 1810 to 31.5 million in 1860, and to more than 74.8 million by 1900. New York, the nation's largest city, had 79,000 residents in 1800, 696,000 in 1850, and 2.5 million at the dawn of the twentieth century. Cities like Chicago, Indianapolis, Louisville, Cleveland, and Baltimore grew by leaps and bounds.

Growth on such a scale would not have been possible without wood; actually, we would not be wrong in calling the Industrial Revolution in America the Wooden Revolution. As the geologist James Hall put it in 1836: "Well may ours be called a Wooden Country; not merely from the extent of [our] forests, but because in common use wood has been substituted for a number of necessary articles." Hall did not exaggerate. Americans were using wood in almost every conceivable way. Fast-growing cities had wooden sidewalks and streets paved with wooden planks, even in busy downtown areas. There were wooden lampposts. Intricate spiderwebs of wooden drain, sewer, and water pipes lay beneath the streets. Until replaced by coal in the 1880s and by oil in the 1890s, firewood was the chief source of energy in the nation's homes, businesses, and factories. Moreover, inventors and tinkerers were constantly finding new uses for wood. Different types of trees were adopted for specific purposes. Rifle stocks were made from black walnut, piano and organ keys from maple, and packing crates from poplar. Policemen carried nightsticks of Osage orange; an extremely hard wood, it was capable of knocking sense into the thickest-skulled lawbreaker. Pine trees yielded turpentine, used in varnish and as a solvent for oil-based paints. When used as a substitute for lamp fuel, turpentine had an unforeseen benefit. Whale oil, a pricey source of near-smokeless lamplight in homes, was in such demand that by the 1860s the sperm whale and other species were being overhunted to the verge of extinction. The availability of inexpensive turpentine sped the decline of whaling, thus helping to save the endangered sea giants. The only drawbacks were turpentine's unpleasant odor and its tendency to explode when improperly handled.[1]

The Wooden Revolution, too, was key to helping America—indeed, the whole of humanity—become better informed. Ever

Turpentine, sourced from pine trees, helped prevent the extinction of whales due to overhunting for their oil, which was burned in lamps. (Date unknown)

since the invention of writing in the Middle East five thousand years ago, there has been a demand for materials to write on. The Bible tells of God's giving Moses the Ten Commandments engraved on two stone tablets on Mount Sinai. But stone "pages" are hard, heavy, and take up a lot of space. Paper was a marked improvement. Papyrus, the earliest paper, was made in Egypt from the white inner tissue of the papyrus plant. In ancient Greece and Rome, people wrote on parchment, made from untanned skins of animals such as sheep and goats. Making parchment, however, took a lot of time and effort, which meant that only the wealthy could afford it. During the Middle Ages, handwritten parchment books were treasured, bequeathed in wills along with money, homes, and land. Monasteries had libraries holding several dozen or even a few hundred books, but kept them under lock and key or chained to reading tables. However, improvements in technology in the 1450s, notably the invention of movable type and the printing press, made books more plentiful than ever before. To meet rising demand, scribes and printers switched from parchment to paper made of linen and cotton rags. Rag paper can last centuries without discoloring or becoming brittle and crumbling to dust.[2]

A printing of the *London Gazette,* a popular rag newspaper in the early 1700s. (1705)

Rags were a valuable commodity in America, as we see from this 1769 advertisement in the *Boston News-Letter:*

Rags are as Beauties, which concealed lie,
But when in Paper, how it charms the Eye:
Pray save Rags, new Beauties to discover,
For Paper truly, every one's a lover.

Each year, the English colonies, and then the United States, imported shiploads of rags from Europe. These were used to make paper for writing and printing: pamphlets, books, handbills, newspapers. Newspapers were popularly known as "rags," not for their trashy content but because of what they were made of. Nevertheless, the supply of rag paper could not keep up with the demand; rag-paper publications remained expensive, beyond the reach of the average person.[3]

All that changed thanks to an unsung hero of modern times. In 1844, a Canadian inventor and poet named Charles Fenerty perfected a method, still used today, of making paper from wood pulp. Due to his invention of a "wood-grinding machine," paper became available in unlimited supply— unlimited, that is, so long as there were enough trees to grind up.[4]

Inexpensive wood-pulp paper led to an explosion of written material, not only for the well-to-do and the educated but for ordinary folks, even the humblest. Wood-pulp paper transformed communications, sped up the transfer of knowledge, and hastened the spread of literacy. Almost anyone could afford to read anything, from "penny dreadful" adventure novels and syrupy romances to scholarly works of history, philosophy, politics, and current affairs. Mass-produced books such as Harriet Beecher Stowe's *Uncle Tom's Cabin* (1852) energized the crusade against slavery, helping to set the stage for the Civil War. Advertising surged, sparking sales, a thirst for new products, business activity, and job opportunities. Above all, in slashing the cost of newsprint, pulp paper gave rise to the modern magazine and newspaper. By the early 1900s, it took a minimum of two hundred acres of forest to make newsprint for the Sunday edition of the *New York Times*. The only drawback to pulp paper is that it is short-lived, turning brown and crumbly after a few decades.

Trees also furnished the means to travel faster than at any time in history. In August 1807, the American engineer and inventor Robert Fulton tested his *Clermont* on the Hudson River at New York City. Skeptical onlookers dubbed the steam-powered vessel Fulton's Folly, betting the engine would explode the moment it got under way. They were wrong: the *Clermont* made the 150 miles to Albany in thirty-two hours, compared to three days by "express" stagecoach. Within a decade, steamboats were navigating the nation's rivers, plowing upstream against swift currents that virtually stymied boats under sail. Regularly scheduled steamboats covered the three-thousand-mile round trip from New Orleans, Louisiana, at the mouth of the Mississippi River, to Louisville, Kentucky, on the Ohio River, in just eleven days. Not only were these vessels built of wood, their iron boilers devoured wood. In the 1850s, for example, a single round trip from New Orleans to Louisville burned six hundred cords of wood. (A cord is a stack eight feet long, four feet high, and four feet wide.) To keep his vessel supplied, a captain had to

"Wooding Up" on the Mississippi by Frances Flora Bond Palmer, depicting a steamboat making a stop at a wooding station. (1863)

make sure he was always within range of an onshore "wooding" station.[5]

Wooding stations were run by "wood-hawks," typically rough men, even outlaws with a price on their heads, who cleared the forest for many miles inland from a river. The English traveler Thomas Hamilton described them in his account of his tour of the States in 1833:

> The steamboats stop twice a day to take in a supply of wood for the engine. These vessels have become so numerous that a considerable number of settlers make it their business to supply them. . . . Outcasts they literally are. Many have fled for crimes, to a region where the arm of the law cannot reach them. Others are men of broken characters, hopes, and fortunes . . . [who] locate where they please, without troubling themselves about any title to the land they occupy. Should a rival in the business of wood-cutting choose to take up his residence inconveniently near, the rifle settles the dispute. One or other becomes food for the vultures, and the market continues uninjured by competition.

During the 1850s alone, woodhawks cleared an estimated 50 million acres of forest, yielding 70 million cords of wood each year.[6]

Yet no invention consumed wood like the railroad train. At first, "trains" were lines (trains) of coupled wagons, commonly at coal mines, drawn by horses along parallel wooden beams termed "rail roads" or "tracks." In 1814, English engineer George Stephenson, considered the father of the railways, built a steam-powered locomotive to replace coal mine horses. Reports of the locomotive's success at drawing heavy loads fascinated Peter Cooper, a New York inventor and engineer. In August 1830, Cooper tested a tiny locomotive, the aptly named *Tom Thumb,* on a thirteen-mile round trip outside Baltimore, reaching a sustained

The steam locomotive revolutionized transportation and commerce. (c. 1939)

essential to binding the nation together. Through purchase and conquest, the United States had obtained land from France and Mexico. In the Louisiana Purchase of 1803, France sold the United States about 827,000 square miles west of the Mississippi River for $15 million, more than doubling the young nation's size. Victory in the Mexican-American War of 1846–1848 led to the annexation of present-day California, Utah, Arizona, and New Mexico. Thus, by 1860 the United States spanned the continent from the Atlantic to the Pacific. Yet overland travel remained slow and dangerous. At an average rate of ten miles a day, the two-thousand-mile journey by wagon from Independence, Missouri, the jumping-off point, to California took about five months in good weather; in winter, migrants risked being trapped by snow in the Sierra Nevada. During the winter of 1846–1847, the Donner Party, a group of pioneers bound for California, became snowbound in the mountains. Of the eighty-nine people who started out,

speed of eighteen miles an hour; a stagecoach traveled at an average speed of about five miles an hour. Before long, "railroad mania" gripped the nation, as business leaders pooled their resources to buy equipment and acquire land.[7]

The federal government, by far the nation's largest landowner, saw railroads as

forty-five survived, largely by eating the bodies of those who had died of starvation. With luck, the sea journey took 198 days to cover the 13,225 miles from New York to Monterey, California, sailing around Cape Horn at the southern tip of South America. This route was also risky; vessels regularly foundered in violent storms, drowning all aboard.

To encourage westward expansion, Congress decided to spur railroad construction with generous grants of federal land on each side of the tracks, varying in width from 20 to 160 miles. The results were astounding. From 30,626 miles of track in 1860, the total rose to 93,269 miles in 1880, 160,592 miles in 1890, and 193,000 miles by 1900, more than in all of Europe and South America combined. This growth made railroads the nation's first big business, privately owned profit-making firms able to influence politics and society as well as the economy. As the rail network expanded, it enabled Americans to master the continent, opening the land to settlement and its natural resources to exploitation. Railroads created a unified national market, so that Texas cattle eventually became steaks in New York restaurants and midwestern pigs ended up as ham and bacon on eastern breakfast tables.[8]

Federal land grants usually consisted of immense stretches of forest, important because the early railroads were incredible tree killers. Indeed, by the mid-1800s, they accounted for one-fifth to one-fourth of the nation's annual timber consumption. In one way or another, every key part of the "iron horse" required generous amounts of wood. Locomotives were made of iron, and there could not have been iron without trees. During the 1850s, iron makers had learned how to remove the impurities from coal so it could be used in making high-quality metal for engines, boilers, bolts, gears, wheels, and tracks. Coal mines, however, needed millions of sturdy wooden beams to shore up their walls and ceilings. Moreover, railroad stations, platforms, loading docks, fences, telegraph poles, and bridges were made of wood.

Some wooden bridges were engineering marvels. Upon seeing such a bridge, the work of engineer Herman Haupt, President Abraham Lincoln observed, "That man, Haupt, has built a bridge, across Potomac Creek, about four hundred feet long and nearly a hundred feet high, over which loaded trains are passing every hour, and upon my word . . . there is nothing in it but beanpoles and cornstalks."

Trestle no. 19 of the A.C. Railroad showcases the importance of wood in the locomotive industry. (c. 1900–1927)

Freight cars and passenger coaches, too, were made of wood. George Pullman, who built the majority of America's sleeping and dining cars, used 50 million board feet of prime lumber every year. (A board foot measures twelve inches wide by twelve inches long by one inch thick.)[9]

Parallel tracks rested on wooden ties, which kept them upright, aligned, and correctly spaced. Each mile of track required up to thirty-five hundred oak or chestnut ties. But until the adoption of chemical preservatives in the late 1890s, exposure to rain and heat caused rapid decay. The need to constantly replace ties made railroads the nation's single largest consumer of wood. In 1873, a trade magazine reported, "Railroad ties last about five years, consequently 30,000,000 ties are used annually for repairs, taking the timber from 150,000 acres." In little more than a decade, that number climbed to 73 million ties.[10]

Railroads and fire were cousins. Until the switchover to diesel and electrical power in the twentieth century, locomotives burned wood and, later, coal to make steam in their boilers. Unavoidably, steady streams of hot embers spewed from their smokestacks. This was one of the hazards passengers faced, along with frequent train wrecks due to equipment failures. During a visit to the United States in 1842, English novelist Charles Dickens described a harrowing night ride. It was summer, and his train sped along with open windows, trailing "a whirlwind of bright sparks, which showered about us like a storm of fiery snow." Several passengers' clothes were singed, and women who tried to shield themselves with umbrellas had the fabric burst into flames inches from their faces. Worse still, it was almost a sure bet that when a train passed through a forest, trailing its cloud of embers, a blaze would result. Such fires raged out of control until they ran out of fuel or were doused by a heavy downpour; nobody tried to put them out. Nevertheless, passengers took fire in stride, an expected hazard of travel, much like today's highway traffic jams and airport delays. Indeed, it may be said that into the early twentieth century, forest fires ignited by the iron horse were as American as apple pie. We will explore their disastrous impact in later chapters.[11]

TIMBER BARONS

As long as they were cut for local use or burned to clear land, trees had no commercial value on the frontier. "Underbrush was fired with wanton carelessness," one old-timer recalled, "and thousands of acres of valuable timber went up in smoke [every year]." The Industrial Revolution, however, created demand for enormous quantities of lumber and, with it, a booming industry. Like any industry at its outset, lumbering attracted ambitious operators, people bent on cashing in on the new opportunities. Accordingly, by the late 1860s, the forests of Maine, New York, and Pennsylvania, once centers of production, were all but stripped, not worth the effort or expense of further "harvesting."[12]

Giant white pine grove in Wisconsin. (Date unknown)

Lumbermen moved their operations to the sparsely populated states bordering the Great Lakes: Michigan, Wisconsin, and Minnesota. These states lay at the heart of the Great Forest. To lumbermen, the Northwoods, as the region was known, rivaled California at the height of the Gold Rush (1849–1855), only the "gold" was not yellow but white—white pine. As a Wisconsin congressman explained, "Upon the rivers which are tributary to the Mississippi, and also those which empty into Lake Michigan, there are interminable forests of pine, sufficient to supply all the wants of [our] citizens . . . for all time to come."[13]

Of all the commercially valuable trees,

the eastern white pine was most desirable. It yielded, a lumberman said, the "most wonderful wood." A mature tree "is of the largest kind we can recollect of having seen," he declared. "Many of the trees were upwards of four or five feet in diameter near the earth, and were very straight and lofty"—straight because natural wildfires had burned away their lower branches, thereby reducing competition for light, water, and nutrients. White pine trees grew so tall, up to 170 feet, that a single one yielded enough wood to build a good-sized family home. The wood, too, was a builder's delight: strong, durable, and fine-grained, it gripped nails firmly and easily took paint.[14]

The early Northwoods lumberman lived in a dog-eat-dog world. With so many operators determined to grab a share of the supply, he faced fierce competition, resulting in inefficiency, waste, and low profits. Eventually, those we may call "the organizers" took matters into their own hands. Their actions were not unique to lumbering;

America's first billionaires—John D. Rockefeller (oil), Andrew Carnegie (steel), Henry Ford (automobiles)—followed precisely the same business model. These single-minded, hard-driving moguls focused on controlling every sector of their industry. They bought up weaker companies, streamlined operations, fixed prices, and maximized profits for themselves, their partners, and their investors. The "timber barons" were no different. As they saw things, money did not grow on trees; it was the trees themselves that grew money and, thus, their fortunes.

Frederick Weyerhaeuser was America's leading timber baron. Born in Germany in 1834, he quit school at the age of twelve, after his father's death, and went to work to help his family. In his early twenties, he immigrated to America, where, after working several years as a day laborer, he found a job at a sawmill in Rock Island, Illinois. The secret of his success, as this classic workaholic later explained, "lay simply in my will to work. I never watched the clock and never stopped

Frederick
Weyerhaeuser.
(c. 1913)

enough to buy his own sawmill and lumber-yard. A highly persuasive man, good-natured yet "sharp as a tack," he formed alliances with other sawmill owners and lumbermen. Step by step, he expanded his holdings. At his death in 1914, the Weyerhaeuser Company, founded in 1900, owned timberlands covering an area larger than the state of Wisconsin. Not only did Weyerhaeuser own the raw materials, he controlled every aspect of the lumber business, from forest to sawmill to market. His properties also included paper mills, steamboats, and hundreds of railroad freight cars. Though historians claim he was the seventh-wealthiest American of all time, the timber baron himself did not know how much he was worth. When a newspaper reporter asked how rich he was, Weyerhaeuser phoned his banker. "There is a man here who has asked me how rich I am. Can you make a rough estimate? No? Too long a job? All right." Putting down the receiver, Weyerhaeuser turned to the reporter and said, "He doesn't know either, can't say offhand."[15]

before I had finished what I was working on." His strong work ethic won the young man rapid promotion, until the owner put him in charge of the sawmill. Weyerhaeuser lived simply, saving his money until he had

LUMBERJACKS

The Northwoods were dotted with logging camps, tiny islands in the midst of an ocean of white pine. Crude affairs, the camps were built to last a couple of seasons, until the area was thoroughly logged, or "cut out," as they said in the business. One camp was much the same as any other. Each had a bunkhouse for the work crew, which numbered from fifteen to sixty men, depending on the size of the operation. There was a stable for the horses, a carpenter's shop, and a blacksmith's forge, where all manner of ironware—horseshoes, axes, saws, chains, pots, pans, kettles—was made and repaired. "Cookie" presided over the cookhouse, a shed where the crew ate. All these buildings were made of rough-hewn logs.[16]

Felling trees was reserved for the cold months, from mid-November through mid-March. This was because the sap was frozen, making the trees easier to cut down, and the heavy logs could be slid on ice instead of having to be dragged through brush and

A "cookie" in an Idaho logging house preparing flapjacks. (Date unknown)

mud. The cold season also provided a workforce of lumberjacks. Originally a Canadian term combining the words "lumber" and "jack," slang for "man" or "fellow," it applied to anyone who worked at felling trees. From spring to fall, many Northwoods lumberjacks farmed. After taking in the harvest, they looked forward to earning extra money and staying active during the winter off-season.

Loggers in front of a logging house. (Date unknown)

(around two dollars a day), but the adventure of living in the wilderness. A jack's poem captures their spirit:

> There's a life that is close unto nature, where
> the soul is happy and free,
> And you live by the brawn of your muscle—
> ah, there is the life to suit me—
> The job in a shipyard is lousy—a paradise
> fit for a tramp.
> So to Hell with a life in the city; I'm off—
> to a logging camp![17]

Some lumberjacks were recent immigrants—Frenchmen, Germans, Irishmen, Swedes, Danes, Norwegians, Finns—hoping to get a start in their adopted country. The most skilled, however, were professionals, largely from Maine and Canada, made jobless when the forests back home were cut out. The majority were young, in their late teens to early thirties. What attracted them to the job was not simply the chance to earn a good wage

Logging work was heavy, demanding strength, stamina, and heart—grit, gumption, pluck, stick-to-itiveness. John E. Nelligan, a Canadian lumberjack in the 1870s, described his American comrades as "those young giants of the North" and "the finest specimens of manhood I have ever seen." "Healthy men," "manly men," and "he-men," they reveled in their physicality. Health and strength, they declared, were divine gifts. They were proud men, and insults, real or imagined, were not to be taken lightly: keeping the crew's respect demanded instant reprisal. This came with fists or the infliction of "logger's smallpox," the holes left in a loser's chest from being stomped by the victor's hobnailed boots. But where women were concerned, the typical lumberjack was respectful, almost prudish. "No man," Nelligan recalled, "could offend, insult, or molest a woman on the street, no man could even speak lightly of a woman of good reputation without suffering swift and violent justice at the hands of his fellows."[18]

Living in camp was never easy, especially for "greenhorns," those new to the job. The lumberjack arrived with the clothes on his back and a duffel bag stuffed with personal items: an extra woolen shirt, woolen underwear and socks, perhaps a Bible and a family photo, a pencil and writing paper, and tobacco for smoking or chewing. Though the bunkhouse had a wood-burning stove, it was never enough on a frigid night. As a result, Nelligan recalled, "the men were forced to lie exceedingly close together in order to keep warm. They would pull the one big blanket over them and pack themselves together as a housewife packs and ties her spoons, back to breast, all facing in the same direction and covered with the same blanket. When one of the jacks would become tired of lying on one side, he would shout 'Spoon!' and everyone would promptly flop over on the other side, eventually landing in the same compact position as before, but facing in the opposite direction." So that no man would have to use the outside latrine on cold nights, each bunkhouse had a "honey bucket," slang for a makeshift toilet.[19]

The bunkhouse reeked of human waste, sweat, damp socks, and dirty bodies. Camps had no bathing facilities, so, Nelligan noted, "no one had a bath from fall to spring. . . . The men washed their hands, their feet, and their faces with snow." This might have removed some of the crusted dirt, but it did nothing about the lice; men's bodies and clothes crawled with the bloodsucking pests.

Lumberjacks spent hours "reading their shirts," picking the vile insects from the seams, where they hid and laid their eggs. "Seam squirrels" too tough to crush between one's fingers were dropped on a piece of tin with a lit candle beneath it. However, only sustained heat, as with boiling every stitch of clothing in a kettle, could bring temporary relief. A louse-free day was like Christmas and Thanksgiving rolled into one. When a Wisconsin lumberjack saw several camp buildings accidentally burn to the ground, he joked: "Well, we got all the men and horses out. Only two million lives lost!"[20]

The workday began before sunrise. At four o'clock, Cookie awoke the camp by beating a gong and shouting, "Roll-ye-out. Roll-ye-out and hear the little birds sing their praises to God. Damn you, get up!" There were two meals a day, to be eaten in absolute silence. "We *eat* in here, *talk* out there," Cookie would growl at anyone who dared utter a word, pointing to the door. A lumberjack stuffed himself, because he expended lots of energy on the job. Breakfast consisted of unlimited buckwheat cakes, potatoes, steak, fried salt pork, and cold beans, washed down with mugs of steaming coffee "black as death" and sweetened with heaping spoonfuls of brown sugar. For supper, the crew had pea soup "thick as mud," boiled potatoes, roast beef, bread and butter, prune or dried-apple pie, and coffee. Nobody ate between meals, not even Frederick Weyerhaeuser. One day, when "himself" wanted a bite in one of his own camps at an off-hour, Cookie refused, saying, "No, Mr. Weyerhaeuser, you can't have a meal now!" Rules were rules, so the boss had to listen to his stomach growl until dinner.[21]

Lumbering was a highly organized operation; each jack had his designated place and task. *Choppers* were the crew's elite, calm men of keen eye and sound judgment. Teams of choppers cut trees down with axes or two-man crosscut saws. The result could be lethal. As the tree began to crackle and shiver, a chopper would cry "Timber-r-r-r-r!" or "Watch out!" or "Widow-maker!" Widow-makers were just that; men could be instantly crushed if a chopper misjudged where the tree would fall. A crew seldom escaped without at least one accidental death during logging season. When a lumberjack "went west," the custom was to bury him on the spot and hang his boots on the nearest tree as a memorial.[22]

Once a tree was down, *barkers* hacked off the branches and stripped away the bark; they left this waste wood, called slash, on the ground or piled into mounds, an invitation to wildfires. *Buckers* then cut the log into manageable pieces for moving, typically sixteen-foot lengths. That done, *teamsters* loaded the logs onto a giant horse-drawn sled with the aid of a pulley, then set out for the nearest river. Since a white pine log sixteen feet long and twenty-four inches in diameter weighs about 1,870 pounds, it was impossible to drag it over bare ground or through deep snow. The only way to move such a heavy object was over a skid road, a slippery ice road. This consisted of parallel ruts made and

cared for by crews of *swampers,* who drove back and forth all night with a water barrel attached to a sprinkling device. The water froze in the ruts, permitting the sled to glide over the ice.[23]

The skid road ended at a frozen river or a stream that flowed into a river. There the teamsters unloaded the logs on the bank or rolled them onto the ice. Just as a rancher identified his cattle by branding them with

A lumberjack crew skidding logs through the snow. (1885)

MICHIGAN LOG MARKS

A collection of unique log marks. (Date unknown)

a distinctive symbol, lumberjacks used a heavy marking hammer to stamp the butt end of each log with the owner's private mark. There were thousands of these; Minnesota alone had twenty thousand registered log marks. Since there were so many outfits, it required imagination, and a gift for the odd and fanciful, to devise a unique mark. Log marks might be initials, words, pigs' heads, keys, beer kegs, bare feet, dollar signs, stars, skulls and crossbones, bells, teapots, and stickmen hanging on gallows. The logs remained in place until the ice melted and they could be floated downstream to a saw-mill.[24]

Come spring, the lumberjacks went home and the *rivermen* took over. As the ice melted, they began the "spring drive." The logs that had accumulated on the bank during the winter, along with those stored on the frozen river itself, were sent downstream on the swift current. Groups of rivermen rode some of the logs; hence they were called "cowboys on wooden horses." But instead of the cowboy's lariat to catch stray cattle, each riverman had a pole sixteen feet long, tipped with a steel point and a hook, used to keep the logs moving and prevent jams from forming. Whenever a riverman boarded a floating log, he took his life into his hands. If he ran into trouble, his comrades could only watch, unable to save him. Any slipup, however small, likely meant drowning or being struck head-on by a speeding log.

The lumberjacks in charge of the "spring drive" had the most dangerous task of all. (Date unknown)

The most dangerous part of the riverman's job was breaking logjams. Once formed at a river bend or sandbar, a jam became a tangled mass, reaching as high as thirty feet and stretching as far as fifteen miles upriver. As a last resort, a few sticks of dynamite could break the jam, but this method damaged too many logs, and logs were worth money. Usually, the crew boss sent an experienced man to break the jam with an ax. A journalist described such a daredevil in action:

He stripped everything, save his drawers. A strong rope was placed under his arms, and a gang of smart young fellows held the end. The man shook hands with his comrades, and quietly walked out on the logs, axe in hand. . . . The man was quietly walking to what might be his death. At any moment the jam might break of its own accord, and also if he cut the [key] log [the one that held the others in place], unless he instantly got out of the way, he would be crushed by the falling timber.

There was a dead silence while the keen axe was dropped with force and skill on the pine log. Now the notch was nearly half through the log; one or two more blows and a crack was heard. The men got in all the slack of the rope that held the axeman; one more blow and there was a crash like thunder and down came the wall, to all appearances on the axemen.

Like many others, I rushed to help the poor fellow, but to my great joy I saw him safe on the bank, certainly sadly bruised and bleeding from sundry wounds, but safe.[25]

When the logs reached the sawmill, workers sorted them according to their markings, and the *tallyman* credited them to their owners' accounts. Other workers then ran the logs through steam-powered circular saws, rapidly spinning toothed disks, each capable of turning out more than forty thousand board feet a day. Chicago was the most profitable market for lumber from the Great Lakes states. Their white pine built much of the "Windy City," which quickly became the nation's lumber capital. Chicago's dealers sorted the lumber and sent it west by railroad, to the unforested prairie states and to the Great Plains beyond. During the nineteenth century, that lumber went into building towns and cities as far west as Colorado and Utah and as far south as Oklahoma and Texas. Tulsa and Oklahoma City, Fort Worth and Dallas, Denver and Salt Lake City: all grew thanks to the bounty of the Northwoods.[26]

But at what a cost! Given the urge to clear-cut, cash in, and move on, the land was bound to suffer. Waterways became polluted with the runoff of soil from lands laid bare by big-time lumbering. Meanwhile, year by year, the material logging crews discarded—slash, deadwood, decaying plant matter—accumulated on the forest floor. Following nature's normal course, wildfires would have cleansed the Northwoods, preventing the buildup of debris and returning essential nutrients to the soil. However, lumbering waste became kindling for infernos that would destroy trees and human lives on a scale never before seen in America. By 1871, the era of the great fires had begun. And the first to suffer their effects were the residents of a Wisconsin logging town called Peshtigo.

A clear-cutting in Missouri. (1938)

PESHTIGO:
THE NIGHT HELL YAWNED

No pen dipped in liquid fire can begin to describe, can paint the scene. Language, 'in thoughts that breathe and words that burn,' gives but the faintest impression of its horrors.

—Luther Noyes, publisher, *Marinette and Peshtigo Eagle,* 1871

FIRES REMEMBERED AND FORGOTTEN

A spectacular urban fire still lives in American memory. On October 6, 1871, scattered fires broke out in Chicago, the proud metropolis boasting the nickname "Young Giant of the Midwest." Throughout the night, horse-drawn steam pumpers, their alarm bells clanging, sped through the streets. Though firemen put out the obvious blazes, they had not eliminated the threat. Embers smoldered unseen beneath heaps of scorched brick, charred timbers, and other debris. Nevertheless, life was beginning to return to normal for the city's 289,000 residents when the wind began to blow—hard. On the evening of October 8, just after nine o'clock, the embers flared, and fire engulfed nearly all of Chicago.

Legend has it that the Great Chicago Fire began in Catherine O'Leary's cowshed at 137 DeKoven Street, not the most desirable address in a city with its share of slums. Afterward, a song recalled the disaster's origin:

Late one night, when we were all in bed,
Old Mother Leary left a lantern in the shed,

And when the cow kicked it over, she winked
  her eye and said,
"There'll be a HOT time in the old town
  tonight."
FIRE, FIRE, FIRE![1]

A journalist later admitted to inventing the cow story, but it remains a favorite in American popular culture, repeated to this day in school textbooks. It is unknown, however, just where or how the blaze began. What we do know is that those who lived through it never got over the experience. Who could forget the flaming deluge roaring down city streets, consuming everything in its path? *Harper's Weekly* reporter John R. Chapin happened to be in town that fateful night. Awakened by the noise, he described the scene from his hotel window: "Niagara sinks into insignificance before that towering wall of whirling, seething, roaring flame, which swept on, on—devouring the most stately and massive stone buildings as though they had been the cardboard playthings of a child."[2]

Mrs. O'Leary and the cow that caused the fire, according to local stories. (Date unknown)

Author Frank Luzerne, another eyewitness, compared the panic that gripped Chicagoans to the retreat of a defeated army:

The crackling of the fire . . . resembled the regular discharge of musketry by an army corps in retreat; but there were still worse evidences of panic than are usually displayed by a routed army, in the hundreds of people, men, women and children, already fleeing to a place of safety, and bearing upon their shoulders such articles of household use as seemed to them valuable at the moment. They were utterly demoralized, and mingled screams of agony, shouts of alarm, prayers and imprecations, with occasional blows right and left, in a jangling noise of words unknown, and gabble without meaning. Eyes blind with blood, and features wildly distorted with terror, people unclad, half-clad, some wrapped in bed-clothing . . . carrying beds, babies, tables, tubs, carpets, crockery, cradles, almost every conceivable thing of household use, formed the most noticeable features of this terrific route.[3]

Chicago saw nineteenth-century America's costliest urban fire, which claimed no fewer than 300 lives, left more than 100,000 homeless, and consumed 17,500 buildings, from lowly cowsheds to stately banks, elegant mansions, and swanky hotels. But newspapers did not always tell the whole story of the disaster. This is because journalists tend to focus on the "big story," the dramatic event that captures readers' attention, tugs at their heartstrings, and sells papers. Nearly overlooked at the time, and all but forgotten

Most newspapers, like this one, focused on the Chicago fire, as it was the "big story." (1871)

today, was a more catastrophic event; it remains, indeed, the deadliest fire most Americans have never heard of. For at the exact moment flames were engulfing Chicago, a fiery tornado 250 miles to the north obliterated the Wisconsin lumber town of Peshtigo in less than thirty minutes.

A SPECK IN THE NORTHWOODS

Built on the east and west banks of the 136-mile-long Peshtigo River, from which it takes its name, the town is located five miles upstream from where the river flows into Green Bay, a "finger" of Lake Michigan, an Ice Age relic poking into the Wisconsin shoreline. Peshtigo Harbor, on the bay, gave steamboats easy access to the town and to the city of Green Bay, forty miles to the south; Chicago lies at the far southern end of the lake. Initially, fertile soil, cheap land, and clean water attracted pioneers to the area. Lumbermen followed, drawn by the vast expanses of white pine.

Famed author Laura Ingalls Wilder was

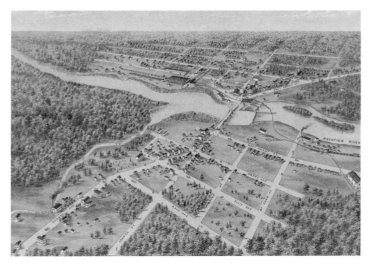

Bird's-eye-view image of Peshtigo before it was ravaged by the fire. (c. 1871)

born in the area four years before the Peshtigo fire. In *Little House in the Big Woods,* her autobiographical children's novel, she recalls the daunting tree world of her childhood:

Once upon a time, sixty years ago, a little girl lived in the Big Woods of Wisconsin, in a little gray house made of logs. The great, dark trees of the Big Woods stood all around the house, and beyond them were other trees and beyond them were more trees. As far as a man could go to the north in a day, or a week, or a whole month, there was nothing but woods. There were no houses. There were no roads. There were no people. There were only trees and the wild animals who made their homes among them. Wolves lived in the Big Woods, and bears, and huge wild cats. Muskrats and mink and otter lived by the streams. Foxes had dens in the hills and deer roamed everywhere.[4]

Peshtigo owed its prosperity to the efforts of a remarkable man. Born in the town of Walton in western New York State, William Butler Ogden was an optimist, supremely confident in his abilities. As he liked to say, "I was born close to a saw mill, was early left an orphan, christened in a millpond, graduated at a log school house, and at 14 fancied I could do any thing I turned my hand to, and that nothing was impossible." It did seem as

William B. Ogden in his old age. (c. 1870)

if Ogden had a golden touch, able to achieve whatever he set his mind to. Good luck he took for granted; he had it in abundance, and assumed he always would. Alert to any chance to make a dollar, he speculated in land, promoted the construction of several railroads, and in 1837 won election as Chicago's first mayor, overseeing the construction of more than a hundred miles of streets.[5]

In 1856, Ogden, by then a multimillion-aire, began looking for opportunities in white pine country. When he first saw the town (then called Clarksville; the name was changed to Peshtigo in 1858, though the origin of the word was, and still is, uncertain), we can imagine, dollar signs flashed before his eyes. The forest began just beyond the last row of houses and ran west and north, seemingly forever. Each winter, no fewer than sixty small-time operators had logging camps in the vicinity. All were located close to streams that fed into the swift-flowing Peshtigo River, ideal for moving logs. Ogden readily adopted the lumber barons' business model. He set up several camps in the forest around Peshtigo. Then he built a sawmill on the Peshtigo River just outside of town, which sent the cut boards to the wooden-ware factory he founded in town. The largest factory of its kind in America, it was five hundred feet long, half as wide, and five stories high. Each day, its workforce turned out items in demand by the rapidly growing na-tion: 45,000 shingles, 5,000 broom handles, 170 washtubs, 50 boxes of clothespins, and 1,500 pails of various sorts. In all, Ogden's businesses employed upward of eight hundred men and boys; apart from the lumberjacks, always seasonal workers, nearly all his employees lived in Peshtigo.[6]

By 1871, Peshtigo had two thousand residents, more or less—likely more, but we cannot know the exact number because scores of people arrived by steamboat every week. Some settled in the town itself, while others went on to clear land for farms in the adjoining settlements of Upper, Middle, and Lower Sugar Bush. Peshtigo also hosted "gandy dancers," laborers from the three camps Ogden set up to build a railroad between the city of Green Bay and the lumber town of Marinette by way of Peshtigo. To house railwaymen on their days off in town, settlers on their way to someplace else, and traveling salesmen, the town had four hotels and boardinghouses boasting clean beds, all-you-can-eat meals, and a host of "modern amenities."

Peshtigo made a good impression on visitors. It seemed to offer everything one might desire. Robinson's meat market also sold oranges and lemons shipped from Chicago, which were considered delicacies, and "ice cream in its season." Harter and Horvath's emporium featured fine clothing, underwear, lace, and embroidery. Peshtigo had a doctor and a practitioner of "painless dentistry." Kelsey and Vierke's drugstore advertised "pure imported wines and liquors for medicinal purposes." It also carried a selection of patent medicines, "miracle drugs" that promised to cure everything from ladies' "monthly discomforts" to bunions, warts, constipation, and "weakness of the nerves." Perry Davis' Painkiller, a blend of "vegetable substances," opium, alcohol, and camphor, was touted as a remedy

Perry Davis' Painkiller was a common multi-use remedy, despite containing ingredients that are illegal or known as toxic today. (Date unknown)

for cramps, heartburn, diarrhea, and "wind in the bowels." Opium, a habit-forming narcotic, was legal and cheap, sold over the counter and by mail order. J. F. Jaques dealt in pianos and organs, symbols of affluence and of their owners' appreciation of life's "finer things." Moreover, the town had a spacious schoolhouse and three churches: Lutheran, Congregational, and Roman Catholic.[7]

Solid citizens turned up their noses at Peshtigo's unsavory elements. On Saturday nights, off-duty railroad crews and lumberjacks from nearby camps came to "paint the town red." They were "powerful thirsty," as no alcohol was allowed on the job, and many sought female companionship. To slake their thirst, there were more than a dozen saloons, which also doubled as gambling dens. To satisfy other needs, they visited brothels staffed by "soiled doves," the polite term for prostitutes. On Sunday mornings, churchgoers scowled at the drunken men reeling along Oconto Avenue, the main drag, or sleeping off hangovers in doorways.

Oddly enough for a place in the midst

of the Northwoods, the one thing Peshtigo lacked was a fire department. When a fire broke out, volunteers rushed to douse it with the Black Hawk, an old-fashioned hand-pumped fire engine that used river water, if the intake hose stretched far enough, or with buckets of well water and pails of sand. All the same, the place was a firetrap. Ogden's sawmill produced so much sawdust that workers could barely dispose of it. Great piles of the stuff accumulated in the mill yard. When these became too high, the excess was dumped into the river, spread over the streets and under the board sidewalks, even piled under house porches. Frugal people filled their mattresses with sawdust; it was clean and soft, and had a pleasant piney scent. To add to the flammables, the storerooms of Ogden's factory were chock-full of barrels of turpentine, paint, varnish, and chemicals for treating wood. Additionally, the smoke-stacks of the factory, sawmill, locomotives, and steamboats belched sparks, which, if the wind was right, became fire hazards.

Peshtigo's luck was about to run out.

THE FIRES OF AUTUMN

Survivors remembered it as a delightful season, that spring of 1871. May and June saw mild, sunny days and starry nights, with rain enough to keep the Peshtigo River high, easily speeding logs down to Ogden's sawmill. But the spring rains passed. As if some commanding unseen power had turned off a faucet, drought fastened its grip on the region. Not a drop of rain fell after July 8, and the summer was a scorcher. Folks grew listless and cranky. "Why the hell don't it rain?" men growled. "You think it'll ever rain again?" The air itself felt menacing; it was so dry, observed a Peshtigo resident, that "if a man touched a match to it, it would burn." This spelled double trouble, for the combination of dryness and heat sucked moisture from everything that held it. Trees and bushes and grass, buildings and barns and rail fences— all became dry as tinder.[8]

Though nobody suspected it just then, the entire region was teetering on the edge of disaster. Many small fires ignited in the woods. We know about them largely thanks to Peter Pernin, the parish priest of Peshtigo and nearby Marinette. Not much is known about the Catholic clergyman, except that he was born in France about 1825. Fortunately, he was a gifted writer, with the ability to describe what he saw and experienced in clear, vivid language. His essay "The Great Peshtigo Fire: An Eyewitness Account" is the fullest eyewitness account of the disaster that befell the town. Written shortly afterward, while the events were still fresh in the author's mind, the essay has been reprinted several times in different formats.[9]

A goodly number of fires, Father Pernin wrote, were due to people's thoughtlessness about the effects of their actions on the environment. Lumberjacks left mounds of slash—leaves, twigs, discarded branches, bark—in and around logging sites. And since gandy dancers aimed to clear land and lay track quickly, because "time is money," they left behind acres of felled trees, their entangled branches forming dense thickets. Hunters, fishermen, and farmers seemed

Wood engraving of Father Peter Pernin. (1890)

oblivious to the danger of wildfire. The priest wrote:

Hunters . . . scour these forests continually, especially in the autumn season, at which time they ascend the streams for trout-fishing, or disperse through the woods deer-stalking. At night they kindle a large fire wherever they may chance to halt, prepare their suppers, then wrapping themselves in their blankets, sleep peacefully, extended on the earth, knowing that the fire will keep at a distance any wild animals that may happen to range through the vicinity during the night. The ensuing morning they depart without taking the precaution of extinguishing the smouldering embers of the fire that has protected and warmed them. Farmers and others act in a similar manner. In this way the woods, particularly in the fall, are gleaming everywhere with fires lighted by man, and which, fed on every side by dry leaves and branches, spread more or less.

Thus far, there had been only surface fires, which did little damage but further dried the vegetation, living and dead. In the mean-time, unseen ground fires smoldered in the humus, the dark organic material that forms on the forest floor when plant and animal material decays. Apparently, nobody was unduly alarmed, because the fires seemed to go out on their own.[10]

By September, townspeople began to pay closer attention. There were many more fires, and they covered a wider area before dying down. Acrid smoke became pervasive, making residents' eyes sting; many also developed hacking coughs similar to those of tuberculosis sufferers. Daytime visibility grew so poor that steamboats on Lake Michigan had to blow their foghorns and navigate by compass. On September 20, Father Pernin and a boy from his congregation were returning from a call at a remote farm. Night was falling. It was silent, save for "the crackling of a tiny tongue of fire that ran along the ground, in and out, among the trunks of the trees, leaving them unscathed but devouring the dry leaves that came in its way, and the swaying of the upper branches of the trees announcing that the wind was rising. . . . We [soon] found ourselves in the center of a circle of fire extending or narrowing, more or less, around us." Fortunately, the youngster's family became alarmed at his failure to return on time. A search party found the pair and led them to safety.[11]

Though this fire died out, relief was only temporary. Saturday, September 23, found Peshtigo in the gravest danger yet. Scattered wildfires erupted around the town, driven by sharp gusts of wind. Father Pernin was amazed at the flames' awesome power and fearsome beauty:

It was a grand sight, the fire that night. It burned to the tops of the tallest trees, enveloped them in a mantle of flames, or, winding itself about them like a huge serpent, crept to their summits, out upon the branches, and wound its huge folds about them. . . . Ever and anon some tall old pine, whose huge trunk had become a column of fire, fell with a thundering crash, filling the air with an ascending cloud of sparks and cinders, whilst above this sheet of flames a dense black cloud of resinous smoke . . . seemed to threaten death and destruction to all below.[12]

But Peshtigo's luck held. By daybreak on Monday, September 25, the wind had died down, and so had the fires. Townspeople breathed a sigh of relief. Cautiously, they began to hope that perhaps the worst was over and what they called the "fire fiend" had "at last come and gone." However, in case it hadn't, Ogden's employees and Peshtigo's homeowners took precautions, placing water barrels at strategic locations around town.[13]

Those precautions came just in the nick of time. Two days later, on September 27, more aggressive wildfires flared up. Terrified residents doused windblown embers with buckets of water and covered their wooden roofs with wet blankets. But, Father Pernin reported, "the wind veered to the south, and cleared away the smoke . . . [so] all is quiet and going on as usual." Nowadays, authorities faced with so unstable a situation would consider ordering the town evacuated. But no one in Peshtigo, at least no one we know about, thought of leaving. A resident explained: "If the wind shifts, we may have to run for it. But if we run, what will happen to all we've built?" They resisted the idea of abandoning the farms, homes, and businesses they'd worked so hard to create.[14]

During the first week in October, wildfires erupted once again. This time, telegraph poles burned and wires melted, cutting Peshtigo off from rapid communication with the outside world. Ominously, Older's Circus had to return to Green Bay when flaming embers ignited several wooden bridges as its wagons tried to cross them. Travelers on the roads at night saw embers glowing red in the darkness. Returning home late one evening, lumberman Isaac Stephenson noticed tongues of flame licking through the woods on both sides of the roadway. Again, the fires

subsided. "We now breathe a little easier," a resident noted, adding, "Peshtigo is yet very far from being out of danger. Unless we have rain soon, God knows how soon a conflagration may sweep the town."[15]

Rain would come, but too late to save Peshtigo. What arrived were gale-force winds and fiery death.

FIRESTORM

Wind was to prove more dangerous than drought. When plants lose moisture, dryness reduces the time it takes for them to ignite. At Peshtigo, at least at first, the saving grace was that many separate fires, severe as any given one might be, could not turn into a full-fledged inferno unless they were driven together by sustained high winds.

Late in the evening of October 7, the leading edges, or fronts, of two enormous air masses—cold air from the north and warm air from the south—collided over Nebraska. Because they had different temperatures and humidity, the fronts did not mix when they met. The cold air, being drier and denser, pushed the moister and lighter warm air upward, creating turbulence—wind—due to the temperature difference between the two air masses. Out on the Nebraska prairies, the resulting winds turned small grass fires into infernos, racing faster "than a galloping horse." By the following evening, farther east, the same high winds blew the Chicago fire onto the pages of history. To the northeast of Chicago, in the Big Woods of Wisconsin, the winds united numerous small wildfires into a raging inferno.

Peshtigo, Sunday, October 8, 1871.

Dawn. Townspeople awoke to the now-familiar smell of burnt vegetation. The air was ominously still, and unusually warm for the season. Respectable folks, as was their custom, dressed in their best clothes and went to services in their respective churches. The not-so-respectable, recovering from Saturday night's "riot and debauch," nursed bruises and hangovers.

Noon. Weird things began to happen.

Ashes fell from the sky "like snow," making eyes sting and tears flow. Forest creatures were seen to act as if moved by some secret knowledge beyond human grasp. Flocks of birds, thousands strong, formed and flew away. Deer came bounding out of the forest, fleeing a menace more lethal than hunters' rifles. Pet cats and dogs left home; they walked down the sawdust-covered streets, now and again looking back, fearful of—what? Father Pernin noticed his pet bird fluttering wildly around its cage, beating its wings against the bars. He also noted people's growing uneasiness. "There seemed," he recalled, "to be a vague fear of some impending though unknown evil haunting the minds of many, nor was I myself entirely free from this unusual feeling."[16]

Night. When the sun went down, a reddish glow appeared way in the distance, above the treetops to the southwest. Around eight-thirty, Father Pernin, fearing the worst, was digging a trench to bury his church's silver candlesticks and other valuables. Looking up, the priest was shocked to see that "the crimson reflection in the western portion of the sky was rapidly increasing in size and in intensity; then . . . I heard plainly, in the midst of the unnatural calm and silence . . . the strange and terrible noise. . . . This sound resembled the confused noise of a number of cars and locomotives approaching a railroad station, or the rumbling of thunder, with the difference that it never ceased, but deepened in intensity each moment more and more."[17]

Around the year 350 BCE, the Greek philosopher Aristotle observed, "Nature abhors a vacuum." By this he meant that empty spaces cannot exist, because they go against the laws of nature. A space must be filled with something, even if that something is invisible, like air. This helps explain wildfire in its most lethal form—the firestorm.

A firestorm is a super wildfire, an elemental force of nature rivaling in destructive power a colossal earthquake, volcanic eruption, tidal wave, hurricane, or tornado. Its basic prin-

ciple is that wind and fire go together. Each feeds the other in a vicious cycle that continues for as long as the fuel lasts: oxygen-rich wind stokes fire, and fire stokes more wind, which stokes more fire, and so on. Indeed, huge fires create their own wind patterns.

When heated air rises, it forms a column. In most cases, if the fire is not large, as with a cookout fire, the column stabilizes a few feet off the ground, rendering it harmless. However, if the fire is massive, the column behaves differently. Rising higher and higher,

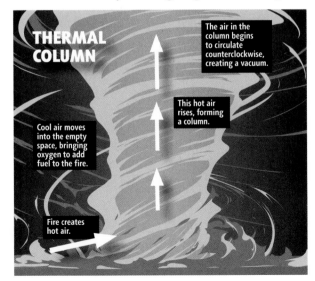

THERMAL COLUMN

The air in the column begins to circulate counterclockwise, creating a vacuum.

This hot air rises, forming a column.

Cool air moves into the empty space, bringing oxygen to add fuel to the fire.

Fire creates hot air.

it starts spinning counterclockwise, just as hurricanes do. This spinning motion creates a partial vacuum at ground level, drawing in cooler air from all directions. The inrushing air acts as a bellows, pumping oxygen into the fire and making the column spin faster and faster, thus drawing in ever more cooler air. When this happens, enormous sheets of flame can be sucked upward by the column, detach from it, and fall back to the ground, splattering "like jelly slopping across the floor." Such a fire can also radiate vast amounts of heat energy, igniting flammable objects even before the flames reach them. Once a firestorm gets going, it takes on a life of its own; nothing human can stop it. It becomes a "hungry beast," gorging on anything flammable, people included, until it starves for lack of fuel or dies when rain deprives it of oxygen. The firestorm that struck Peshtigo was the first ever recorded in North America, but not the last.[18]

The firestorm struck at nine-thirty in the evening, when most townspeople had already gone to bed. Strong winds fanned the lingering wildfires, merging them into a wall of flame five miles wide and half a mile high, advancing at speeds of a hundred miles an hour, the same as the sustained winds of a Category 2 hurricane. Within seconds, crown fires erupted in the forest canopy, each tree igniting its neighbors in a chain reaction, thus feeding the wind and further raising the temperature. Pine sap instantly melted, bubbled, and expanded, causing trees to explode and send flaming splinters in all directions. Upon reaching temperatures of two thousand degrees Fahrenheit, the firestorm was as hot as a crematorium, the chamber in which dead people's bodies are burned.

The first thing Peshtigans saw was the sky ablaze. Immense ribbons of flame whipped overhead, randomly dropping on the town. Afterward, most survivors were at a loss to describe their impressions in mere words. Those who tried used terms like "masses of sheeted flame," "whirling slab of fire," "tornado of fire," and "hurricane of fire." The terrific force of the wind picked up thousand-pound wagons and uprooted giant trees, turning them into missiles. A house was torn from its foundation and hurled through the air "a hundred feet," before it exploded, scattering flaming debris like buckshot.[19]

What followed can serve as a case study in how humans react when abruptly thrust into a life-and-death situation. As in Chicago that night, the moment residents realized what was happening, they instinctively tried to flee. Peshtigans, startled awake by the noise outside, headed for the river, not knowing what they would find when they arrived. Getting there, however, was another matter. It meant running a gauntlet of fire, literally, because the pine sidewalks and houses lining the streets were ablaze. Father Pernin joined the refugees. "People seemed stricken dumb by terror," he wrote. "We all hurried blindly on to our fate." Years ago, as a college professor, I read parts of his essay to a class, city kids who'd never seen any-

Artist Mel Kishner's conception of the terrorized people of Peshtigo fleeing toward the river. (Date unknown)

thing larger than a house fire; it left a deep impression. On September 11, 2001, as I watched TV clips of people fleeing the collapsing buildings of New York's World Trade Center, I couldn't get the priest's words out of my mind.[20]

Wherever one turned, tragedy marked every step of the way. Hundreds of refugees headed across the wooden bridge over the Peshtigo River. Father Pernin watched as "those who lived in the east were hurrying towards the west, and those who dwelt in that west were wildly pushing on to the east so that the bridge was thoroughly encumbered with cattle, vehicles, women, children, and men, all pushing and crushing against each other so as to find an issue from it." A wild melee ensued. Moments after the crowds met, the bridge burst into flames and collapsed, sending everyone tumbling into the frigid water.[21]

Meanwhile, the firestorm engulfed the main part of Peshtigo, on the west bank of the river. A survivor, a Civil War veteran who'd cringed under fierce artillery duels, later described the scene in a report to the Wisconsin State Assembly:

From the ground to hundreds of feet above the tree tops, [it] seemed at times to be a mass of sheeted flame, rolling in tremendous billows, and passing with a continuous roar, loud as the loudest thunder or artillery! Beyond, and ahead of the main volume of flame, [it] seemed as if whole acres of flame would flash out in the air almost instantaneously, lighting up the country with a fierce lurid glare.

In his dash for life, a four-year-old boy was crushed beneath the hooves of runaway horses. A couple rushed down smoke-filled Oconto Avenue, its sawdust paving afire in countless places. Scarcely able to see their hands before their faces in the thick smoke, the husband gripped his wife's arm. Without warning, he tripped and fell, releasing his hold. Fumbling in the darkness, he rose, grabbed her by the waist, and pulled her toward the river. As he turned to say how lucky they were to reach the bank alive, a gust of wind momentarily cleared the smoke. "My God," he yelled. "You're not my wife. I've saved the wrong woman!" He never found his wife or her remains.[22]

Some sacrificed themselves to save loved ones. Days earlier, newlywed J. G. Clemens, a housepainter, had promised his mother-in-law to protect her daughter with his life.

Illustration of the Peshtigo fire. (1871)

He meant it. While racing down a street, flames licking at them, the couple realized they were doomed. Just then, a buckboard pulled up. Clemens lifted his bride aboard, shouting to the stranger to get going—fast. But when she reached to help her man climb up, he shook his head. There was no point stressing the horse more than necessary, he cried. As the driver whipped the animal forward, she turned, only to see Clemens fall. She demanded that the driver stop, but he refused, saying, "If we stop, we'll die." Though she tried to jump out, he grabbed her wrist, holding it until they reached the riverbank.[23]

Most of those who made it to the river were dazed and exhausted. Father Pernin, however, kept his head. The priest was on the bank, pondering what to do next, when again the wind shifted, briefly clearing the smoke. What a scene! "The banks of the river as far as the eye could reach were covered with people standing there, motionless as statues, some with eyes staring, upturned towards heaven, and tongues protruded. The greater number seemed to have no idea of taking any steps to procure their safety, imagining, as many afterwards acknowledged to me, that the end of the world had arrived and that there was nothing for them but silent submission to their fate." But he knew better; after all, God helps those who help themselves. "Without uttering a word," the priest recalled, "I pushed the persons standing on each side of me into the water. One of these sprang back again with a half-smothered cry, murmuring: 'I am wet'; but

immersion in water was better than immersion in fire."[24]

Though standing neck-deep in the river, survivors remained exposed to the firestorm raging overhead. "I saw nothing but flames; houses, trees, and the air itself were on fire," Father Pernin wrote. "Above my head . . . I saw nothing but immense volumes of flames . . . rolling one over the other with stormy violence." To add to the horror, Ogden's woodenware factory erupted with volcanic fury, sending flaming debris—beams, buckets, barrels, shingles, tubs, clothespins—raining down on people's heads. And when Ogden's sawmill blazed up, people had to dodge flaming logs floating downstream. Along with the logs swam a cow with a woman holding on to one of its horns. All the while, gusts of wind blew sheets of flame over the river, forcing people to duck under the frigid water every couple of minutes.[25]

Few of those who failed to make it to the river, or were caught in the open, lived to tell about their ordeal. We can only imagine what they saw and how they felt in their final moments of life. So-called fire balloons, globe-shaped objects ten or more feet across, whirled overhead, fell to the ground, and burst with a loud bang, showering those nearby with a burning substance that stuck to their flesh like glue. There was no telling where one of these glowing horrors might land. When a farmer named Lawrence made it with his wife and four children to the center of a large field nearly half a mile from the forest, they thought themselves safe. With trees blazing all around, they lay flat on the ground, panting but unharmed. Then a fire balloon burst in their midst, leaving only charred bones and ashes. While nobody can say for sure what these things were made of, the best guess is that they were glowing pockets of vaporized pine sap ignited upon contact with oxygen. Survivors of later firestorms occasionally mentioned similar objects.[26]

So intense was the firestorm's radiated heat that some people simply combusted,

burst into flames, even though the fire never touched them. One survivor's account tells how a certain Mrs. Demerau and her husband, a farmer, made it to a clearing. They were sitting on the ground, watching the woods burning around them, when the poor woman shrieked, "Nelson! I'm on fire." No sooner had the words left her mouth than her entire body flamed like a torch. Elsewhere, farmer Phineas Eames was awakened by a bright light shining through his bedroom

A Mel Kishner painting depicting the citizens trapped in outlying areas. (Date unknown)

window. Seeing that "the whole heavens seemed one vast wave of fire," he roused his wife and children, a young boy named Lincoln and a baby girl. In desperation, the family ran toward a clearing, his wife carrying the infant in her arms. Suddenly, what he would describe as a "wave of living fire" engulfed them. The whole family fell to the ground, covered in flames. Eames blacked out. Wakening to the deafening sound of wind, his clothes still smoldering, he said he heard a voice in his head, "distinct and clear," telling him, "Get up; get up, and look for your children." Eames found his wife and daughter, dead. Searching further, he came upon "a little form, roasted to a crisp." Supposing it was Lincoln, he cried out, "Oh, my boy." He later recalled, "I had no desire to live . . . and, in agony of spirit, I prayed to go too. But was not allowed to die."[27]

Women and girls seemed especially susceptible to fire. For the nineteenth-century American woman, long hair worn piled high, knotted into a bun, twisted into braids, or hanging loose was the height of fashion. Yet hair and fire are a wicked combination, as sixteen-year-old Helga Rockstad found. The Peshtigo resident was running toward the river, her waist-length blond hair trailing behind, when lumberjack John Cameron saw her head erupt in flames. The next morning, all that remained on the spot where Helga fell were two nickel garter buckles and a little mound of fine gray ash. What's more, women often have a higher content of fat in their bodies than men. And since fashion also dictated that they wear several layers of clothing, they were well insulated—too well insulated. Once ignited, their clothes acted like a metal tube enclosing a candle, focusing the heat inward. In the case of Mrs. C. R. Towsley of Lower Sugar Bush, "intensely hot human 'fat drippings' caused her body to combust."[28]

As the night wore on, the firestorm surged east and north of Peshtigo. To the east, it leaped to the Door Peninsula on the shore of Green Bay, igniting the settlements of New Franken and Robinsonville and the town of Williamsonville. As it sped north, approaching Marinette on the Michigan border, it came to a chain of low hills. These had been formed by boulders and sand left by the retreating Pleistocene ice sheet thousands of years before. Now they saved human lives. Upon reaching this barrier, the fire swung around both sides of the hills in search of fuel. Weakened by the detour, it continued northward, skirting Marinette and jumping the wide Menominee River into Michigan, where it destroyed several small settlements. Both Marinette and Menominee, its sister town in Michigan, had close calls. A resident of Marinette remembered how "we struggled all night in the blinding smoke and intense heat, not knowing how soon the seething fringes of the fire would close in upon us." Except for the loss of several buildings, the towns survived, and no lives were lost. Meanwhile, at Peshtigo, the firestorm followed its natural life cycle. As it gobbled up the last morsels of the area's fuel supply, the air cooled and the wind slackened. By 3:30 a.m., October 9, it was calm.[29]

Survivors faced challenges, physical and emotional, common to the aftermath of all devastating events. Now the horror took on new dimensions. With the wind gone, the smell of death hung in the air, sharp and nauseating. "The stench rising that morning," recalled survivor James Monahan, "was so powerful that we could not bear it. The smell of burned flesh was so sickening that many of the women, after escaping from the river, fainted." It would be like that until the burial details completed their grisly work.[30]

Startled awake by the roaring firestorm, many had gone into the river wearing only their nightclothes. Afterward, all emerged from the frigid water into the even colder air, the temperature having fallen overnight. His teeth chattering, Father Pernin felt chilled to the bone. Since the sand onshore was still warm, he removed his wet shoes and dug his feet into it, which gave some relief. For many of his companions, however, their hours of immersion brought on hypothermia, a condition that occurs when the body loses so much heat that its temperature falls to a dangerous level, even causing death. What's more, daylight revealed the full extent of their loss. Survivors, stunned and trembling, gathered in tiny groups, asking questions, all the while dreading the answers:

"Have you seen my wife?"

"Have you seen my husband?"

"My children, have you seen them?"

"Has anyone seen my mother?"

As the day wore on, however, they had some consolation: a heavy downpour doused the remaining fires burning across the region.[31]

RECKONINGS

Relief efforts got under way at daybreak, October 10. The first volunteers to reach the stricken town came from Marinette and Menominee. Many were Civil War veterans, no strangers to scenes of violent death. But what they saw at Peshtigo was beyond their experience. It shocked them, unnerved them, left them traumatized.

Strewn about the countryside around Peshtigo were stacks of scorched trees "up-rooted and twisted" by the wind. In one location, the firestorm had melted sand into a sheet of glass. (On July 16, 1945, at Alamogordo, New Mexico, the desert floor around the test site of the first atomic bomb was also turned into green glass by the explosion's heat.) In the "Bushes," the three outlying farm settlements, those who'd sought shelter in their wells had boiled alive, like lobsters thrust into bubbling kettles.[32]

Searchers found human remains in various stages of decomposition scattered in the woods and fields. "For more than a week," wrote lumberman Isaac Stephenson, "we found bodies or parts of bodies. . . . We had collected and interred one hundred and thirty-nine, some of them whole, some merely ghastly fragments. In many cases, however, there was nothing left of human beings other than a streak of light ashes which would scarcely have filled a thimble. In others the bones as well as the flesh had been consumed and only the teeth remained. . . . Sometimes the bodies of the victims lay in groups.

Near the [Ogden] factory ten men were discovered lying on their faces within the space of twelve feet, with their hands covering their eyes," suggesting they died together, all at once. The firestorm also exhibited strange behavior, as with the bodies of a Mrs. Tanner and her two toddlers, a boy and a girl. The children's clothes had been burned off, leaving them naked and scorched, but their silky blond hair was untouched. Elsewhere, there were bodies of victims the fire had not touched; they likely died of shock, heart failure, or suffocation by carbon monoxide, an odorless, colorless, tasteless gas formed during the burning process. Some deaths must have been exceptionally painful. Superheated air can still contain trace amounts of oxygen. Breathing it in burns away the delicate linings of the nostrils, mouth, and throat. Farther down the airway, the lungs are seared so that, in effect, the victim is cooked alive from inside.[33]

Peshtigo was gone. All that remained of the once thriving town was "a seared and blackened ruin" of smoldering rubble and heaps of scorched bricks. As if the firestorm had a freakish sense of humor, it melted metal objects into weird shapes. "The iron tracks of the railroad," Father Pernin noted, "had been twisted and curved into all sorts of shapes. . . . All the rest was a desert the desolation of which was sufficient to draw tears from the eyes of the spectator." The wind had tossed his church bell fifty feet from the ash heap of the building it once graced; "one half was now lying there intact, while the other part had melted and spread over the sand in silvery leaves." Fellow searchers found in the ruins of a hardware store sixty dozen iron axes melted together, and kegs of nails in the same condition. Packets of spoons were fused, stovepipes melted into fist-sized balls, and brightly colored glass plates turned into baseball-sized blobs. A man was found dead, his clothing and body not even singed, but with a pants pocket containing pennies melted together.[34]

Nobody will ever know the exact costs

of the night hell yawned. What history calls the Peshtigo fire was really an inferno that consumed the town and its neighboring settlements, along with eleven smaller Wisconsin and Michigan towns. There was no systematic body count, only estimates based on human remains recovered and accounts by survivors of missing family members. The best guess is that 1,500, possibly 2,500, perished in Peshtigo and the surrounding

The memorial marker in the Peshtigo Fire Cemetery honoring the countless unnamed victims. (2007)

farm settlements, a total at least five times higher than in the Great Chicago Fire. No fewer than 600 residents and visitors died in Peshtigo itself. Today, a mass grave in the cemetery outside the Peshtigo Fire Museum holds the remains of 350 unidentified men, women, and children. Additionally, the deadliest firestorm in American history destroyed 1.28 million acres of prime forestland, an area about twice that of Rhode Island, containing an estimated one billion trees.[35]

The burning of the telegraph line delayed full-scale relief operations. Since the nearest functioning telegraph terminal was in Green Bay, a lake steamer had to carry the news there. That took two days. When the news reached the executive mansion in Madison, the state capital, Governor Lucius Fairchild, a one-armed Civil War hero, was away and unreachable. But his wife, Frances, was at home. The First Lady was a born leader with a commanding presence, and it was said that "all obeyed her" unhesitatingly. Though she lacked any legal authority, Frances Fairchild took charge, issuing orders and dictating telegrams. She sent government clerks to homes in Madison with orders to "bring all the blankets you can"—and warm clothing, medicines, and food. These she sent northeast by railroad to Green Bay. This was a pioneer effort, for government disaster relief was virtually unknown in the America of 1871. Once the furor over the Chicago fire died down in the national press, newspapers finally turned their attention to Peshtigo. Though none of the major ones sent reporters to the stricken area, opting to run rewritten accounts from local Wisconsin papers, their coverage had an impact. Benjamin Franklin Tilton, editor of the *Green Bay Advocate,* was astonished when "food and clothing began to pour [in] . . . first by the carload, and then by the trainload. There came cooked provisions and bread apparently enough to feed the people of the State, until we were obliged to cry 'enough.'" Nevertheless, when aid workers brought supplies to remote farms, it was often too late. In one case, they found a

Governor Lucius Fairchild, pictured with his wife, Frances. (c. 1870)

young girl dead of starvation; she'd been the only member of her family to have survived the firestorm.[36]

Peshtigo recovered slowly and with difficulty. The winter of 1871–1872 was among the coldest on record. Those who chose to remain eked out a shaky existence in hastily constructed huts, surviving on relief supplies. Come spring, when farmers tried to put in a new crop, billions of armyworms, the caterpillar stage of a destructive species of moth, emerged from deep in the soil where the fire hadn't reached. The crawling green hordes stripped the fields bare, so there were no crops in 1872. It was better in 1873, though much of the land around Peshtigo remained a dead zone; decades would pass before it fully recovered its fertility.

Peshtigo's heyday was over. William Butler Ogden gave up on it as a bad investment; he did not rebuild his businesses there, and he never returned. There was still timber left in the Big Woods, but it would not last much longer. By the early twentieth century, the most profitable trees, the white pines, were just about exhausted. After leaving the area burned up and cut out, the big lumber outfits pulled up stakes, shifting their operations westward, to Washington, Oregon, and California. According to World Population Review, Peshtigo has a population of 3,339, not even twice that of 1871. Today, it is a community centered around agriculture, light manufacturing, and retail.

THE HINCKLEY HORROR OF 1894

The great tragedy was that the victims died in vain. Not for many years were the American people ready to do anything much to prevent disasters like that at Peshtigo.

—Stewart Holbrook, "Fire Makes Wind: Wind Makes Fire," 1956

DARK LEGACY

The Peshtigo disaster might have given Americans pause, prompting them to rethink their attitudes toward the environment. Sadly, it barely registered in the national consciousness. The ruined town was, however, remembered in a way none at the time could have imagined or thought fitting. In 1941, as the nation drifted toward entry into World War II, the U.S. military collected any scrap of information it could find about firestorms. By then, the airplane had come into its own as a death-dealing bomber. And so Pentagon planners wanted to learn all they could about Peshtigo and firestorms—how they start, how they behave, and how to keep them going to cause maximum loss of human life and infrastructure damage. Later, those lessons were applied to the firebombing of German and Japanese cities. In July 1943, American and British bombers attacked Hamburg, Germany's chief seaport, with thousands of high-explosive and incendiary bombs, igniting the war's first man-made firestorm and killing more than forty thousand civilians in one night. Military historian Martin Middlebrook's description of the raid, based on multiple survivors' accounts and official fire department reports, sounds eerily like stories from Peshtigo:

Even above the crashing noise of the high-explosive bombs, the people could hear the howling of the [firestorm] "like a devil laughing." . . . [Survivors] all talk of the tremendous force of the hot, dry wind against which even strong men were sometimes unable to struggle. . . . Anything light was immediately whipped away, bursting into flames as it went if it was burnable. Branches were torn off trees; even whole trees were forced over and their roots dragged out of the ground. What appeared to be "bundles of flames" or "walls of fire" sometimes shot out of a burning building and along a street. There were "fiery whirlwinds" which could snatch a person in the street and immediately turn that person into a human torch while other people, only a few yards away, were untouched. The wind was always accompanied by clouds which looked like "a blizzard of red snowflakes" and all survivors remember the shrieking, howling of the storm as it raced through the streets. . . . Most of the bodies were blackened and shriveled to half their normal sizes, like mummies, but others were unburnt, although all their clothes, except their shoes, had disappeared.[1]

The town of Hamburg, Germany, was bombed by Allied Forces during World War II. A man-made firestorm caused vast destruction. (c. 1942–1945)

Dozens of Japanese cities suffered the same fate. In the early hours of March 10,

1945, wave upon wave of B-29 bombers dropped tens of thousands of incendiaries on Tokyo. The resulting firestorm swept the Japanese capital, leaving more than a hundred thousand people dead, a million homeless, and sixteen square miles a wasteland of ashes and twisted metal. Accounts of the aftermath of these raids are as horrific as anything reported from Peshtigo.[2]

Wisconsin did nothing to avert another Peshtigo. Wasteful logging methods continued as long as there was enough white pine to cut profitably. And the state's forests continued to burn, experiencing at least one serious wildfire, though no firestorms, each decade from 1880 to 1910. That half a million acres of prime forestland went up in smoke in any given year was not deemed unusual; a year that saw "only" a hundred thousand acres lost to wildfire was almost regarded as a blessing. How many lost their lives in these fires is unknown, though the number was surely nowhere near the toll in and around Peshtigo.[3]

THE GREAT MINNESOTA FIRE

Neighboring Minnesota had its own Peshtigo experience. Located in Pine County, near the Wisconsin border, the lumber town of Hinckley was home to twelve hundred people, most of them immigrants from Sweden. It was a nice place to live. The *Hinckley Enterprise,* the local paper, boasted in four-inch letters: "HINCKLEY IS A CITY THAT IS *RICH* IN GOOD SCHOOLS AND CHURCHES. ITS PEOPLE ARE BOLD IN ENTERPRISE, FIRM IN PURPOSE, LIBERAL IN SUPPORTING PUBLIC MEASURES, MORAL IN THEIR LIVES, WARM IN THEIR HOSPITALITY, AND EVER GLAD TO HELP YOU CLIMB THE LADDER OF SUCCESS."[4]

The paper had good reason to brag. Gleaming with prosperity, Hinckley had five hotels, three churches, a barbershop, a bookstore, a jewelry shop, a two-story brick schoolhouse, Axel Hanson's Opera Hall, and Lindstrom's Confectionery, which featured a popular new drink called Coca-Cola. Cowan's Drugstore sold everything from bandages to beauty aids. Like Peshtigo's drugstore, Cowan's carried a full line of patent medicines, such as Strong's Headache Killer and Wilson's Electric Belt for Women, at only three dollars a magical cure for "female weakness . . . general debility, heart disease, malaria, liver disease, kidney disease, and constipation."[5]

Hinckley was nicknamed "the Town Built of Wood," and its prosperity rested on the surrounding forest of white pine. Most families had at least one member working for the Brennan Lumber Company, which ran a major logging operation and high-capacity sawmill. As in Peshtigo, too, the mill produced so much sawdust that workers simply dumped it into the millpond, spread it on vacant lots, and heaped it into dozens of thirty-foot-high mounds. In the surrounding forest, lumberjacks, as was their custom, left behind tree stumps and piles of slash—wildfires waiting to happen. Settlers, as usual, set fires to clear land for cultivation. Two railroads, the Eastern Minnesota and the St. Paul & Duluth, had their own depots in town. Though the trains often spewed sparks, the fires they ignited were usually isolated; if they failed to go out on their own, they smoldered, coming to life when the wind picked up, only to die down when it tapered off. A veteran trainman reflected the popular attitude. He was blasé, explaining, "We have had to run through smoke time and time again every year. There have always been more or less forest fires in Minnesota."[6]

The economy of "the Town Built of Wood" relied on the white pine logging industry. (1885)

The year 1894 was different. Beginning in mid-July, prolonged drought and sweltering heat gripped the eastern part of the state. Lumber and debris baked in the heat. Living vegetation lost moisture, turning brown and brittle. At the Brennan sawmill, freshly cut planks were piled in the adjacent lumberyard; it held some 12 million board feet, every inch tinder-dry. Scattered fires flared in the woods, marshes, and foliage beside the railroad tracks. A pall of smoke hung overhead, and some days the sun had an eerie yellowish color. A St. Paul, Minnesota, newspaper saw the writing on the wall, observing, "Unless a heavy rain comes soon, there may be a great loss sustained."[7]

No rain came. Instead, on the afternoon of Saturday, September 1, a stiff breeze blew from the southwest, fanning smoldering embers into open flames. With hot air shooting skyward and cool air rushing in to fill the vacuum at ground level, a firestorm erupted. Over a mile wide, it did not strike Hinckley at first, but overran the villages immediately in its path. Among these was Pokegama, nine miles to the south, where all 179 residents perished within minutes. A traveler remembered how "the waves of fire rolled forward with unimpeded destruction, setting on fire everything burnable a whole mile before itself. . . . The flames came steadily near, long, wiggling like snakes . . . spitting hissing sparkling bunches of fire before itself. And behind the fearsome, rolling wall of fire . . . the cyclone broke down with a so unbelievable strength, so that the ground by the foot of the line of fire was white as the charcoal in the forge under the bellows pressure of air. . . . While these horrors played out, the fire flew rolling, twisting, unceasingly forward towards Hinckley."[8]

Other than the reddening sky and smoke rising in the distance, residents had no warning of the approaching firestorm until it arrived. The effect on Hinckley was as if a torch had been thrown into a gasoline tank. At about five o'clock in the afternoon, the town literally exploded. Panic! "A nameless fear overcame everyone," a survivor wrote, "and a frenzy, indescribable and wild. . . . All reason, all thought appears in some seconds to have abandoned the unfortunate city residents, who now ran like crazy people around each other without a single clear thought upon *which* means of salvation they should seek for their lives." Nevertheless, scores of residents had the presence of mind to flee to a water-filled gravel pit in the center of town; these managed to survive. At least 126 others fled to a swampy patch just outside town. Scarcely had they leaped into the putrid muck when "a sea of fire" engulfed the place, killing everyone. The moment the fire struck, an eyewitness recalled, "there was one piercing cry of mortal anguish, and then all was still, the literal stillness of death itself."[9]

Meanwhile, at the Eastern Minnesota Railroad depot, engineers William Best and Harry Powers hurriedly coupled five coaches of a passenger train and three boxcars of a freight train together. With a locomotive at either end facing opposite directions, they could be moved forward or backward as the engineers desired. Best began to move the train backward when, as expected, he saw hundreds of townspeople rushing to climb aboard. They were in bad shape. Many of the women were barefoot and rumpled, often carrying small children in their arms. "It was at this juncture," Best recalled, "that excited men pushed women and children from the coaches in their mad haste to get in themselves." Seeing this, several brawny railroad workers taught these fellows manners—with their fists.[10]

Though Best waited for as many as possible to board—about five hundred in all—time was running out. It grew incredibly hot. The air shimmered. The paint began to bubble and melt, running off the cars; many of the wooden rail ties were smoldering. As Best backed out of the depot, his last glimpse of Hinckley was heartrending: "Houses were burning so rapidly that one could see bedroom sets and other contents of the rooms. The fire would seem to burn the sides right off the buildings, revealing the contents in the glare. Buildings seemed to melt rather than burn in the fierce glow. We backed rapidly away from this scene of ruin and death . . . [and] saw people running toward the train, and beckoning us to stop. But it was useless to think of it, for they were too far away from us, and I turned my head that I might not see them in their distress." Everyone lucky enough to make it aboard Best's train survived.[11]

Scores of fugitives ran northward, too, along the tracks of the St. Paul & Duluth Railroad. It was hellish. Many were nearly naked, their clothes torn to shreds or smoldering. Every few yards, tongues of flame lashed out from the woods, felling two or three at a time. All of a sudden, the rest, expecting the same fate at any moment, saw a headlight coming toward them. Though engineer James Root had driven his passenger express through dense smoke for forty miles, he had no idea that he was heading into an approaching firestorm. Upon seeing the fugitives, Root

jammed on the brakes in the nick of time. As the train screeched to a stop, a woman holding her two daughters by the hand cried, "For God's sake, will you save us?" While the fugitives clambered aboard, Root decided to reverse direction and make for Skunk Lake, a shallow marsh six miles up the line. Moments later, just as the train began to move, "a great hurricane of fire bore down and struck the train." The heat grew so intense that glass windowpanes melted, allowing flames to lick through the passenger cars. The excruciating heat drove one man out of his mind. Screaming, he leaped out a window, only to vanish into the flames.[12]

John Wesley Blair, an African American porter, kept his head. Blair, said the official report, "stood at his post . . . passing water as coolly and collectedly as if he were on a summer excursion. When the passengers were lying . . . with their faces down, Blair stood up in the midst of the flames playing a fire extinguisher on the women and children whose clothing took fire." All the while the

John Wesley Blair (far right), here pictured with fellow railroad men, was cool and collected as he heroically saved the lives of his passengers. (1894)

porter spoke softly, soothingly, calming them and sustaining their courage. The symbolism of Blair's heroism is important. The 1890s was a time when Jim Crow rode tall in the saddle. Though the Civil War had officially ended slavery, formerly enslaved people and their kin still bore heavy burdens. Soon after emancipation, Southern legislatures passed hundreds of Jim Crow laws. That nickname was inspired by an 1840s minstrel show clown played by a white man in blackface, with bright red lips, dancing to the banjo tune "Jump Jim Crow!" Racists used the Jim Crow character to represent all Blacks as ignorant, cowardly, and shiftless. Blair's behavior, his decency, his commanding presence, gave the lie to such notions.[13]

The train approached Skunk Lake, which was more a marsh than a lake. As it began to cross the Skunk Lake bridge, the wooden planks caught fire and flames leaped through the windows, igniting many of the wicker seats. A boy named Otto turned to his father, asking, "Have we got to die, Papa?" A heavy-set man bolted out of his seat and barged down the aisle, shouting at the top of his voice, "We are all going to heaven together," then collapsed, whimpering.[14]

Root was not ready to go to heaven just yet. Though in great pain, with his hands burned and his face cut by flying glass, the engineer jammed on the brakes, a signal

THE HINCKLEY HORROR OF 1894 • 109

for everyone to get out. Passengers hardly needed encouragement. " '*Skunk Lake! Fly for your lives!*' was now called out through the cars," a survivor wrote, "and quicker than can be described, we all threw ourselves out of the burning train and jumped down into the marsh. . . . This was . . . our saving, although it hung by a hair, for the boundless heat and the dangerous masses of smoke, which immediately after our stepping down into the marsh, began to envelop us, was close to killing many. We . . . buried ourselves in the mud up to the chin and covered the face and head with the wet mass."[15]

Not everyone could exit the train on their own. A man named Albert Speyer became a lifesaver that day. As Speyer raced toward the swamp, he stopped in his tracks, calling to a friend, "Did you not hear a child cry?" The friend heard only panicky screams and cracking fire. Speyer, however, trusted his own ears. He wheeled around, ran back to the train, kicked away burning debris, and entered a car, vanishing amid the smoke and flames. Onlookers gasped, thinking him a goner. However, after a minute or two, Speyer staggered from the car. His hair was singed, and his clothes were reduced to smoldering rags. But he held a bundle in his arms—a little girl wrapped in his coat. "I got her out anyway alive!" he cried triumphantly. It was later learned that relatives had put her aboard the train alone at Duluth, so there was no one to look after her when the fire came. Apparently, nobody interviewed Speyer about his life story, so apart from this heroic deed, nothing is known about this Good Samaritan.[16]

Skunk Lake deserved its name; the people sat for seven hours, chin-deep in its stinking muck, until the firestorm exhausted itself. All survived. Afterward, rescue workers found 418 bodies in and around Hinckley; the remains of others were never found. To add to the horror, the blaze destroyed twelve other area towns and laid waste to 350,000 acres of prime timber.

Communications had dramatically improved since 1871, so Hinckley's fate quickly

Firefighters stand beside a steam fire engine in this image of the Hinckley firehouse taken sometime before the fire of 1894. (Date unknown)

became front-page news. On Tuesday, September 4, reporters from just about every major newspaper in the United States and Canada began arriving by train. Hinckley was the "big story." Suddenly, regional telegraph lines were abuzz with the lurid details and weepy "human interest" stories. "It Was a Hamlet of Horror," shrieked the *Duluth News Tribune.* Not to be outdone, the *Minneapolis Tribune* described waves of fire that "Dance in Ghoulish Glee, Leaving Hundreds of Charred Corpses in Their Wake." Even the sedate *New York Times* titillated readers with an account of how "The Dead Lie in Heaps at Hinckley."[17]

By Wednesday, September 5, massive amounts of aid had begun to pour into the stricken area. A tent city sprang up as a temporary shelter, feeding station, and distribution hub for relief supplies. At the same time, the disaster brought out some of the worst of human nature. The news reports and relief effort attracted hordes of thrill-seeking tourists, who descended on the place by the trainload. As the *Duluth News Tribune* noted, "There was a mad rush by passengers from the cars to see the nine bodies which lay close to the tracks. Prominent among the . . . most persistent in the attempt to gain a view of the blackened and distorted trunks were several mere girls. They got a close view and one of them turned deathly sick and would have fallen but for some helping hands that escorted her back to the chair car. The sight was too horrid for her, as it was for many of the men." However, not everyone came just to sightsee; there were also the disaster vultures. They combed through the wreckage, grabbing anything that attracted their attention to keep or to sell: coins fused together by intense heat, scorched bits of clothing, lumps of glass melted into odd shapes.[18]

Though Hinckley was rebuilt, its best days lay in the past. In time, eastern Minnesota's white pine was exhausted, and since the land was not suited to farming, the town languished. As of 2021, according to World Population Review, Hinckley had 1,942 residents, just 600 more than when the firestorm struck more than a century earlier. Hospitality, food service, and retail are its chief industries. The town's current slogan is "Relax . . . Have Fun!" Each year, the Hinckley Fire Museum, located in a plain wood-frame

Hinckley's Main Street the morning after the fire. (1894)

building, attracts a certain number of curi-
ous vacationers and tour groups willing to
pay the five-dollar admission fee. A monument and mass grave are on Fire Monument
Road.[19]

Tragic as the Peshtigo and Hinckley firestorms were, the public soon lost interest.
Nevertheless, in certain quarters, the fires
helped spur a reexamination of long-held attitudes. But before returning to forests and
wildfires, we must take a detour to explore
what environmental historians have called
"America's war on wildlife" and the crusade
to save our natural heritage.

AMERICA'S WAR ON WILDLIFE

The wild things of this earth are not ours to do with as we please. They have been given to us in trust, and we must account for them to the generations which will come after us to audit our accounts.

—William T. Hornaday, *Our Vanishing Wildlife,* 1913

WAR ON WILDLIFE: BISON

The driving forces in America's war on wildlife were money, military "necessity," women's fashion, and just plain willfulness. Bison and birds, above all the passenger pigeon, were the main victims. Though both existed in such vast numbers as to be thought unlimited, within just a few decades, one was driven to the edge of extinction and the other vanished entirely. Their fate is testimony to humanity's ability to alter the natural world quickly, permanently, and for the worse.

Commonly known as the buffalo, the American bison is native to the Great Plains, a sprawling grassland of 1.3 million square miles, reaching from Canada to Mexico and from the Mississippi River to the foothills of the Rocky Mountains. The buffalo is the largest land animal in North America; a full-grown bull weighs sixteen hundred pounds, stands six feet at the shoulders, and is ten feet long from tip of snout to tip of tail; cows are slightly smaller. In the early 1540s, Spanish explorers described the buffalo as *un animal feo y fiero*—"an animal ugly and fierce."

A social animal, the buffalo roamed the Great Plains in immense herds, some extending from horizon to horizon, grazing on the nutritious grass.

A herd of buffalo on the Great Plains. (c. 1904)

People found themselves at a loss for words to describe the numbers they encountered. In 1794, a trader named Duncan McGillivray spoke in biblical terms of animals "as numerous as the locusts of Egypt." Fifty years later, artist John James Audubon thought it "*impossible to describe or even conceive* the vast multitudes of these animals." In May 1871, five months before the Peshtigo firestorm, Colonel Richard Irving Dodge drove a buckboard near the Arkansas River in southern Kansas.

"The whole country," the colonel wrote, "appeared one mass of buffalo, moving slowly northward." That single herd "was about five days passing a given point, or no less than fifty miles deep. From the top of Pawnee Rock, I could see from six to ten miles in almost every direction. The whole space was covered with buffaloes, looking at a distance like one compact mass." Though we will never know the exact number, in 1929, famed naturalist Ernest Thompson Seton estimated that in 1800 there had been no fewer than 75 million buffalo in North America.[1]

The buffalo was central to the culture of the Plains tribes: Lakota, Cheyenne, Blackfoot, Comanche, Crow, Kiowa, and others. Their songs, dances, and stories celebrated the animal's generosity in offering itself as food for them. Indeed, the animal that the Lakota called *tatanka* was the tribes' staff of life. While they hunted it primarily for food, they relied on it in hundreds of other ways. They said that everything a person needed except drinking water and wood came from *tatanka.* Women fashioned its hide into lodge coverings, blankets, and all manner of clothing, from gloves to moccasins. They twisted its dried muscle fibers into sewing thread; men used the tough fiber for bowstrings. Its coarse hair became rope, its tail a flyswatter; the hollow horns made excellent cups and storage vessels. Hooves were boiled into glue, and bones shaped into needles, awls, knife blades, spearpoints, and skin scrapers. "Buffalo chips," piles of dung, lay everywhere. Even when it rained, chips stayed dry on the inside, making them an ideal all-weather fuel for heating and cooking. Whites said steaks cooked over chip fires had a strong but pleasant "bite." Though Native Americans hunted tens of thousands of buffalo each year, they did not make a serious dent in the herds, as the number of calves easily made up for the losses.

The coming of the white man changed everything. Whites might kill buffalo for no reason other than the thrill of bringing down a large moving target. To pass the time on long train rides, passengers shot the lumbering beasts from open windows. (By 1876, a train called the Transcontinental Express could cover the twenty-nine hundred miles from New York City to San Francisco in just eighty-three hours.) Professional hunters earned good money by shooting buffalo for their tongues, served as delicacies in eastern restaurants, and for their coats, favored for warm robes and blankets. In 1870,

Wood engraving showing buffalo being shot from a passing train. (c. 1872)

a Pennsylvania tannery devised a method of turning buffalo hide into top-grade leather for shoes, furniture, and drive belts, which connected steam engines to factory machinery. Before long, hides were fetching $3.50 apiece, a dollar more than the average factory worker earned for a ten-hour day. As a result, hide hunters slaughtered vast numbers of "stinkers"—slang for buffalo—skinned them, and left the ground littered with their rotting carcasses. Sitting Bull, a Lakota war leader and wise man, was aghast at such callousness. He called the slaughter "a death-wind for my people."[2]

Sitting Bull was right. To open the Great Plains to white settlement, the U.S. Army helped the hunters with free ammunition, information, scouts, and military escorts. When the tribes resisted, the army did not defeat them in open battle, because they knew the country so well and escaped rather than fight against long odds. Instead, commanders launched nighttime cavalry raids on sleeping encampments, shooting people of all ages and sexes, burning food stores, and running off horses, making hunting virtually impossible. Faced with starvation, the tribes yielded and moved to reservations, basically open-air prisons where they subsisted on government handouts. By 1884, the buffalo was tottering on the edge of extinction, with scarcely a thousand scattered survivors where there had once been tens of millions.[3]

That year, a wealthy New Yorker named Theodore Roosevelt visited the North Dakota Badlands. Wherever the future twenty-sixth president of the United States turned, he saw evidence of the recent slaughter. He wrote in *Hunting Trips of a Ranchman* (1885):

The extermination of the buffalo has been a veritable tragedy of the animal world. . . . No sight is more common on the plains than that of a bleached buffalo skull; and their countless numbers attest the abundance of the animal at a time not so very long past. On those portions where the herds made their

A man stands on top
of a mountainous
pile of buffalo skulls.
(c. 1892)

last stand, the carcasses, dried in the clear, high air, or the mouldering skeletons, abound. . . . A ranchman who . . . had made a journey of a thousand miles across Northern Montana, along the Milk River, told me that, to use his own expression, during the whole distance he was never out of sight of a dead buffalo, and never in sight of a live one.[4]

Nevertheless, at this time in his life, Roosevelt thought the slaughter a "blessing." Using racist language, he explained that it "was the only way of solving the Indian question. As long as this large animal . . . existed, the Indians simply could not be kept on reservations, and [so] its disappearance was the only method of forcing them to . . . abandon their savage mode of life." Like so many whites, Roosevelt regarded Native Americans as "savages," because their beliefs and lifestyles differed from those of their supposed racial "betters." In later years, he would go all out to protect the remaining buffalo, as we will see in the next chapter, but he did nothing for First peoples. In fact, Roosevelt said, "I don't go so far as to think that the only good Indians are the dead Indians, but I believe nine out of ten are, and I shouldn't like to inquire too closely into the case of the tenth."[5]

THE END OF THE PASSENGER PIGEON

The "Lord of the Plains" was not the only endangered species—merely the biggest. As the buffalo slaughter reached its peak in the 1880s, the war on birds began in earnest. Americans killed birds for fun, food, and profit. Guns were readily available, sold over the counter in hardware stores to anyone able to pay the price. The 1897 Sears, Roebuck mail-order catalog advertised a wide variety of firearms in the $24.50 to $93.57 price range (between $727 and $2,545 in 2019 dollars). "Shooting" was a favorite pastime, a way to relax and socialize. The activity was considered an American birthright, and no license was required to own a gun or hunt with it. Hunting was justified by the biblical idea that God made mankind master of the natural world. And so, as a naturalist wrote in 1886, the "sport" followed from the notion of "birds as things made to be killed." A shooter agreed, saying, "They're our'n to use"—and, if need be, to use up.[6]

Sport hunters bet on how many birds they could bring down within a set time. A Maine lighthouse keeper described the result of banging away at sandpipers, birds that feed on snails, mussels, and other creatures that live along the shoreline. "They form in flocks and sit on the shore," he wrote. "Gunners come and slaughter them awfully, for it is no trick to fire into a big flock of them and wound a large number. After the gunners have been here, my children bring in many wounded ones, some with broken wings or legs shot off, or eyes shot out."[7]

Market hunters killed for a living. Home-makers, notably in the South, favored rob-ins for pies and stews. The tasty birds were inexpensive—five cents a dozen—and easily caught. Rather than shoot robins in flight, hunters took them at night, while the birds were asleep in their roosts. A man would climb a tree with a flaming torch, blinding the startled birds. He'd then seize one, pull off its head with a twist of the wrist, drop it into a sack, and quickly grab another. Poultry markets displayed bunches of robins hung up with strings through them "like onions." One might also find hanging beside them meadowlarks, blackbirds, sparrows, thrushes, and even the occasional woodpecker. "Egg-ers" specialized in furnishing grocers with the eggs of wild birds. When it came to peli-cans and seagulls, they'd row out to the is-lands where the birds nested. To make sure only fresh eggs were taken, they'd smash all the eggs they found, then return a few days later to collect the newly laid ones.[8]

"Today," naturalist William T. Hornaday wrote in 1889, "nothing that wears hair is too humble to be skinned and worn." Seal, fox, martin, otter, mink: all were used in wom-en's clothing. The same applied to feathers. From the ostrich fans that cooled ancient Egyptian pharaohs to the plumed helmets of Roman centurions and medieval knights, feathers have been used to signify rank and social status. From roughly the 1880s to the 1920s, birds, too, were prized by fashionable European and American ladies. Dubbed "fly-ing gems" for their iridescent feathers, tiny hummingbirds were set into earrings, neck-laces, and brooches. Swans were symbolic of Venus, the Roman goddess of love, beauty, and desire. Their down, the soft, fluffy feath-ers, made ideal powder puffs and trimmings on dresses. Killing so graceful a bird, a natu-ralist noted, was "like shooting an angel."[9]

American hunters killed an estimated five million birds each year to adorn women's hair, hats, and dresses. Centered in New York

City, the trade in fancy feathers was far more profitable per unit than that of white pines. In 1915, for instance, the long, delicate feathers of the snowy egret, native to southern coastal marshes, were worth almost twice their weight in gold. Egret feathers fetched thirty-two dollars an ounce; gold went for nineteen dollars an ounce. The golden yellow wings and iridescent green neck feathers of the greater bird of paradise, imported from the South Pacific island of New Guinea, and snow-white ostrich plumes from Africa were so valuable that dealers charged whatever they pleased; some considered them more desirable than diamonds.[10]

Leading newspapers and magazines hyped feathers as status symbols and their wearers as trendsetters. It was reported that one lady with a taste for the color red "had the whole front of her dress made up of the red breasts of robins." A New York newspaper noted, "Mrs. Stanton Whitney had her gown of unrelieved black looped up with blackbirds; and a winged creature, so dusky that it could have been intended for nothing but a

A woman wearing a "chanticleer" hat adorned with bird feathers. (c. 1912)

crow, reposed among the curls and braids of her hair." The same paper enthused over how "Miss Brady looked extremely well in white, with a whole nest of sparkling, scintillating birds in her hair, which it would have puzzled an ornithologist to classify." To be sure,

Frank M. Chapman of the American Museum of Natural History was astounded by the displays he saw on Manhattan streets. During an afternoon stroll in 1896, he counted 700 hats, of which 542 were decorated with the feathers of forty different species, including bluebirds, red-headed woodpeckers, Baltimore orioles, meadowlarks, and snowy owls. Not all women were content with feathers: *Harper's Bazaar* in 1879 noted that some bonnets "employ butterflies and foliage as well as the feather."[11]

What finally ended the feather trade was not poorly enforced international agreements or such acts of Congress as the Lacey Act of 1900 and the Migratory Bird Treaty Act of 1918, but a change in women's fashions in the 1920s. This was the Jazz Age, when American women won liberties and rights, such as voting in national elections, once thought forever out of reach. Along with rights came "liberated" clothing styles, notably, looser-fitting garments. New hairdos like the bob were shorter, and therefore unsuited for large, overly elaborate hats. As plain, bell-shaped cloche hats became all the rage, the feathered hats of yesteryear vanished, and with them the demand for exotic feathers.[12]

It was different with the passenger pigeon.

John James Audubon, the foremost nineteenth-century painter of birds, did not think the passenger pigeon, a species numbering in the billions, could possibly be driven to extinction, and certainly not within a single human lifetime. He was wrong. The process began in the early 1870s, just as the Great Buffalo Hunt got into full swing and the great forest fires began. The development of a nationwide telegraph system alerted hunters to nesting sites, while the expanding railway network enabled them to reach the huge colonies easily and then send their "bags" quickly to market. The pigeon's juicy flesh was said to make good eating; its fat could be melted down for soap and candles.[13]

"This hunting is easy," an observer wrote. "Women can take part with pleasure since there is neither fatigue nor danger of being wounded." Market hunters set out to kill the most birds in the shortest time. They blasted the airborne flocks with double-barreled shotguns, and snared hundreds at a time in huge nets hung between tall poles set in the ground. To lure birds into a net, hunters used stool pigeons, captured birds, their eyelids sewn shut, fastened to movable sticks to attract attention. Hunters also suffocated birds by burning sulfur beneath their nests,

Illustration of a hunter with feathers in her hat, called *The Woman Behind the Gun*, by Gordon Ross. (c. 1911)

and poisoned them with whiskey-soaked corn.[14]

A typical slaughter took place in May 1871, five months before the Peshtigo firestorm. The "feathered tempest" arrived in Wisconsin, blotting out the sun. For some reason, the flocks favored the Badger State; it had five towns named Pigeon Creek, three Pigeon Lakes, and three Pigeon Rivers. One breeding colony that spring covered much of the southern two-thirds of the state; it was 125 miles long and 6 to 8 miles wide, and held an estimated 136 million birds. News of the colony brought hunters by the hundreds from across the region. They happily laid waste to the colony. Within a few short weeks, the shooters left behind countless broken nests and maggots feeding on dead squabs. Meanwhile, millions of slaughtered adult birds were sent by train to eastern markets, where they sold for as little as fifteen cents a dozen.[15]

It went on like this for the next two decades. But with adult birds dying faster than the next generation could replace them, the passenger pigeon entered an irreversible death spiral. Martha (named after George Washington's wife) was the last of her kind. She died in her cage in the Cincinnati Zoo on September 1, 1914. Years later, the Wisconsin Society for Ornithology dedicated a bronze memorial plaque to the extinct bird. It reads, in part, "This species became extinct through the avarice and thoughtlessness of man."[16]

Obviously, the nation was squandering its natural heritage and, thus, its precious resources—and perhaps also losing its soul in the process. The crisis seemed most severe in the forests. Decades before the rise of the lumber barons, keen observers had noted that the forests, and the wildlife within them, were shrinking at an alarming rate. As early as 1823, novelist James Fenimore Cooper warned that Americans were "felling the forests as if no end could be found to their treasures, nor any limits to their extent." But before anything could be done, Cooper realized, his countrymen had to understand—*truly* understand—that a crisis existed. Doing so required a change in outlook, nothing less than rejecting timeworn attitudes and accepting fresh ideas about nature and mankind's place in it.[17]

VII

CHANGING MINDS

Here is your country. Cherish these natural wonders, cherish the natural resources, cherish the history and romance as a sacred heritage, for your children and your children's children. Do not let selfish men or greedy interests skin your country of its beauty, its riches, or its romance.

—Theodore Roosevelt, twenty-sixth president of the United States

GEORGE PERKINS MARSH

Changing minds became the mission of one of America's greatest though least-known geniuses. George Perkins Marsh (1801–1882) was born in Woodstock, Vermont. His parents let him roam freely as a child, and he spent his days "almost literally in the woods." Though he was the son of a judge and was trained as a lawyer, Marsh's driving passions were philology (the study of languages), scientific literature, and history. An avid reader, Marsh built a personal library of over twelve thou-

sand volumes, and taught himself twenty languages so he could read them. Entering politics, he served two terms as a congressman from Vermont, then became a professor of English at Columbia University in New York. In 1861, President Abraham Lincoln named Marsh U.S. minister to the newly formed Kingdom of Italy, a post he held until his death.[1]

Whenever possible, the diplomat took breaks from his official duties to travel through the lands bordering the Mediterranean Sea. Those trips were eye-openers. According to his treasured books, the

ico and Peru, yet it, too, collapsed. Why? Historians blamed the standard villains: internal political disputes and needless foreign wars, which wasted lives, corrupted morals, and devoured wealth. During his tours, however, Marsh noticed something else—something these places had in common. Once heavily forested, all had been stripped bare and the majority of their people impoverished. The underlying cause, he decided, was "man's ignorant disregard for the laws of nature."[2]

Marsh may well have been the first American to raise the alarm in scientific terms about the long-term impact of man's activities on the environment. In 1864, at the height of the Civil War, he presented his findings in book form. *Man and Nature; or, Physical Geography as Modified by Human Action* became an instant sensation, going through multiple printings in the United States and England within a year. The reason for the book's success was that it was far more than a scholarly study of deforestation. It made readers think, for the author advanced a brand-new way of

Portrait of George Perkins Marsh. (c. 1850)

ancient civilizations of Greece and Rome, Egypt and Syria, Palestine and North Africa, though once prosperous and glorious, had fallen into decay. Likewise, in modern times, the Spanish Empire had ruled gold-rich Mex-

viewing nature. Marsh's big idea, as the title suggests, is that human action modifies—changes—the environment in fundamental ways. He also questioned an age-old belief grounded in the Bible. As we have seen in chapter 2, the book of Genesis teaches that God made the world for mankind. Having been created in the divine image, humans were supposedly separate from, and above, the natural order. It followed, therefore, that the Almighty had given His chosen creatures license to conquer and use "wild nature" as they saw fit.

Marsh's book appeared five years after Charles Darwin's *On the Origin of Species,* which set forth the theory of evolution through natural selection. Marsh mentioned this important work several times in his own book, but it did not affect his thinking in any major way. Instead, Marsh focused on man's impact on the natural world. The author asked readers to think about "whether man is of nature or above her." Though Marsh did not answer the question directly, *Man and Nature* explains that all life is part of an interconnected web, and that changes in one part of the system affect other parts. "All nature," the author declared, "is linked together by invisible bonds, and every organic creature, however low, however feeble, however dependent, is necessary to the well-being of some other among the myriad forms of life." Take the lowly mosquito, a pest if there ever was one. It, too, plays an essential role, because it feeds trout, which also eat the parasitic insects that destroy the eggs of salmon, which people harvest for food.[3]

Marsh insisted that because humanity is able to change the environment, it is a force of nature in its own right—a harmful force. "Man," he declared, "is everywhere a disturbing agent. Wherever he plants his foot, the harmonies of nature are turned to discords. . . . Of all organic beings, man alone is to be regarded as essentially a destructive power." Owing to human vanity, greed, and ignorance, "the earth is fast becoming an unfit home" for mankind. Indeed, the human species was easily its own worst enemy. Left unchecked, its excesses were bound to bring about "the depravation, barbarism, and perhaps even extinction of [our] species."[4]

In Marsh's view, Americans' worst offense was their reckless attack on forests. By destroying woodlands, they were courting disaster. Mother Nature is bountiful, yet she is also unforgiving; it may take a long time, but she always "avenges herself upon the intruder" who abuses her generosity. Abusing forests, Marsh continued, severed the delicate strands that hold the web of life together. The results are far-reaching. Loss of tree cover reduces evaporation, thus decreasing rainfall in the affected area. The "well-wooded and humid hills" dry out, and wind carries loose soil away, reducing fertility. When it does rain, the land cannot absorb the water, resulting in flooding, which leaches nutrients from the remaining soil, further decreasing fertility and crop yields, in turn leading to poverty and famine. What's more, summers in deforested areas tend to be hotter and drier, increasing the frequency and severity of wildfires.[5]

Even so, Marsh thought, there was hope. As nations went, the United States was very young; its natural resources, though depleted, were still immense. The author urged his countrymen to learn from the errors of the past: "Let us be wise in time, and profit from the errors of our older brethren!" *Man and Nature* was like a pebble cast into a still pond; its "ripples" stimulated discussion, changed minds, and motivated reformers.[6]

JOHN MUIR

Not all reformers thought alike. While adopting Marsh's main ideas, they came at the problem from different angles. John Muir (1838–1914) was born in Scotland, one of eight children. His family immigrated to Wisconsin when he was eleven years old. Rebelling against his strict Protestant upbringing, he left home at the age of twenty to make his way in the world. That was not easy: the young man tried his hand at various

Portrait of John Muir. (c. 1902)

occupations, among them farming, sheep-herding, and managing a sawmill, all without satisfaction or success. The problem, Muir came to realize, ran deeper than earning a living. "I was tormented with soul hunger," he recalled years later. "I was *on* the world. But was I *in* it?"[7]

Muir became a vagabond, seeking, as we say, to "find himself." One thing was certain, however: he wanted nothing to do with violence. So, during the Civil War, he avoided being drafted into the Union Army by fleeing to Canada. There he lived as a fugitive, roaming the forest north of Lake Huron, refusing to contact family and friends for fear of being exposed as a draft dodger. Nor did Muir care for Black people, for whose freedom the Union side was fighting. While he

CHANGING MINDS • **129**

described some Black people snobbishly and condescendingly as "well trained" and "extremely polite," he held strong racist views, regarding the majority as lazy. He wrote that "one energetic white man, working with a will, could easily pick as much cotton." This was nonsense. Muir had never picked cotton under the blazing sun, and he had never seen any other white people doing so, either.[8]

In 1868, Muir wound up in California. At first, he despised the Golden State. Already, enormous tracts of land had been spoiled by human activity. Forests were being clear-cut and meadows plowed under without regard to the ecological damage. Gold miners used fire to clear wildland and aid prospecting; the more plant cover they destroyed, the easier it was to find gold-bearing outcrops. In the mountains, prospectors' use of high-pressure water hoses was turning slopes into muddy rubble, and the runoff polluted streams. Because of logging, Muir wrote, the San Joaquin Valley, today among the world's most productive agricultural areas, "wears a weary, dusty aspect, as if it were a traveler new-arrived from a wasting journey." Railroads were ruinous. "Every train rolls on through dismal smoke and barbarous melancholy ruins. . . . The sky is black and the ground is black, and on either side, there is a continuous border of black stumps and logs and blasted trees appealing to heaven as if still half alive. . . . I saw six fires started by sparks from a locomotive within a distance of three miles."[9]

Eventually, Muir made his way into the Sierra Nevada, a mountain range running along the eastern edge of California. Paradise! In Yosemite Valley, carved by Pleistocene glaciers, the pure air perfumed by pine and cedar, the wildlife, the soaring granite cliffs, and the thundering waterfalls all delighted him. Muir built a one-room cabin and lived in it on and off from 1868 to 1874. Unlike America's original European settlers, who detested wilderness, he reveled in it; lying alone at night was like being surrounded by friends, for "every leaf seems to speak." Being in "God's wilderness" was akin to a religious experience, as Muir felt himself, spiritually and physically, becoming one with nature. "You cannot feel yourself," he wrote. "Presently you lose consciousness of your own separate existence; you blend with the landscape, and become part and parcel of nature." Later in life, Muir would return to Yosemite for shorter stays, to unwind and reconnect with nature.[10]

Yosemite's only drawback, Muir felt, was the Native American inhabitants he came across. They disgusted him. He saw them as "dirty and unclean." Indeed, "a strangely dirty and irregular life these dark-eyed, dark-haired, half-happy savages lead in this clean wilderness." Muir cringed at the sight of Native American women, for he thought them "clots of filth" compared to the wild animals. Of one woman he wrote, "Her dress was calico rags, far from clean. In every way she seemed sadly unlike Nature's neat well-dressed animals, though living like them

on the bounty of the wilderness." Muir has been romanticized as a lover of nature, but he held deeply racist attitudes about First peoples, who were the original stewards of the land.[11]

Above all, Muir felt himself kin to the forest. The man loved trees as deeply as any human ever had. "American forests! The glory of the world!" he gushed. "The forests of America, however slighted by man, must have been a great delight to God; for they were the best he ever planted. . . . For many a century after the ice-ploughs were melted, nature fed them and dressed them every day; working like a man, a loving, devoted, painstaking gardener; fingering every leaf and flower and mossy furrowed bole; bending, trimming, modeling, balancing, painting them with the loveliest colors . . . and ever making them more beautiful as the years rolled by." Muir never acknowledged that it was only white Americans who had slighted the land.[12]

During his time in Yosemite, Muir

thought deeply about mankind's place in nature. Like George Perkins Marsh, he came to believe that living beings are interconnected, and that harming one inevitably harms others. But unlike the scholarly Marsh, who thought in scientific and historical terms, Muir focused on rights and the human spirit. For him, Mother Nature played no favorites; all living beings have as much right to live and thrive as people do. The tragedy was that spiritual "dis-ease," a gnawing unease brought on by the stress of city living and the pursuit of the almighty dollar, blinded so many Americans to the source of true happiness.[13]

Muir took to heart Jesus's saying in Matthew 4:4: "Man shall not live by bread alone." In other words, material things—inanimate, spiritless objects—are never enough for a healthy life; people need beauty as much as bread. Muir used emotional, almost biblical, language to urge Americans to turn to wilderness as medicine for the soul. Beset by "the stupefying effects of the vice of over-industry and the deadly apathy of luxury," he wrote, "tired, nerve-shaken, over-civilized people" must return to nature "to get rid of rust and disease." Let them go to the forests, "God's first temples," and there "touch nerves with Mother Earth." For in "God's wildness is the hope of the world, where the galling harness of civilization drops off, and wounds heal."[14]

Painting of Yosemite Valley. (c. 1871)

Muir became an activist, spreading his message through speeches, articles, and books. A start had already been made; in 1872, Congress established Yellowstone National Park, the model for all others in the world. Located in Wyoming, Montana, and Idaho, it was officially designated "a public park or pleasuring ground for the benefit and enjoyment of the people." Muir did not think that one "pleasuring ground" was enough. As a result of a lobbying campaign by him and several influential friends, in 1890 an act of Congress made Yosemite America's second national park, and also the first federal land ever set aside explicitly for forest protection. In 1892, Muir took the lead in founding, and became the first president of, the Sierra Club. Based in California, the Sierra Club remains dedicated to raising public awareness of the need to preserve our natural heritage.[15]

The activist had faith in the federal government—more faith than many Americans do today. Muir believed that its power, if wisely and morally directed, was an instrument for good. In an 1897 article for the *Atlantic Monthly,* a leading magazine for "genteel" folk, he wrote, "Any fool can destroy trees. They cannot run away; and if they could, they would still be destroyed—chased and hunted down as long as fun or a dollar could be got out of [them]. . . . Through all the wonderful and eventful centuries since Christ's time—and long before that—God has cared for these trees, saved them . . . but He cannot save them from fools—only Uncle Sam can do that."[16]

Muir called himself a "preservationist." A certain amount of timber, he recognized, must be cut "for every right use"; that was just common sense. Preservation, however, referred to keeping great swaths of unspoiled natural environments in their original state, just as God made them, so the "dis-eased" could reconnect with nature. Nevertheless, that was asking a lot at a time when so many believed that "the business of America is business," and that Uncle Sam should interfere as little as possible with private initia-tive.[17]

GIFFORD AND THEODORE

Others saw a very different role for government. To them, the question was twofold: How to use federal power to promote the nation's economic progress in the here and now? And how to do so while saving wilderness for the long-term profit and enjoyment of future generations? Their answer was not Muir-style preservation, but "conservation," keeping as much wilderness as possible from abuse and exploitation, while using it to create economic value. In short, conservationists wanted to use the nation's natural heritage, but use it wisely. Chief among these was Gifford Pinchot (1865–1946), a.k.a. the father of the conservation movement.[18]

Though the United States had no titled nobility, Pinchot was an aristocrat, born to wealth and privilege. His grandfather Cyrille, the founder of the family's fortune, was a timber baron who'd clear-cut forests in Pennsylvania and New York. Cyrille's son, James, struck out on his own, becoming a leading importer and manufacturer of fine wallpapers to beautify the homes of the nation's elite. A sensitive man, James was troubled by what he described as his father's "sins" against the environment. Because of

Gifford Pinchot, the father of the conservation movement. (c. 1914)

men like Cyrille, he explained, the forest that had once been home to the passenger pigeon, deer, and other animals "has largely disappeared." James taught his eldest son, Gifford, that the Pinchots were bound by what the French call *noblesse oblige,* or "nobility obligates," the belief that society's "best elements" have a duty to serve the public good. Without a doubt, James felt, God had charged people like his family with higher purposes than making money. Business was fine, in its place. However, James would add, "no man can make his life what it ought to be by living it merely on a business basis. There are things higher than Business."[19]

The boy spent countless hours wandering in the woods around Grey Towers, his grandfather's estate near Milford, Pennsylvania. "I loved the woods and everything about them," he recalled. There he learned to catch brook trout and painted turtles. There, too, it became his "firm intention to become a naturalist." To foster his interests, when Gifford turned seventeen, his parents gave him

a copy of George Perkins Marsh's *Man and Nature.* He took the book to heart; not only did it form the framework of his view of the natural world, but it fit neatly into his father's teaching about *noblesse oblige.*[20]

Gifford grew into a six-foot-two-inch noodle of a man, long-legged and long-armed, with a thin face, blue eyes, and a high-pitched voice. An "odd bird," he slept on the floor of his room and, in the morning, had his valet throw cold water in his face. When he was twenty and about to leave for Yale University, his father asked him an "amazing question for that day and generation": How would Gifford like to become a forester? As yet, not a single American had chosen forestry as a profession. "I had no more conception of what it meant to be a forester than the man in the moon," he wrote. "But at least a forester worked in the woods and with the woods—and I loved the woods and everything about them. . . . My Father's suggestion settled the question in favor of forestry."[21]

Because American universities had no

programs in forestry when Pinchot graduated from Yale in 1889, he enrolled in the National School of Forestry in Nancy, France. Having cut down most of their own forests in centuries past, Europeans, determined to save the remainder, set up specialized schools to study and teach about their care and use. France led the way. Unlike Americans, the French rigidly controlled their forests. Government-certified foresters, thoroughly trained professionals, treated trees as a crop, deciding which and how many could be "harvested" annually. Accordingly, France's forests were almost like formal gardens, "divided at regular intervals by perfectly straight paths and roads at right angles to each other." People from nearby villages were allowed to take away every scrap of deadwood, every fallen branch "down to the size of a pencil," which they could use themselves or sell for firewood. Fires in these managed forests were rare, and never erupted into firestorms.[22]

On returning to the United States in Oc-

tober 1890, Pinchot set up shop as a "consulting forester," a job title he invented for himself. Before long, wealthy businessmen, among them longtime family friends, began hiring him to manage their private forests. One was railroad tycoon George W. Vanderbilt, owner of Biltmore, an immense estate in North Carolina. Disciplined and businesslike, Pinchot had no interest in forests as refuges for spiritual renewal. In a none-too-subtle jab at John Muir, he called the "mere preservation" of beauty "sentimental nonsense." In Pinchot's view, "Forestry is Tree Farming. . . . To grow trees as a crop is Forestry"—nothing less and nothing more. However, two key questions demanded answers. First: How best to use natural resources such as forests without destroying them? And second: Who should benefit from nature's bounty?[23]

Pinchot did not think big business was serving the nation well. Powerful corporations called trusts controlled major sectors of the economy: railroads, banks, metals, oil, timber. These he branded "special interests," a term coined in the 1890s to highlight the greed and wastefulness of the few. Accountable only to their boards of directors and stockholders, the titans of industry threatened to undermine and, Pinchot feared, ultimately overthrow democracy by turning their economic power into political power by corrupting Congress, state legislatures, and courts. The result would be oligarchy, the public-be-damned rule of small, selfish groups for their own profit and pleasure.

For the forester, therefore, conservation went beyond safeguarding natural resources of economic value; it was vital to preserving democracy and liberty. Pinchot wrote:

> The central thing for which Conservation stands is to make this country the best possible place to live in, both for us and our descendants. It stands against the waste of the natural resources which cannot be renewed. . . . It believes in prudence and foresight instead of reckless blindness . . . and it demands the complete and orderly development of all our resources for the benefit of all the people, instead of the . . . exploitation of them for the benefit of a few. . . . Conservation . . . holds that the people have not only the right, but the duty to control the use of the natural resources, which are the great sources of prosperity. And it regards the absorption of these resources by the special interests, unless their operations are under effective public control, as a moral wrong. Conservation is the application of common-sense . . . for the common good.[24]

America's forests were Pinchot's main concern. "What," he asked, "will happen when the forests fail?" With reckless lumbermen and wildfires doing massive damage, the outlook seemed grim. He worried that the tragedies Marsh had described in *Man and Nature* would repeat themselves in his own country: soil erosion, polluted streams, floods, droughts, fertile lands turned into man-made deserts. Likewise, wood-dependent industries such as building, mining, railroads, and shipping would crumble with the onset of a "timber famine," throwing millions out of work. Time was short, Pinchot warned, for "the forests have already begun to fail, as the direct result of the suicidal policy of forest destruction which the people of the United States have allowed themselves to pursue."[25]

Pinchot's arguments attracted a following. In 1898, the thirty-three-year-old was offered a government position: chief of the Division of Forestry. The impressive title implied that this agency supervised the nation's forest reserves. It did not. Created seven years earlier by the Forest Reserve Act of 1891, the reserves had been carved out of the public domain and withdrawn from sale and settlement. The aim was not to protect forests so much as watersheds, areas that drain into rivers. Under the act, Presidents Harrison, Cleveland, and McKinley had placed 50 mil-

lion acres of forestland in the reserves. By some bureaucratic idiocy, the reserves were under the Department of the Interior, which managed federal properties but employed no foresters. The Division of Forestry was a tiny agency within the Department of Agriculture, but it had no authority over the forest reserves. The only job of its dozen clerks was to gather statistics about forests and handle inquiries from the public. Pinchot, however, was hardly the sort of person to sit still and accept things as they were. On taking charge, he lobbied Congress to increase his division's budget and expand its workforce, but that was it: he could not go any further. What he needed was someone with "pull," a person at the pinnacle of power who could get things done. Luckily, his talent for networking took him into the orbit of a human dynamo named Theodore Roosevelt (1858–1919).[26]

In 1897, Pinchot joined the New York–based Boone and Crockett Club, named for frontiersmen Daniel Boone and Davy

Theodore Roosevelt, in his late twenties, wearing his hunting gear. (c. 1885)

Crockett. Founded in 1887 by Roosevelt, who was its first president, the club appealed to prominent people (men only) in business, politics, science, and the military; famed Civil War generals Philip Sheridan and William Tecumseh Sherman were charter members. At first, the club aimed to preserve big game—moose, elk, mountain lions, grizzly bears—for hunting. Like "TR," as friends called him, club members were keen hunters, though not, they claimed, "game butchers," who killed for the thrill of taking a life. According to TR, the true hunter was a sportsman who savored the total wilderness experience. Such a man—a man like himself—felt "the joy of the horse well ridden and the rifle well held; for him the long days of toil and hardship, resolutely endured, and crowned at the end with triumph." Due largely to the club's efforts and those of its ally, the American Bison Society, several dozen of the few remaining buffalo were sent to the Bronx Zoo, bred, and relocated to protected sites in Oklahoma, Montana, Nebraska, and South Dakota. Their descendants are the buffalo today's tourists see in Yellowstone National Park. The club steadily expanded its mission to protecting other endangered species, forests, and historic and scenic places.[27]

Pinchot's timing was perfect; he befriended TR at just the right moment in his political career. The New Yorker had already been a rancher and cowboy in the Dakota Badlands, where he saw the results of the buffalo slaughter. In 1898, he burst onto the national scene, a man sizzling with energy. Capitalizing on his fame as a hero of the Spanish-American War, in which he'd led a cavalry unit called the Rough Riders, Roosevelt returned home to be elected governor of New York that fall. From there, he went on to run as William McKinley's vice president on the Republican ticket, and after McKinley's assassination in 1901, Roosevelt became the twenty-sixth president of the United States.

TR and Pinchot were kindred spirits. Brash and self-assured, neither was shy about his athletic prowess. During TR's brief residence in the governor's mansion in Albany, the forester had an open invitation to visit. Their private meetings were often more like good-natured brawls than polite chats over afternoon tea. Stripped to the waist, they'd wrestle on the ornate carpets; the stocky TR

always got the better of his lanky opponent. But when it came to boxing, the long-armed Pinchot had the advantage. After one bout, he boasted, "I had the honor of knocking the future President of the United States off his very solid pins." Later, TR and "Giff," each packing a Colt six-shooter, would give the president's Secret Service detail the slip

President Theodore Roosevelt (left) and Chief Forester Gifford Pinchot on a river steamer in Mississippi. (c. 1907)

to go skinny-dipping in the Potomac River. After one swim, Pinchot returned home wet and scruffy. As he went up to his room, Mary McCadden, his childhood nurse and housekeeper, took one look and snapped, "Drenched! You've been out with the President!"[28]

When it came to the environment, Pinchot and the president dreamed the same dreams. Both had absorbed the lessons of Marsh's *Man and Nature.* TR was also a nature enthusiast. His father, Theodore Sr., had been a founder of the American Museum of Natural History, and as a boy, TR studied birds with a passion. Moreover, he was a respected naturalist in his own right. Leading naturalists, whom TR often invited to the White House, dedicated their books to him. They regarded him as an authority on North American mammals; out of respect, a newly discovered elk—*Cervus roosevelti*—was named in his honor. A lifelong birdwatcher, TR gleefully reported his sightings to ornithologist Frank M. Chapman. In 1907, the president claimed to have seen two, possibly three, passenger pigeons! If so, these were among the last survivors of their kind in the wild.[29]

While Gifford Pinchot was the father of the conservation movement, Theodore Roosevelt was the conservationist president. Part of the credit for this must go to Pinchot's rival, John Muir. The president and the preservationist were not close friends, but they were acquaintances. Though Muir did not know much about birds, which disappointed TR, his knowledge of trees, plants, and glaciers more than made up for this lack. In May 1903, Muir invited TR on a four-day camping trip in Yosemite National Park. The president's servants laid a pile of woolen blankets on the ground for him to sleep on, then went away, leaving the two men alone. Muir simply put down tree branches and wrapped himself in a canvas sheet. TR was enchanted. "The first night was clear," he recalled, "and we lay down in the darkening aisles of the great Sequoia grove. The majestic trunks, beautiful in color and in symmetry, rose round us like the pillars of a mightier cathedral than ever was conceived even by the fervor of the Middle Ages." Another night, while sitting around the campfire before turning in, Muir pressed his guest to add Yosemite Valley to the national parks. It was an easy sell; indeed, Muir got more than he asked for.[30]

Not only did TR enlarge Yosemite National Park, he went on to sign legislation establishing five more national parks: Crater Lake, Oregon; Wind Cave, South Dakota; Sullys Hill, North Dakota; Mesa Verde, Colorado; and Platt, Oklahoma. The only drawback was that, in the effort to protect wilderness, Native Americans were seen as interlopers. Of course, this was ridiculous; Native Americans had lived on these newly created parklands for thousands of years. Nonetheless, between the 1870s and 1930s, they were expelled, some might say "ethnically cleansed," from Yellowstone, Yosemite, and Glacier National Park, which was created by Congress in 1910, after TR left office.[31]

President Roosevelt made his first move to protect wildlife in 1903, after Frank Chapman told him about Pelican Island, a speck

President Theodore Roosevelt (left) and John Muir on Glacier Point at Yosemite. (c. 1903)

of land in Florida's Indian River. Plume hunters were ravaging the island's colonies of pelicans, egrets, and other waterbirds. Outraged, the bird-loving president asked an aide, "Is there a law that will prevent me from declaring Pelican Island a Federal Bird

Reservation?" Told that there was not, and that the island was actually federal property, TR snapped, "Very well then. I so declare it." Roosevelt would create fifty-one more bird refuges, plus four national game preserves, areas where wild animals could not be hunted, or hunted only in a controlled way for sport and to keep their numbers in line with the available food. The president also cajoled Congress into passing the Antiquities Act of 1906, to save "historic landmarks, historic and prehistoric structures, and other objects of historic or scientific interest." These sites included the Grand Canyon, Arizona; Chaco Canyon, New Mexico; the Petrified Forest, Arizona; and Devils Tower, Wyoming.[32]

The forests were never far from TR's thoughts. Like Pinchot, he was coldly practical, thinking forests should be used as resources, not as refuges for the spiritually "dis-eased." Whether he wholly believed this or not is an open question; personally, TR found nothing more restorative than a time-out in the forest, hunting or bird-watching.

Pelican Island, the country's first national wildlife refuge. (c. 1905)

But the president, advised and prodded by the forester, made his priorities clear in his first State of the Union message, in 1901. "The fundamental idea of forestry," he told Congress, "is the perpetuation of the forests for use. Forest protection is not an end in itself; it is a means to increase and sustain the resources of our country and the industries which depend on them. The preservation of our forests is an imperative *business* necessity." Accordingly, TR set aside by executive order 150 million acres of forestland to be managed for purposes such as timber production, water and wildlife protection, grazing, and outdoor recreation. For the right to use the forest reserves, grazers and lumbermen had to pay annual fees to the government.[33]

But Pinchot was still frustrated. So long as the forests in the public domain were under the control of the Interior Department, and the Division of Forestry part of the Agriculture Department, he was powerless to bring about the changes he thought essential. The president understood. In 1905, he proposed, and Congress agreed, to transfer the forest reserves to the U.S. Department of Agriculture and rename Pinchot's division the Forest Service.

The new agency's mission was (and is) to maintain healthy and productive forests and grasslands for use by present and future generations. In 1907, to win broad popular support by making the conservation cause more personal, the forest reserves were renamed "national forests." Pinchot was finally able to put his ideas into effect. Roosevelt declared that Americans owed the forester a debt of gratitude. "Gifford Pinchot," TR wrote in his autobiography, "is the man to whom the nation owes much for what has been accomplished as regards to the preservation of the natural resources of our country. He led, and indeed during its most vital period embodied, the fight for the preservation through use of our forests."[34]

In many ways, we still live with the Pinchot legacy, both the good and the bad.

THE WORST FOREST FIRE EVER: THE BIG BLOWUP OF 1910

It was the largest forest fire in American history. Maybe even the largest forest fire ever.
No one knows for sure, but even now, it is hard to put into words what it did.

—Jim Petersen, "The 1910 Fire," 1994

THE FOREST RANGER

The earliest volunteers for the Forest Service were believers. To a man—only men were recruited, and only white men at that—they saw their chief as a prophet, a genius, unselfish and pure. Proud of the nickname "Little GPs," they seemed to have been cast in the same mold as Gifford Pinchot. Utterly devoted to him, nearly all in their early twenties to early thirties, they felt themselves "chosen" for public service. The boss had personally trained groups of them in the woods around Grey Towers,

his family's Pennsylvania estate. Others were graduates of the Yale School of Forestry (today's Yale School of the Environment), founded in 1900 with a grant of $150,000 from Pinchot and his father, James. Back then, that was a huge sum, equivalent in buying power to $4.6 million in 2019.[1]

These young idealists had not signed up for the money. Little GPs earned $60 a month, or $720 a year, in 1910; top pay for a factory worker was $400 a year, while an accountant earned $2,000, a dentist $2,500, and a mechanical engineer $5,000.

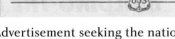

MEN WANTED!

A RANGER MUST BE ABLE TO TAKE CARE OF HIMSELF AND HIS MULES UNDER VERY TRYING CONDITIONS; BUILD TRAILS AND CABINS; RIDE ALL DAY AND ALL NIGHT; PACK, SHOOT, AND FIGHT FIRE WITHOUT LOOSING HIS HEAD . . . .

ALL THIS REQUIRES A VERY VIGOROUS CONSTITUTION. IT MEANS THE HARDEST KIND OF PHYSICAL WORK FROM BEGINNING TO END. IT IS NOT A JOB FOR THOSE SEEKING HEALTH OR LIGHT OUTDOOR WORK . . . .

INVALIDS NEED NOT APPLY!

Advertisement seeking the nation's first forest rangers. Note how women and people with disabilities were excluded from consideration at that time. (c. 1905)

Though the government provided the ranger's work gear—an ax, a notebook, and a pamphlet of regulations—he had to pay for everything else. There was no regulation uniform, so the ranger wore blue jeans, a wool shirt, a felt hat, and hobnailed boots. As a symbol of his authority, he had a tin badge with a pine tree logo and the words "Forest Guard, U.S.D.A. Forest Service."[2]

No ranger expected an easy life amid the beauties of nature. This was because the Forest Service watched over nine geographic districts, called regions, each comprising several states and covering all national forests and grasslands. Rangers patrolled on horseback or watched from lookout towers atop high hills. Region 1, the most challenging, consisted of 41 million acres in twenty-two national forests spread over four states: all of Montana, northern Idaho, part of eastern Washington, and a sliver of South Dakota. There were never enough trained men to cover this enormous region; even if there had been, there were few trails, let alone roads, to give access to the most densely wooded sections. If wildfire broke out in a remote area, it burned until the fuel ran out or it rained.

Forest Service badge worn by a ranger. (c. 1943)

Neither were Region 1 rangers respected by area residents. Quite the opposite: they were heartily detested. Pioneers had come a long way, crossed a continent in search of a better life in the West. They aimed to settle wherever they wished and do whatever they thought best with the land, including the national forests. This was not as outlandish as it may seem to today's ecology-minded Americans. After all, pioneers reasoned, national forests *were* public lands—the law said so. And weren't they members of the public? But the government, embodied in the Little GPs, kept telling them what they could and could not do with "their" property.

Government does not exist in a vacuum. Its every action, however well intended, is bound to create winners and losers. So-called wildland reforms, while perhaps gratifying to easterners and to Washington bureaucrats, often harmed "little people," a.k.a. pioneers. For example, as we've seen, conservationists like Theodore Roosevelt thought national forests should be saved not only for the enjoyment of future generations but also for their contribution to economic prosperity in the here and now. As a result, the government leased grazing and lumbering rights in national forests. Each year, for a fee, ranchers were allowed to graze a certain number of cattle for a certain time, and lumbermen could cut a certain number of trees in a given season. These leases, as we might expect, went to the already-haves, those who could afford to pay or slip bribes into the pockets of the right officials. As if that were not enough, in the eyes of the law, a pioneer's felling trees in a national forest for fuel or a log cabin was "timber theft." Shooting deer to feed one's family was deemed "poaching," a throwback to medieval forest laws, punishable by fines and jail time. If a farmer near the border of a national forest burned trees to clear his own land and the fire spilled across the boundary, regulations treated the accident as "arson." Not surprisingly, forest rangers did not make many friends by enforcing the law. As one old-timer explained, "We were extremely unpopular as rangers. . . . We never knew when a bullet might meet us in a thicket or on the trail." Not that rangers were defenseless; as peace officers, they carried firearms. Even so, a hunter shot a ranger to death in Montana in 1907; the shooter claimed he'd mistaken the man for a deer, but nobody who wore the pine tree badge fell for that hooey.[3]

As if threats of murder were not bad enough, the Forest Service had enemies in high places. President Roosevelt earned a reputation as a "trustbuster" because he

An early forest ranger with his horse and equipment. (c. 1910)

sought to break up what he termed "lawless" corporations that abused the public to further their own selfish interests. His activism triggered a backlash. Big business, through generous political campaign contributions and bribes, had allies in Congress, who fought TR over his most ambitious proposals, especially when they involved valuable natural resources. Among his opponents was the powerful Speaker of the House of

Representatives, Illinois Republican Joseph G. Cannon. "Uncle Joe," as everyone called him, saw no reason to spend congressional time and taxpayer dollars on "harebrained" conservation schemes. In a stunning display of ignorance, Cannon dismissed environmental concerns by saying he would spend "not one cent for *scenery*."[4]

Uncle Joe and his cronies felt that TR and Pinchot had gone too far. Pinchot, especially, rubbed politicians and business tycoons the wrong way. In politics, as in much else in life, personality shapes attitudes. Unfortunately, Pinchot often came across as a patronizing, pompous, self-righteous know-it-all. Creation of the national forests was the last straw. Vengeful congressmen began to pick the Forest Service apart, ignoring its requests for updates to legislation and cutting its budgets. To make matters worse, TR, the forester's main supporter, left the White House in March 1909, at the end of his second term. William Howard Taft, TR's successor, despised Pinchot, calling him "a good deal of a crank" and a fanatic who thought only of "his Cause." Taft lost no time in dismissing him. Deprived of its guiding spirit, and with opposition mounting in Congress, the Forest Service seemed doomed after only five years of existence. What saved it was the very thing foresters and conservationists feared most: wildfire.[5]

BATTLING WILDFIRE

Pinchot's attitude toward wildfire would shape Forest Service policy for generations. As early as 1899, in *A Primer of Forestry*, a popular work aimed at educating the nation, he wrote that of all "the foes which attack the woodlands of North America, no other is so terrible as fire." But thanks to the miracles of modern science, humans no longer had to view forest fires "simply and solely as acts of God, against which any opposition was hopeless and any attempt to control them not merely hopeless but childish." In truth, he declared with absolute certainty, forest fires were "wholly within the control of men," for the methods of eliminating them were "fully within our reach." In this, as time would tell, Gifford Pinchot was wrong—totally, terribly, tragically wrong.[6]

Nevertheless, the methods he favored were based on knowledge of the fire triangle as it applied to forestry. We recall that the triangle has three elements, all of which must be present for fire to occur: fuel, heat, and oxygen. If any of these is absent, it is impossible to have fire. On the other hand, if a fire is already burning, removing a single element will make it go out.

Rangers were taught to apply these principles to battling the various types of wildfire. A localized surface fire, for instance, is similar to a campfire; you put it out by scattering its fuel with rakes and shovels, then drowning the flames with water or covering them with soil to cut off the oxygen. A larger blaze calls for a fire line, or a firebreak, to "starve" the fire by blocking its access to fresh supplies of fuel. This is done by scraping down to the bare ground around a fire, thereby holding it

in place while it exhausts the available fuel. Dealing with a fast-moving blaze requires backfiring, or counterfiring—in effect, fighting a large fire with a smaller one. As we have seen, such blazes are driven by wind, but they also create their own wind pattern. If a fire is set just in front of an advancing one, it will be sucked into the original blaze, whose heat is rising so rapidly that it creates a partial vacuum at ground level. When

Forest ranger using canvas as a method of early firefighting. (c. 1908)

the two fires meet, the original blaze cannot advance because there is no more fuel left, the backfire having already used it up. While backfiring can stop an aggressive blaze in its tracks, there is the danger of it getting out of hand and spreading on its own. These methods apply only to "normal" wildfires. As ever, a full-fledged firestorm is in a class by itself. Once this monster gets going, it takes on a life of its own; nothing humans can do will slow it or put it out.

When it came to wildfire, the forest rangers' mission clashed with the pioneers' interests. Whether or not they put it into so many words, pioneers favored "the Indian way." In the East, we recall, Native Americans repeatedly set fire to woodlands. So, too, in the West; over the centuries, in the Sierra Nevada, for example, they'd fired the pine forests thousands of times. Those fires were beneficial, not harmful. In 1887, the poet and frontiersman Joaquin Miller described the process and its outcomes: "In the spring . . . the old [women] began to look about for the little dry spots of headland or sunny valley, and as fast as dry spots appeared, they would be burned. In this way the fire was always the servant, never the master. . . . By this means, the Indians always kept their forests open, pure and fruitful, and conflagrations were unknown." Basically, selective burning, in the right place and at the right time, greatly reduced the risk of firestorms, and this practice is still used today by many Native Americans.[7]

Forest rangers detested these practices, and they were not shy about saying so—loudly. Since Gifford Pinchot taught that fire was the forest's worst enemy, it followed that anyone who deliberately set one, for whatever reason, was an ignoramus at best, an evildoer at worst. As we might expect, those who relied on burning answered in kind. There are reports of pioneers' resentments from as far back as the 1890s, when Congress created the forest reserves. In 1897, the European-trained forester John Bernard Leiberg described the refusal of "pioneer arsonists" to sit still for government interference with their livelihoods:

> It has been a common occurrence to hear such remarks as, "If the Government intends to guard and preserve the timber from fires and prevent unlimited cutting, we will try to burn up what is left as soon as possible"; or, "Since the reserve has been set aside, every prospector carried an extra box of matches along to start forest fires with." These sayings were not made in a spirit of bravado, but with the conviction that the course outlined was the proper one to pursue to show their disapproval of Government interference in what they have heretofore considered their rights, namely to cut, slash, or burn, as convenience or fancy might dictate.[8]

Leiberg was right; these were *not* idle threats. In April 1910, forest ranger William W. Morris reported a series of "grudge fires" set in Idaho's Coeur d'Alene National Forest by irate homesteaders. And they were not alone. That spring, as usual, when the snow melted, the forests in and around Region 1 were besieged by silver prospectors, loggers, rail camp crews, shepherds, and hunters who set fires, then let them burn when they moved on. Though forest rangers fought all the fires they could get at, their gravest challenge came that fall. History knows what happened as the Big Blowup, or the Big Burn, of 1910.[9]

FIRE, FIRE, EVERYWHERE

If the Peshtigo firestorm was the deadliest in American history, the Big Blowup was the largest. And while the Peshtigo disaster failed to spur a reexamination of the nation's attitude toward wildfire, the 1910 disaster shaped official Forest Service policy for the rest of the twentieth century and beyond.

The Big Blowup came as a surprise to everyone. The winter of 1909–1910 had been one for the record books. Region 1 was brutally cold and buried in snowdrifts of twelve feet or more. The sharp snapping of snow-heavy tree limbs echoed through the still forests. By April, the snow had melted, the runoff flowing into streams and rivers, but the expected spring rains never came. In their place, the most severe drought anyone could remember set in. July brought day after day, week after week, of unrelenting heat. "There was a burning dryness in the air," a prospector wrote home. "Everywhere the heat was intense and stifling." The combination of drought and heat sucked moisture from vegetation, turning forests into tinderboxes.[10]

Ignition—the sparks—came from several sources. Bolts of dry lightning, from electrical storms that produced lightning and thunder but little or no rain, struck trees, setting them ablaze. Mounds of loggers' slash, campfires left by careless hunters, and intentional fires set by low-life rangers called firebugs deepened the crisis. Not surprisingly, the worst offenders were the railroads. By 1910, eastern companies were converting to steam engines that used oil as their fuel, but western firms still favored the cheaper coal. Rail lines laced Region 1, including the national forests. And wherever they ran, locomotives spewed sparks into the air. By late July, regional papers were filled with alarming news: "another fire started along the railroad track," a wooden bridge "caught fire from a spark from a freight train," and "almost every passenger train sets fires." To fight the blazes, companies hired spotters to patrol their tracks with handcars and assigned line crews to douse any fires. These measures were just about useless. Before long, other trains came along, spewing sparks into tinder-dry forests.[11]

In late July, rangers reported as many as two thousand flare-ups, small and large, across Region 1. Overwhelmed, the Forest Service appealed directly to the White House for assistance. On August 8, President Taft ordered thirty infantry companies, totaling four thousand soldiers, to the fire lines. This was a massive effort, for in 1910 the total

"Buffalo Soldiers" of the Twenty-Fifth Infantry, out of Fort George Wright. (Date unknown)

strength of the U.S. Army was a mere 81,251 officers and men, including large bodies of troops stationed in the Philippine Islands. The force sent to the fire zone included the "Buffalo Soldiers" of the Twenty-Fifth Infantry, the army's first peacetime all-Black regiment. Originally formed to police the Plains tribes, they became the go-to outfit for other missions. During the 1910 fires, these men gave a good accounting of themselves, evacuating homesteaders to safety. Their actions earned praise from all. One ranger, Thaddeus Roe, said his "attitude toward the Black race has undergone a wonderful change."[12]

Desperate for yet more hands, the Forest Service scoured the cities of Missoula and Butte, Montana, and Spokane, Washington, for temporary workers. Though many

Trains brought in volunteers from every walk of life to help fight the fire. (1910)

men dutifully volunteered, others went only because the government offered to pay 25 cents an hour, a generous sum at the time. Most volunteers, though willing enough, had no experience in the woods. Many others were down-and-outs, "bums and hoboes" who couldn't have cared less if forests burned. As ranger Elers Koch put it, "We had to gather together such men as we could from the streets, the saloons, and the freight train[s]. . . . When we loaded a crew of fire fighters on the train[s], we always expected most of them to be drunk, and consequently hard to handle." In all, the Forest Service deployed ten thousand men in Region 1's forests. Even if they had been up to the task, there were not nearly enough of them to deal with what lay ahead.[13]

Wildfires raged throughout July and into August. It was touch and go; exhausted ranger teams appeared to be holding their own, only to have fresh blazes erupt when the wind picked up. By August 11, Wallace, Idaho, lay directly in the path of a surging wildfire. Built in a narrow valley surrounded by steep mountains, the city of three thousand serviced the world's most productive silver-mining district, hence the nickname "Silver Capital of the World." Wallace was a good place to live. "It seemed like a toy city," a ranger recalled, "clean and spotless, and very much up to date, with fine homes and fine people." The city had railroad yards, machine shops, a wide variety of stores, a well-equipped hospital, a hotel, a brewery, a fire department, a police force, and more saloons than regular folks thought it should.[14]

As the fire approached Wallace from the west, newspapers reported, "dense smoke [buried] the [city] making it impossible to see objects 200 yards away." Showers of burning pine needles fell onto rooftops. Though homeowners and the fire department doused many fires, they were about to be overwhelmed when the wind suddenly died down. By August 19, the tide seemed to have turned, as conditions across Region 1 markedly improved. Though scattered fires still raged in the mountains, city residents heaved a sigh of relief.[15]

The next day, Saturday, August 20, all hell broke loose. A change in the weather was the culprit, as an unseasonal cold front came roaring out of Oregon. Gale-force winds, blowing at seventy-five miles an hour, tore across northeastern Washington, northern Idaho, and western Montana. Nature took its course: wind made fire, and fire made wind. The advancing front pumped oxygen into scattered wildfires, creating not one but multiple firestorms, each evidently larger than those that destroyed Peshtigo and Hinckley. Before a firestorm reached a town, it announced its presence in ominous ways. First, the air literally tingled, "as though the whole world was ready to go up on spontaneous combustion." Moments later, recalled Ranger Koch, "the mountains roared." Townspeople likened what they heard to "the sound of a thousand trains rushing over a thousand steel trestles" and to the "roar of Niagara Falls." Clouds of black smoke rose skyward, moving with the wind currents in the upper atmosphere. To the west, the smoke was so thick that ships five hundred miles out on the Pacific Ocean could not navigate by the stars. To the east, the smoke was visible as far away as Watertown, New York. Soot from the fires landed on Greenland glaciers.[16]

Among the religious, these firestorms conjured visions of the end of days, of the planet cracking open and its molten core gushing to the surface. Based on interviews with survivors and official reports, Idaho author Betty

Goodwin Spencer penned the most vivid account of the Big Blowup we have:

> The forests staggered, rocked, exploded, and then shriveled under the holocaust. Great red balls of fire rolled up the mountainsides. Crown fires, from one to ten miles wide, streaked with yellow and purple and scarlet, raced through treetops 150 feet from the ground. . . . The wind uprooted even the monster trees and flung them through the air like matchsticks. The heat of the fire and the masses of flaming gas created whirlwinds that mowed down mile-wide swaths of pine and fir and cedar in advance of the flames. . . . Public domain or private property, timbered land or farmland, bordered a forest or lay between two forests. Cities and small towns also were adjacent to or between forest lands. But the fire, aroused and propelled by the wind, disregarded all boundaries with a magnificent disdain. It swept over all the country—over national forests, over mountain crags, over low-lying hills, and over the brown plains. It leaped gullies and ravines and mile-wide river canyons. In ranger parlance, it "took everything out clean."

Whole towns—Taft, De Borgia, Haugan, Tudor—vanished beneath rolling waves of fire. Some people survived by blind luck, being at the right place at the right time. For instance, an evacuation train with a thousand people from the town of Avery crossed a burning bridge and made it into a tunnel, where it escaped the fiery deluge that engulfed everything outside.[17]

The exploits of individual ranger crews became Forest Service legends. Even today, more than a century later, to read about them is at once terrifying and elevating, testaments to human courage in the face of nature's wrath.

On the afternoon of August 20, Joe B. Halm, a twenty-five-year-old ranger and a former football star at Washington State Col-

The town of Wallace in the aftermath of the fire. (c. 1915)

lege, was leading a seventy-man crew. They had just finished mopping up a surface fire along the headwaters of the St. Joe River in northern Idaho when the wind picked up and a crew member, wild-eyed and panting, dashed out of the underbrush shouting, "She's coming! The whole country's afire!" Already, the sky had a red glow, and embers the size of a man's arm began falling. Instantly, Halm ordered his men to grab whatever supplies they could carry and follow him to a low sandbar, barely thirty feet across, in the middle of Bear Creek, one of the St. Joe's many tributaries.[18]

The firestorm came. Tongues of flame leaped over the cowering men. The flames, coupled with the sound of exploding trees, were terrifying. "We're not going to stay here and be roasted alive. We're going," a man shrieked. But Halm would have none of it;

panic, he knew, was suicide. Abandoning the sandbar meant certain death in the woods. Drawing his pistol, Halm barked, "Not a man leaves this camp. We'll stay in this creek and live to tell about it."[19]

They lived. By daybreak on August 21, the wind had shifted, at least along this stretch of the St. Joe, and the fire gradually subsided. "Dawn broke almost clear of smoke," Halm recalled. "Such a scene! The green, standing forest of yesterday was gone; in its place a charred and smoking mass of melancholy wreckage. The virgin trees, as far as the eye could see, were broken or down, devoid of a single sprig of green. Miles of trees—sturdy, forest giants—were laid prone. . . . Save for the minor burns and injuries, all [my men] were safe."[20]

Meanwhile, Edward C. Pulaski fought his own desperate battle. At forty, the ranger was "the Old Man," among the oldest members of the Forest Service. The great-grandson of Casimir Pulaski, the volunteer Polish cavalryman who'd saved George Washington's life during the Revolutionary War, "Big Ed" stood six foot three and had a sterling reputation. According to a performance report, "Mr. Pulaski is a man of most excellent judgment; conservative, thoroughly acquainted with the region." He'd mentored Joe Halm as a rookie forest ranger.[21]

Pulaski recalled that on the morning of August 20, while he and his forty-five-man crew were working the fire line at Placer Creek ten miles southwest of Wallace, "a terrific hurricane broke over the mountains." With trees burning all around, he decided to make a dash for Wallace, only to find the trail blocked "by raging, whipping fire." Realizing that their only hope of survival lay in reaching an old mine tunnel he knew about, Pulaski led the way through the smoke. As they ran, a burning tree fell, crushing a man. Luckily, the rest of the crew, along with two horses carrying supplies and blankets, reached the tunnel. Seconds later, the firestorm turned the site into "a raging furnace." In reality, the tunnel was just a trial shaft, a hundred or so feet long, that prospectors had abandoned when they found no silver ore, but it still had all the earmarks of a death trap. The opening was barely wide enough for the men and horses to squeeze through. Puddles of muddy water dotted the floor.[22]

With the firestorm raging outside, the heat drew the cool air out of the tunnel, replacing it with hot, smoky air. Pulaski ordered his crew to lie flat on the floor, facedown, to conserve the breathable air. Stressed to the breaking point, several men began weeping and cursing. One fellow shouted, "Oh, Lord!" Another lost it, yelling that he was getting out come hell or high water. He did. The last Pulaski saw of him, he was running toward the burning forest and certain death. Moments later, Big Ed drew his pistol. "The next man who tries to leave this tunnel," he swore, "I will shoot." They hugged the floor.[23]

Pulaski guarded the tunnel's mouth, which he covered with blankets. When the mouth's wooden support beams ignited, he carried water in his hat from the puddles to keep the blankets wet. In the process, his hands and face were badly burned. Finally, he passed out, as did all his companions. Hours later, the firestorm had passed and the air began to cool. It was about five o'clock in the morning of August 21. Big Ed remembered awakening to a voice calling, "Come outside, boys, the boss is dead." Pulaski replied, "Like hell he is." Before leaving, he ordered a head count. Five men and both horses lay dead of smoke inhalation; thirty-eight men survived.[24]

Forest ranger Edward C. Pulaski, his forty-five-man crew, and two horses sheltered in this muddy mineshaft. Five hours later, all but five men and the horses emerged, injured but alive. (c. 1910)

The return to Wallace was another kind of ordeal. Mad with thirst, the crew tried to drink from Placer Creek, only to find it choked with ashes and the water too hot to swallow. They staggered onward, tripping on smoldering roots, clambering over burning logs, feeling their way through drifting smoke. Covered with dirt and soot, their boots burned off their feet and their clothes in shreds, they crawled on hands and knees when walking got too difficult. Big Ed was in awful shape. "I was blind and my hands were burned from trying to keep the fire out of the mine," he recalled. Pulaski never fully recovered; the firestorm left him with facial scars, impaired vision, and weakened lungs. Yet he remained in the Forest Service, retiring in 1929, only to die in a car crash two years later. He left behind a legacy of heroism and (as we will see) the pulaski, an invention that became an essential tool in the modern forest ranger's kit.[25]

Wallace passed through its own fiery ordeal. Dawn on August 21 saw flames topping the mountains south of the city. The valley below, a survivor said, resembled a "deep bowl . . . completely lined with seething flames." The wind strengthened, sounding like "a storm at sea," and burning embers fell. It was time for nonessential people to leave.[26]

Hours earlier, as the situation worsened, the Northern Pacific and Union Pacific railroad companies assembled five rescue trains. Mayor Walter Hanson's plan was to evacuate Wallace's women and children, sick and elderly, while all able-bodied men stayed to fight the blaze. However, no one had planned for panic. "I have been in panics," said Carl Getz, a visitor from Seattle, "but the one at Wallace was the worst I have ever seen." Conditions at the depot became chaotic as dozens of men scrambled to board the trains, pushing aside women, some carrying infants under wet towels. Trainmen had their hands full, struggling to keep order, and not a few men made it to the coaches and boxcars. As a pregnant woman began to board, "an obnoxious bruiser" elbowed her. That did it! Several trainmen grabbed him, threw him to the ground, and beat the daylights out of him. When other men rushed to board a train, police officers treated them "in a manner that showed them they had better remain," according to the *Idaho Press.* "A few caresses with huge clubs the officers carried was the most convincing argument." The trains took around two thousand evacuees to Spokane, Washington, and Missoula, Montana. Though a third of Wallace went up in flames, and two lost their lives, the men who remained saved the rest of the town by backfiring.[27]

The firestorms left as quickly as they'd come. By midmorning on August 22, the wind died down. Temperatures in Region 1 plummeted, and on August 24 soaking rains broke the drought, smothering any remaining patches of fire. People rejoiced in the downpour. "We were glad to get wet," one said, grinning from ear to ear, "for we knew our long fight was over."[28]

It had been a costly fight. Over the course of two days, the Big Blowup claimed the lives of seventy-eight firefighters and seven civilians. As at Peshtigo and Hinckley, the fire had transformed some of the dead into tiny heaps of gray ash; others, still recognizable as human, lost fingers, ears, and arms when burial parties touched their remains. The material loss was immense, with hundreds of homes, farms, ranches, sawmills, and mining camps totally destroyed. In all, "the red demon from hell" incinerated more than three million acres of private and national forests, an area the size of New Jersey, making it the largest wildfire ever recorded in America. Like their forest home, wildlife suffered dreadfully. Onlookers saw flocks of flaming birds falling out of the sky. For weeks afterward, riverbanks stank from the rotting remains of dead trout. A ranger described one sight that still tugs at our emotions: "If you could see a little black bear clinging high in a blazing tree and crying like a frightened child, you could perceive on a very small scale what happened to the forest and its creatures."[29]

The Big Blowup was history. But the battle over its meaning and the way forward had just begun.

A Forest Service ranger surveys the damage after the Big Blowup. (c. 1910)

AFTERSHOCKS

The ashes were still cooling in Region 1 when the blame game began. Though ousted from his post, with the Forest Service apparently doomed, Gifford Pinchot turned the catastrophe into a public relations triumph. Intent on shaping public opinion, he seized the moral high ground, framing the event in terms the average citizen could understand—no, *feel*. The Big Blowup arose, he declared, from a clash between heroes and villains. Following his lead, conservation groups and reform-minded journalists portrayed forest rangers in emotional terms. In speeches and articles, they portrayed them as selfless men prepared for any sacrifice in the sacred cause of safeguarding America's natural heritage. "The Forest Fire Fighters," by famed western poet Arthur Chapman, captures the tone:

The wind sweeps off the spire-like peak,
And is whirling the cinders high;

While down in the stifling, deadly reek,
We struggle, and all but die.

We have felled the trees in the fire's path,
Till our hands are bleeding and sore;
But always it speeds, with a hiss of wrath,
And leaps the barrier o'er.

We have fought it back, with blaze 'gainst
  blaze,
And yet has the foe slipped past;
But slowly we yield, in the choking haze,
Till the victory's won at last.

Small pay do we get, and thanks are gruff,
When we've fought the foe to his knees;
But, after all, the reward's enough,
When we hear the wind in the trees.[30]

In Pinchot's eyes, the villains were venge-ful congressmen, moral idiots bought by special-interest dollars. Had those "public enemies," those scoffing misers, done their duty and not sought to destroy his beloved Forest Service, it would have had the means

to prevent, or at least to gain early control of, the firestorms! "For the want of a nail, the shoe was cast, the rider thrown, the battle lost," he told a reporter for *Everybody's Magazine*, a mass-circulation weekly headquartered in New York. "For want of trails the finest white pine forests in the United States were laid waste and scores of lives lost. It is all loss, dead irretrievable loss, due to the pique, the bias, the bullheadedness of a knot of men who have sulked and planted their hulks in the way of appropriations for the protection and improvement of these national forests." Theodore Roosevelt agreed. In a public let-ter, the former president declared that what the rangers had done was enough to "make Americans proud of having such a body of public servants." Those who'd lost their lives, TR continued, should not be allowed to have died in vain. Still, politicians, as was (and is) their habit, excused themselves by claiming that they'd only been looking after the tax-payers' interests by scrimping on conserva-tion expenditures![31]

Pinchot's heroes-versus-villains tactic

won the battle for public opinion. In doing so, it also won a bitter debate. Until the Big Blowup, pioneers and even a few foresters had argued for following the example of Native Americans, seasonally using fire to cleanse woodlands, preventing them from becoming overgrown. Pinchot and his allies' publicity campaign resolved the matter. His insistence that forest fires were "wholly unnecessary," and that "a fire in the forest is the same kind of thing as a fire in the city," led to the only logical conclusion. All that was needed to prevent future Big Blowups was early detection, speedy response by skilled professionals, and sensible rules about disposing of lumbering debris. Congressional opponents, smarting under the withering criticism, decided they had to take action. Early the next year, Congress adopted legislation—the Weeks Act of 1911—calling for stamping out all forest fires. Wildfire had effectively become a national enemy, as menacing as any foreign foe.[32]

The Forest Service took wildfire prevention as its gospel; both natural and man-

Forest fire prevention poster stressing personal responsibility for protecting forests, created by the federal Works Progress Administration. (c. 1936–1939)

made fires were to be eliminated from the nation's woodlands. Period! As Congress increased its budget, the agency expanded its operations. It cut trails through the woods, built more lookout towers on high ground, pre-positioned firefighting equipment at strategic points, and installed telephone lines for rapid communication. In 1935, the agency adopted the "10:00 a.m. rule": all wildfires, regardless of how remote they were, had to be put out by ten o'clock the morning after they were first detected.

This rule went hand in hand with publicity campaigns to educate the public about the evils of wildfire. The campaigns' mascot, Smokey Bear, made his debut in 1944. Over the years, millions of posters depicting the savvy bear saying "Only You" and "Only *You Can Prevent Forest Fires!*" were placed in forests, campsites, and schools. "Smokey the Bear," a song by Steve Nelson and Jack Rollins, touted the conservationist bear and his message:

> *With a Ranger's hat and shovel*
> *and a pair of dungarees*

> *you will find him in the forest*
> *always sniffin' at the breeze.*
> *People stop and pay attention*
> *when he tells 'em to beware,*
> *'cause ev'rybody knows that*
> *he's the Fire Preventin' Bear. . . .*

> *If you've ever seen the forest*
> *when a fire is running wild,*
> *and you love the things within it*
> *like a mother loves her child,*
> *then you know why Smokey tells you*
> *when he sees you passing through,*
> *"Remember . . . please be careful . . .*
> *it's the least that you can do."*[33]

Hollywood taught children to dread wildfire. In 1942, Walt Disney Studios released *Bambi.* Adapted from the 1923 novel *Bambi: A Life in the Woods,* by Austrian writer Felix Salten, this feature-length cartoon scolded adults for abusing woodlands. The story recounts the life of Bambi, a fawn befriended by Thumper the rabbit, Flower the skunk,

Smokey Bear imploring individuals to prevent forest fires. (c. 1989)

and other charming forest creatures. They live together happily until tragedy strikes in the form of hunters, who kill Bambi's mother and leave their campfire untended, igniting a horrific firestorm. Animated in color, a recent innovation, the scene of Bambi and his father fleeing through the flames is unforgettable. I saw *Bambi* when it was first released; my friends and I were six and seven. The fire scene was so graphic that we hid behind our jackets, peering at the screen for just a few seconds at a time. Lesson: all wildfires are bad, and good people have a sacred obligation to prevent them at all costs.

Time, however, would teach a different lesson. For the Forest Service's cure proved to be as bad as the disease itself. Attempting to eliminate natural fires from woodlands was disastrous, costing lives and untold bil-

lions of dollars. Ironically, preventing fire at all costs was the formula for bigger, hotter, and faster wildfires.

BIGGER, HOTTER, FASTER

Fires are outrunning us. We're trying harder than ever to put them out, and they're continuing to win, more and more, every year. We think that we as humans should be able to dominate this phenomenon of wildfire. And in reality, we can't. . . . This is a natural phenomenon that is similar to the ocean in that it is really big, that it is much larger than us when it really gets going.

—A. Park Williams, climatologist, 2018

FIGHTING WILDFIRE TODAY

American environmental scientists have noted an alarming trend. We have, most agree, entered a new era of wildfires. In every year since 2000, an average of 71,300 fires in U.S. forests have burned an average of 6.9 million acres, more than twice the annual acreage lost in the previous decade (3.3 million acres). Aside from the lives and property destroyed, always a tragic waste, the financial costs of fighting wildfires have skyrocketed. Whereas in 1985 the federal government spent nearly $240 million on suppression alone, by 2015 the price tag was $2.1 billion, rising to $3.1 billion in 2018, $1.59 billion in 2019, and $2.27 billion in 2020.[1]

This, observers say, is not supposed to be happening, given the advances in all aspects of fighting wildfires. To be sure, if Big Ed Pulaski could wondrously return from the grave, he would scarcely recognize his profession. In the century since the Big Blowup of 1910, Forest Service people have become better trained, better organized, better informed, and better equipped than ever before.

The people on the front lines are more diverse than in Pulaski's day. No longer a white male monopoly, the Forest Service recruits from all backgrounds and ethnicities. In October 2018, Vicki Christiansen, a twenty-six-year veteran of wildland firefighting, became the nineteenth chief of the Forest Service. Taking over from Christiansen in 2021, Randy Moore became the first African American chief. Moore supervises 25,000 permanent employees, who guard 193 million acres in 154 national forests and 20 grasslands in 43 states and Puerto Rico.[2]

Since the 1970s, women have taken part in all aspects of Forest Service work, notably the management of hotshot crews. So called because they attack the hottest spots of wildfires, hotshots are an elite rapid-reaction force similar to the military's Special Operations troops. Highly trained, they are organized into twenty-person crews. To qualify as a member, one must meet the most rigorous physical standards. These include running a mile and a half in under eleven minutes and doing forty sit-ups in sixty seconds, twenty-five push-ups in sixty seconds, and four to seven chin-ups, depending on the candidate's body weight. The hotshots' main job is to get to a blaze quickly and contain it. The big idea, as always, is to eliminate one side of the fire triangle: fuel, oxygen, or heat. This is commonly done by building a firebreak around the blaze, confining it while it uses up the available fuel.[3]

Native Americans are still extremely involved in firefighting today. For many it is a rite of passage, but there is also considerable community pride invested in firefighting crews and their accomplishments, almost to the level of sports competition. Thanks to twentieth-century advances in technology, wildland firefighters are better able to do their jobs. Nowadays, meteorologists, specialists in weather forecasting, employ a battery of sensitive instruments to track changes in wind force, temperature, and humidity in fire-prone areas. In addition, artificial intelligence (AI), interconnected computer systems able to perform tasks that previously required human intelligence, such as calculating and map reading, now aid firefighters. Should a blaze erupt, state-of-the-art computers linked to orbiting satellites can create real-time maps of its location, direction, and speed. Nevertheless, humans are still in control. As forest ecologist Edward Smith explains, "Nothing is going to completely replace the human brain to make decisions, but AI can help us make better decisions." At the same time, advances in electronics such as portable telephones and radios keep firefighters in touch with each other in the field and with their headquarters, enabling them to coordinate their efforts for maximum effect.

Though battling wildfire is inherently dangerous, science has made the job as safe as possible. While the firefighters of 1910 wore ordinary work clothes, their descendants are, effectively, "knights of the forest." Like medieval knights clad head to toe in

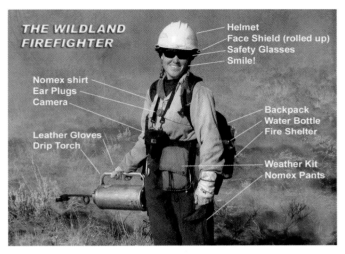

The vital elements of a firefighter's uniform.

steel armor, they go to battle wearing PPE—personal protective equipment—made of fire-resistant materials. To safeguard against falling branches, the firefighter wears a hard hat made of lightweight (less than 15.5 ounces) fiberglass, strong and heat-resistant. The hard hat also has special clips for attaching goggles to shield the wearer's eyes from smoke, dust, and small flying objects. Shirts and trousers are made of cotton treated with flame-resistant chemicals. They fit loosely, allowing the wearer to move about freely, and are bright yellow for easier visibility in smoky conditions. Leather boots, designed for traction on steep and uneven terrain, have non-skid soles. While there are scores of designs, a firefighter's gloves usually have an outer layer of kangaroo leather for flexibility and inner layers of Nomex, a synthetic flame-resistant fiber used to insulate against heat.[4]

Last but not least, today's wildland firefighter carries two lifesaving pieces of equipment. The first, a respirator, is a breathing apparatus that provides oxygen and protects airways and lungs from hot gases. The second, a pup tent–like shelter, offers protection from extreme heat when the firefighter is overrun by wildfire. Packed in a zippered carrying case, the shelter is made of bonded layers of aluminum foil, fiberglass, and woven silica, a mineral component of sand. Despite their obvious advantages, these devices have limitations. Journalist Brian Mockenhaupt explains:

Fire shelters are the final defense against the unexpected . . . [and are able to] deflect up to 95 percent of a fire's radiant heat. The shelters aren't nearly as good, though, at withstanding the convective heat from hot gases, or direct contact with flame. At 500 degrees, they start to delaminate. At about 1,200 degrees, the foil starts to melt; at 1,400 degrees, the fiberglass starts to break down; and at 2,200 degrees, the silica breaks down. But well before a shelter breaks down, the temperatures inside it have probably already risen to fatal levels. Human beings can breathe air up to 300 degrees Fahrenheit, but only for a very short time. Most firefighters killed in burn-overs die not from burns but from the superheated air. A single breath can cause suffocation.

Tragically, nineteen hotshots died near Yarnell, Arizona, in June 2013 when waves of wildfire rolled over their shelters.[5]

Like their comrades, these heroes used the traditional hand tools of their profes-

A prototype fire shelter, post-burn. (2015)

firefighters began using the pulaski as early as 1913, and fell in love with it straightaway. Before long, it became indispensable; tens of thousands of them were deployed. The tool is especially valuable in creating firebreaks, sections of land cleared of vegetation to contain advancing wildfires. Crews chop down trees with the ax side, then dig ditches with the hoe. "Every time a firefighter hefts a pulaski," says historian Stephen J. Pyne, "he or she is retelling the story of the Great Fires" of 1910.[6]

sion: axes, hoes, rakes. In addition, they carried the invention of a ranger whose name is heard wherever Americans fight wildfire. The pulaski was the brainchild of Big Ed Pulaski. After the Big Blowup, the ranger, his wounds still raw, set out to develop a single tool that could do several things. The result, which bears his name, combines an ax and a hoe on a single handle, allowing the user to chop or dig with just a flip of the wrist. Except for the addition of a lightweight thirty-six-inch fiberglass handle, the design has remained unchanged since its inventor's day. Wildland

Better yet, the modern wildland firefighter relies on types of heavy equipment unavailable when the Forest Service was young. If a fire is accessible by road, trucks carrying crews and equipment race to the scene; if not, bulldozers may clear the way. Mechanical pumpers can douse the blaze with water piped from nearby lakes or rivers.

The airplane has become a major addition to the firefighters' arsenal. During World War 1 (1914–1918), early planes, little more than motorized kites made of wood, wire, and canvas, flew combat missions and observed enemy activity on the ground. Immediately after the war, in 1919, the U.S. Army used its two-seater scout planes to locate wildfires in remote areas; army pilots flew the aircraft, while the Forest Service furnished the observers. One drawback: since these planes were not equipped with radios, firefighters could get the information only when the observers landed, a dangerous lag in response time.[7]

During the 1930s, the Soviet Union pioneered the training of paratroopers to fight behind enemy lines. Because the Communist nation also had vast forests in Siberia, and thus the fires that inevitably go with them, the Soviet air force experimented with "parachute firemen." Specially trained teams were sent to fight fires in otherwise inaccessible places, with striking success. After too long a delay, the United States followed the Soviet lead. By the early 1940s, it was training "smokejumpers" at the Army Airborne School at Fort Benning, Georgia. Like their Soviet counterparts, our smokejumpers parachute from planes into areas near forest fires

in remote areas. From there, they move to the blaze and try to prevent it from becoming a conflagration.[8]

Smokejumpers consider themselves the elite of the elite: no wildland firefighters are as highly trained, and none are exposed to more hazardous conditions. When the alert

A smokejumper parachutes into the forest. (c. 1943–1944)

sounds, the mixed-sex crews suit up. Here, too, the Soviet Union was ahead of the United States; in 1936, Zoya Trukhina was named the world's first female smokejumper. Deanne Shulman became America's first female smokejumper in 1981. Regardless of their sex, every volunteer wears the standard yellow firefighter's suit under a jumpsuit made of materials resistant to cuts, scrapes, and punctures from trees and other hazards in the drop zone. Strong as it is, the jumpsuit can withstand temperatures of two thousand degrees Fahrenheit for a maximum of just *four seconds*. Standard-issue fire gear is worn under the jumpsuit.[9]

Having landed after parachuting from a height of fifteen hundred feet, an extremely dangerous feat in itself, smokejumpers discard the outer suits, link up, and retrieve their gear, which is parachuted in separate metal containers holding two days' worth of supplies: sleeping bags, shelters, food, water, pulaskis, saws, first aid kits, walkie-talkies, and other necessities. That smokejumpers live dangerously is proven by the fact

that thirty-two have died in the line of duty since 1940. The worst single loss occurred in August 1949, when twelve lost their lives fighting the Mann Gulch Fire in Montana's Helena National Forest. Norman Maclean's *Young Men and Fire* is a heart-pounding account of this tragedy.[10]

Smokejumpers and other wildland firefighters are backed up by specialized aircraft. Aerial supertankers are cavernous vessels, each designed to drop 12,000 gallons of retardant at a time. The raspberry-red stuff seen falling from such planes is a mixture of water, to wet down the target area, and a chemical retardant containing phosphate fertilizer, to slow the fire and lower its temperature. Federal use of retardants has risen sharply in recent years, from roughly 8.5 million gallons in 2012 to 39.3 million gallons in 2018.[11]

Though highly effective, says Timothy Ingalsbee, executive director of Oregon-based Firefighters United for Safety, Ethics, and Ecology, "these chemicals do not have a benign effect on the environment." Depending

U.S. Air Force reserve crews drop fire retardant from a C-130 Hercules. (Date unknown)

on where retardants are used and how strong they are, they can be toxic for wildlife and humans. Studies have shown that a single dose landing in a stream can kill fish wholesale; for this reason, the Forest Service has banned retardant use within three hundred feet of lakes and waterways. Nevertheless, there is no controlling the shifting wind, which may carry the brew to ecologically sensitive sites. Helicopters are most effective for pinpoint water drops. Pilots can dip buckets dangling from retractable cables into lakes and rivers, then hover over the fire to empty up to twenty-six hundred gallons of water on it.[12]

CLIMATE CHANGE

Despite the many advances in equipment and methods, today's wildland firefighters face two challenges Big Ed Pulaski's generation could not have imagined. The first is climate change due to global warming. The second is the effects of the Forest Service's own policy of snuffing out wildfires as soon as they are detected. We will examine each in turn.

The study of climate change relies on many different scientific disciplines: biology, botany, ecology, oceanography, meteorology, climatology. Despite this complexity, there is almost universal agreement among experts that rising global temperatures are on track to have dire results as the twenty-first century progresses. As James G. Speth, former dean of the Yale School of the Environment, warns: "Climate change is the single greatest threat that societies face today." When did this threat arise? Why? How does it influence today's wildfires? What can be done about it?[13]

Weather and climate, we recall, are not the same. "Weather" refers to warm and cool, dry and moist, the conditions experienced by a locality over a period of days or weeks. "Climate" refers to the average of conditions over long intervals of time, such as the Pleistocene Epoch. Ice ages have come and gone. Due to natural causes still not fully understood, certain regions experienced the "Little Ice Age," beginning in the fourteenth century and lasting roughly four hundred years. During the coldest period, between 1645 and 1717, average winter temperatures in Europe and North America were as much as thirty-five degrees Fahrenheit lower than today. European rivers remained frozen solid far into spring. Glaciers in the Alps grew and advanced, obliterating Swiss and Italian villages in their path. Travelers shunned places where, as one put it, "ice and frost are [more] common since the creation of the world." The ice was so thick on the Baltic Sea that one could walk from Sweden to Finland. Polar ice expanded far south into the Atlantic Ocean, virtually ending trade between Iceland and Europe. Until the Little Ice Age ended in the 1850s, winters were uncommonly frigid and summers cool and damp, causing crop failures, famines, and population declines. Widespread anxiety may have led to the search for scapegoats, people to blame for the worsening conditions. This in turn might help explain the "witch craze," the horrific persecution of so-called witches, chiefly women, in Europe and America, which peaked in the 1600s.[14]

We face the opposite situation. The problem today is climate change resulting from global warming, defined as "a significant increase in Earth's climatic temperature over a relatively short period of time as a result of the activity of humans." As George Perkins Marsh observed in *Man and Nature,* mankind is a force of nature in its own right. Following in Marsh's footsteps, today's scientists believe human activities are the basic, if not the sole, cause of climate change. In this regard, studies of ice core samples tell a fascinating story. Ice cores are cylinders of ice drilled out of a glacier, then preserved in laboratory freezers for study. Like a tree with its annual growth rings, an ice core can reveal the climate conditions of the distant past. Snow builds up, one layer atop another, and under the pressure of its own weight, the snow eventually turns to ice. As this happens, ice crystals capture tiny bubbles of air that contain samples of Earth's atmosphere. By chemically analyzing these samples, some dating back eight hundred thousand years, researchers can measure changes in the amounts of certain atmospheric gases over time and compare them to modern levels.[15]

Ice cores reveal that the composition of Earth's atmosphere began to change around the 1830s, in the early stages of the Industrial Revolution, when machines gathered in factories began replacing human muscle power in a substantial way. The Industrial Revolution has proven to be a mixed blessing. To begin with, its more efficient production methods made available more consumer goods at lower prices, thereby creating job opportunities and dramatically raising living standards for most people, though not for all at once. Those who benefited lived longer, healthier lives in more comfortable and san-

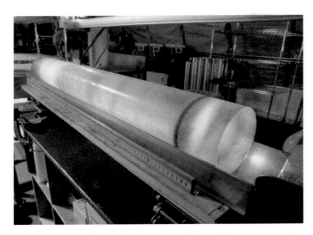

The dark band in this ice core from West Antarctica is a layer of volcanic ash that settled on the ice sheet approximately twenty-one thousand years ago. (Date unknown)

itary conditions than ever before in human history. However, the new industrial machinery required cheap, abundant fuel. Wood was inefficient; it simply could not generate the heat energy needed to sustain industry and transportation at peak efficiency. As a result, inventors turned increasingly to fossil fuels as a power source. Coal, oil, and natural gas are called fossil fuels because they have formed in Earth's crust, over millions of years, from the decomposed remains of plants and animals.

Nowadays, most of the energy we use comes from fossil fuels; in the year 2019, the United States got eighty percent of its energy from them. Trains, planes, automobiles, ships, industry, the military, heating, lighting, and electrical appliances: all require fossil fuels. So does agriculture, which depends on nitrogen-rich fertilizer, a product made chiefly from natural gas. Similarly, polyester, the most common artificial fiber used in the manufacture of clothing, is produced by a chemical reaction involving oil, coal, air, and water. Medicine is heavily reliant on plastics, also made from oil and natural gas, for everything from tubing to syringes, bandages to pill casings, surgical gloves to disposable gowns—to mention just a few items. The downside is that the heavy use of fossil fuels affects the environment through global warming.

The science is not complicated. Our sun's rays pass through Earth's atmosphere and strike the planet's surface. Most of this energy—about seventy percent—is absorbed by the land and vegetation. This is good; without these warming rays, Earth would go into a deep, deep freeze, making life as we know it impossible. But there can be too much of a good thing. Normally, the other thirty percent of the heat reaching Earth is reflected back into space by snowfields, ice sheets, clouds, and ocean surfaces, which act as gigantic mirrors. This essential process balances the constant heat radiating from the sun, preventing the planet from overheating.[16]

As early as the 1820s, scientists understood that certain gases can trap heat, but they saw no danger in that. With the dawn of the computer age in the 1950s, however, scientists gained the ability to gather, analyze, and compare historical data pointing to the effects of "greenhouse gases." These include water vapor, methane, ozone, and, above all, carbon dioxide released during the burning of fossil fuels. A greenhouse is a glass building in which delicate plants are grown to shield them from the cold. Heat in the form of sunlight enters the building, warming the plants, soil, and air. But because the glass roof is solid, the excess heat cannot escape unless the gardener opens a few panels from time to time, thus preventing an unsafe buildup. While plants need carbon dioxide to make food, too much of this heat-absorbing gas acts like a closed greenhouse roof on Earth's atmosphere. By trapping excess heat rising from the planet's surface, the gas prevents it

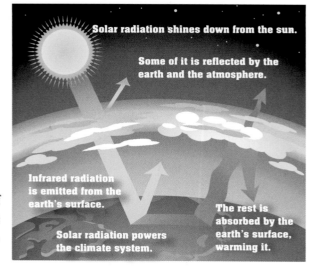

Illustration of the greenhouse effect.

from bouncing back into space. Over time, the heat accumulates, chiefly in the oceans, which influence weather conditions on land. The result is climate change due to global warming. This is happening right now. The world's weather bureaus have been tracking global temperatures since the 1870s. Over the last fifty years, climate scientists report, "the average global temperature has increased at the fastest rate in recorded history. And the trend is accelerating." What's more, over a 134-year period, sixteen of the hottest years worldwide have occurred since 2000, a truly ominous development.[17]

A 1968 study conducted for the oil industry by the Stanford Research Institute warned that "man is now engaged in a vast . . . experiment with his environment, the earth," one that "may be the cause of serious worldwide environmental changes." This is a polite understatement. The unregulated burning of fossil fuels and the buildup of greenhouse gases in the atmosphere threaten to create conditions simi-

lar to those at the end of the Pleistocene. Back then, as miles-high glaciers melted, sea levels rose, drowning Beringia and submerging low-lying coastlines. In our day, the immense Antarctic ice sheet has been losing more than 134 billion tons of ice every year since 2000. According to a 2019 United Nations report, sea levels, which rose globally by 7.5 inches in the twentieth century, could rise another 36 inches (3 *feet*) by the end of the twenty-first.[18]

In the worst-case scenario, the effects of global warming go far beyond drowning shorelines and islands. Given that warm air holds more moisture than cool air, climate change plays a role in extreme weather events, fueling more powerful hurricanes, heavier downpours, and worse flooding. Similarly, global warming triggers feedback loops, in which an action produced by an ecological system intensifies that very system. Hotter and drier conditions, for example, contribute to longer and more intense wildfire seasons. Inevitably, more wildfires push more smoke pollutants into the air, which blacken ice sheets, which absorb more sunlight, causing the ice to melt even faster.

Equally important, global warming hastens the spread of disease. Until the arrival of Europeans, we recall, the Americas were isolated from Old World epidemics. Since Native Americans had never experienced smallpox, for example, they had no acquired resistance to it, and thus died in untold numbers. Global warming is creating a similar situation. Insect-borne diseases are advancing into temperate North America from their places of origin in Central and South America, gaining a foothold in populations that have rarely or never been exposed to them. Moreover, higher temperatures and longer breeding seasons let mosquitoes and ticks carry infections such as malaria and Lyme disease farther afield. It is the same with Chagas disease, a lethal heart condition brought on by a minute parasite transmitted by kissing bugs, insects native to Central America nicknamed for their habit of biting people near the lips.[19]

While deliberately setting wildland fires to clear land for farming and grazing yields more food, it also increases the chances of pandemics, outbreaks of disease that affect multiple countries or the world. This is because forest clearing exposes people to highly infectious diseases caused by viruses such as SARS and Ebola, some of which have jumped to humans from wild animals that live in dense tropical forests. According to *Scientific American,*

Three quarters of the emerging pathogens that infect humans leaped from animals, many of them creatures in the forest habitats that we are slashing and burning to create land for crops . . . and for mining and housing. The more we clear, the more we come into contact with wildlife that carries microbes well suited to kill us—and the more we concentrate those animals in smaller areas where they can swap infectious microbes, raising the chances of novel strains. Clearing land also reduces biodiversity, and the species that survive are more likely to host illnesses that can be transferred to humans. All these factors will lead to more spillover of animal pathogens into people.[20]

There is also a connection between global warming and natural forest fires. Though warm air holds moisture, extremely hot air does the opposite. Environmental scientist Dana Nuccitelli explains: "With these hotter, drier conditions extending late into the year, wildfires have become larger, and they spread faster, cause more damage, and are more difficult to contain." Given these facts, it seems hardly accidental that the ten warmest years ever recorded in the United States, all of which have occurred since 2005, have also coincided with an increased threat of wildfire. Yet we must be careful in our conclusions. Nobody, after all, can (as yet) point to

a specific weather event, let alone a specific wildfire, and say that it was caused solely by global warming. But as history tells us, severe droughts and heat waves triggered earlier firestorms: Peshtigo, Hinckley, and the Big Blowup. Climate change skeptics have argued that those catastrophes occurred many decades before global warming became a problem anyone was aware of, and so it cannot be to blame for the current rash of wildfires. This is faulty logic: being unaware of something does not mean it does not exist.[21]

Though the vast majority of fire scientists believe global warming is a grave threat that must be addressed by the world community, they question its role in recent fire events. It is, they claim, only one factor in the increasing severity of wildfires. They point to recent Department of the Interior findings that as many as ninety percent of American wildfires are caused by people, and are thus preventable. Most of these fires result from negligence, sparks from broken power lines, and arson. Another human cause, according to today's firefighting community, stems from the policy, dating to the Big Blowup, of trying to prevent each and every wildfire. According to fire ecologist Sasha Berleman, "We have 100 years of fire suppression that has led to this huge accumulation of fuel loads." In other words, efforts to eliminate all fire from forests have led to a huge buildup of older trees, unhealthier trees, dead trees, and debris on the forest floor. As a result, the inevitable fires are larger, hotter, and costlier than they would have been if allowed to burn according to nature's timetable. The results of this misguided policy are best seen in the West, notably in California.[22]

THE GOLDEN STATE BURNING

On September 28, 1542, a three-ship expedition—*San Salvador, La Victoria,* and *San Miguel*—sailed along the California coast under the flag of Spain. Led by Juan Rodríguez Cabrillo, its mission was to find the legendary Seven Cities of Gold, whose very buildings were said to be encrusted

with the precious metal. While the expedition members explored the coast, the ships lay at anchor in an enormous bay, which the expedition's chronicler dubbed Bahia de los Fumos, or Bay of the Smoke. All around the bay, the crews saw smoke billowing into the sky, likely from burning chaparral, shrubs that favor areas with mild, damp winters and hot, dry summers. Today, the renamed San Pedro Bay is the site of the Port of Los Angeles, the West Coast's busiest seaport.[23]

Though wildfires are nothing new in California, they have never been as severe as in recent years. The Golden State is the nation's most wildfire-prone, followed by Texas, Colorado, Arizona, Oregon, and Idaho. Half of the twenty largest recorded fires in California history occurred from 2018 through 2022.[24]

It is a well-known fact that fires in forests with widely spaced trees are likely to stay on the surface, burning themselves out without causing long-term damage. This is the kind of fire Native Americans once set to promote agriculture and prevent megafires, another term for firestorms. According to ethnoecologist M. Kat Anderson, "Legends about destructive fires reflect the almost universal belief among California Indian tribes that catastrophic fires were not a regular, natural occurrence, but rather a rare punishment" for offenses against the spirits that rule the natural world. Today, global warming, coupled with the anti-fire policies in place since 1910, has turned California's forests into powder kegs. Ironically, the most severe fire threats are in the national forests of the Sierra Nevada, once John Muir's model of an earthly paradise. Nowadays, many places in these forests are overripe and overgrown, standing invitations to megafires. Moreover, a recent Forest Service report estimates that 129 million trees in the region have been killed by drought and invasive bark beetles, which breed in living and dead trees, adding more fuel to future fires.[25]

What we may call "human ecology" has made the situation worse. California's popu-lation has risen from 24 million in 1980 to almost 40 million in 2020. There is much to like about this state: its sunshine, its stunning scenery, its magnificent beaches. Even so, local zoning laws, often pushed through by environmentalists to protect endangered species and keep favored locations as pristine as possible, have hampered construction of affordable housing. The resulting shortage has forced would-be homeowners

California wildfires as seen from the International Space Station, approximately 250 miles above Earth. (2018)

to build away from the main population centers, in areas closer to the state's already stressed forests. In firefighter jargon, the term for those areas is WUI, pronounced "wooey," short for "wildland-urban interface." Up through the year 2010, Californians built more than 2 million homes in the state's most fire-prone locales. Worse, over the next thirty years, no fewer than 1.6 million more homes are expected to go up in areas authorities consider at "very high fire risk."[26]

In terms of wildfire, the year 2018 was record-shattering. "The old records belong to a world that no longer exists," says meteorologist Martin Hoerling, correctly. Droughts and heat waves, likely intensified by climate change, cropped up across the globe. Europe sizzled under a heat wave that the French, Italians, and Spaniards dubbed "Lucifer." Greece went into mourning as scorching heat and high winds fueled blazes that claimed eighty lives; raging fires drove residents of seaside towns along the Aegean into the shallows for safety. Blistering heat and wildfires raged in Sweden as far north as Lapland, a wilderness area home to reindeer herds largely inside the Arctic Circle. "I have not seen anything like it," said farmer Anders Edberg. "It makes you feel small. Nature is powerful and strong. Fire is powerful." And "down under," temperatures spiked to 114 degrees Fahrenheit in parts of Australia. Fruit growers reported that the pits in peaches got so hot that they cooked the fruit from the inside! On the island of Tasmania, just south of mainland Australia, fifty-six wildfires burned on a single day, pushing firefighters to the limit, forcing them to choose where to devote their energies. In a model of understatement, the government announced, "There has been a long-term increase in extreme fire weather, and in the length of the fire season, across large parts of Australia."[27]

It has only gotten worse. By any measure, Australia's 2020 fire season was disastrous. "Nature is closing in," noted one report. "Fueled by climate change, and the world's re-

A kangaroo hops past a burning house in New South Wales, Australia, during the 2020 fires.

fusal to address it, the fires that have burned across Australia are not just destroying lives, or turning forests as large as [some] nations into ashen landscapes." The fires have forced Australians to imagine the unimaginable. "What many of us have witnessed this fire season," says journalist Damien Cave, "does feel alive, like a monstrous gathering force threatening to devour what we hold most dear on a continent that will grow only hot-

ter, drier and more flammable as global temperatures rise." Unless people awaken to the menace of climate change, adds political scientist Robyn Eckersley of the University of Melbourne, "we're doomed."[28]

In the United States, 2018 witnessed 51,898 wildfires burning 8.51 million acres, chiefly in the West. The Golden State fared worst. July was its hottest month on record, with temperatures five degrees higher than normal. Death Valley had the hottest month ever recorded on Earth, with a daily average of 108 degrees Fahrenheit in the shade, at times spiking to 125 degrees in the shade.[29]

The Carr Fire, two hundred miles north of San Francisco, erupted on July 23. By the time it was fully contained on August 30, it had become the sixth most destructive fire in the state's history, killing seven people, consuming at least a thousand homes, and destroying 207,000 acres of woodland, an area larger than New York City. The blaze started when a truck blew a tire and the metal rim scraped the road, sending sparks into dry brush. At times, the Carr Fire became a megafire, creating its own wind, leaping an eight-lane highway, even melting aluminum boats on a lake.[30]

The Camp Fire, named after Camp Creek Road in Butte County, began on November 8 in overgrown brush a hundred miles north of Sacramento, the state capital, and raced southwest through steep canyons that acted as funnels. As in the Carr Fire, humans were the immediate cause; the usual culprits of wind, heat, and low humidity did the rest. For decades, Pacific Gas and Electric (PG&E), the utility company that serves California, has run its electrified power lines through wildlands; it has no choice, because by law it must supply all communities, including those in the wildland-urban interface. The problem is that strong winds rip wires off their poles, creating showers of sparks. As in the early days of the railroad, those sparks set fire to nearby trees and brush. From mid-2014 through 2017, damaged PG&E power lines ignited no fewer than fifteen hundred wildfires. Though most were put out within an hour or so, some spread rapidly, stoked by sustained winds. In 2017, PG&E equipment was responsible, says an official report, for at least seventeen major wildfires.[31]

The Camp Fire turned Paradise into hell. Located in the foothills of the Sierra Nevada, this Northern California town of twenty-six thousand, once a favorite of middle-class retirees, was set in a wooded area accessible by four county roads lined with tall pine trees. Fire was no stranger in Paradise. Every year, small wildfires ignited in the dry, dense foliage of the canyons on either side of town, without causing serious damage.

The Camp Fire was different. The experiences of Paradise residents are reminiscent of the Peshtigo firestorm 147 years earlier. "It got darker and darker," David Russell recalled. Then the world burst into flames. "I looked out my back window," Vinnie Terranova told a local radio station, "and I [see] this wall of flames about a mile long coming towards us that was not there ten minutes earlier. . . . It was everywhere at once." The fire grew at the rate of one football field every second. Amber Paton and her family joined their neighbors, running for their lives. "Family upon family just running down the street. . . . Flames on both sides. It was crazy," she recalled. Escaping by auto was a matter of luck. Traffic jams on the roads out of town, obscured by smoke and with fire on both sides, forced motorists to abandon their vehicles. "It was

hell on earth getting out of there," said Ben Raulerson. Not everyone did. By the time it was over, on November 25, the Camp Fire had claimed eighty-eight human lives, three more than the Big Blowup of 1910, and reduced 153,000 acres of woodland, 14,000 homes, and 530 commercial buildings to ashes. Ground-based firefighters were all but powerless. Indeed, the rising heat columns even forced the water bombers to fly too high to drop their payloads.[32]

Firefighters observe the ruinous damage in Paradise, California, after the Camp Fire swept through. (2018)

While the 2019 fire season was not as extended or deadly as the previous year's, it brought misery to millions of Californians. Determined to reduce the danger from equipment failures in high winds, PG&E shut off the electricity in threatened areas, sometimes for several days. As a result, food spoiled in refrigerators, air-conditioning failed in nursing homes, schools closed, and hospitals had to switch on emergency generators to preserve refrigerated medicines and perform emergency surgeries. Near Los Angeles, however, high winds dropped a tree branch onto a power line, causing sparking. The resulting fire endangered the Getty Museum, a treasure house of paintings and sculptures valued at billions of dollars.

Elsewhere, 2019 saw a repeat of the previous year's disasters. Wildfires raged in such ecologically diverse places as Alaska, the Amazon rain forest in Brazil, and South Korea. During one week in November, more than 120 wildfires burned across four Australian states. "We're starting to see unprecedented conditions," said Joëlle Gergis, a climate scientist at the Australian National University. "We had bush fires starting as early as winter—and by the time spring came around, we had fires in subtropical rainforest." Government scientist Richard Thornton agreed. "Something is clearly changing," he told reporters. "And the climate is driving all of that."[33]

FIRES OF 2020

The year 2020 seemed to confirm these dire conclusions. Starting in August, California suffered its worst wildfire season on record, with 9,639 fires burning an area of 4,177,855 acres, roughly the size of the state of Rhode Island, destroying or damaging 10,488 structures and claiming the lives of thirty-three people. To make matters worse, the disaster occurred in the midst of a persistent drought and heat wave, at the very time a COVID-19 pandemic was spreading fear and death across the nation, sapping its spirit and draining its medical resources.[34]

Lightning seems to have been the chief

culprit in igniting these blazes. On August 16 alone, a monstrous electrical storm hit California. Over the course of three days, lightning struck the Golden State no fewer than eleven thousand times. Leading climate scientists agreed that, given California's ecological history, the 2020 wildfires may well have been exacerbated by climate change due to human-caused global warming. David Romps, director of the Berkeley Atmospheric Sciences Center, declared: "To cut to the chase: Were the heat wave and the lightning strikes and the dryness of the vegetation affected by global warming? Absolutely yes. Were they made significantly hotter, more numerous, and drier because of global warming? Yes, likely yes, and yes." *Likely* yes, but, we note, not definitely so in every instance. Daniel Swain, a climate scientist at the University of California, Los Angeles, cautions that it's hard to assess whether climate change played a role in sparking the fires in Northern California.[35]

What is beyond any doubt is the fires'

human impact. For residents of fire-stricken communities, the experience was horrendous, a living nightmare. Wildfires swept wine country, a scenic area of vineyards and wineries north of San Francisco. Erupting on September 27, the Glass Fire, named for a 610-foot slope called Glass Mountain, ravaged Sonoma and Napa Counties. The best efforts of hundreds of firefighters were

Wildfires have been getting more intense; here, the Federal Emergency Management Agency captures an image of a raging wildfire. (Date unknown)

unable to contain it for nearly a month, until October 20. During that time, flames charred 67,484 acres, destroying or smoke-ruining grape crops worth tens of millions of dollars. Dave Eggers, one of the San Francisco Bay Area's best-known writers, witnessed the cataclysm. "It looks like an active volcano," he recalled in an article for *New Yorker* magazine. "An enormous plume of gray-white smoke billows from Glass Mountain's wooded peak." Eggers, overcome by despair, concluded: "It's not right, any of this. The fact that it gets harder every year, that fires get more frequent, bigger, deadlier. The fact that we have to count on volunteers, and firefighters from Colorado, Texas, Mexico, Australia. The exorbitant expense. There aren't enough people, there aren't enough planes and bulldozers and trucks. There's too much fire. We can't keep living like this."[36]

HARD CHOICES

What can be done to prevent future megafires? This is a big question about a complicated subject, so there can be no easy, one-size-fits-all answer. For sure, part of the answer lies in ending our dependence on climate-changing fossil fuels and developing alternative sources of energy, not a goal to be accomplished cheaply or quickly or without political opposition. But the answer also lies in rethinking our approach to wildfire. As Forest Service researcher Mike Battaglia explains, "A forest is like a lawn. You have to cut your lawn every week." By "cutting," he means returning fire to our woodlands—and doing it big-time. With regard to California, Jeff Brown, manager of a field station in the Tahoe National Forest, insists, "We need to be burning close to a million acres each year, just in the Sierras, or it's over."[37]

By the 1930s, ecologists had begun to question the policy of snuffing out wildfires as quickly as possible. During the 1950s, forest managers started experimenting with a method that would have appalled Gifford Pinchot. They tried "prescribed," or "controlled," burning, intentionally setting fires and allowing naturally occurring ones to burn themselves out. The goal was to reduce the threat of megafires by thinning overgrown forests and consuming the debris accumulated on their floors. In 1978, the Forest Service officially abandoned the no-burn-ever policy. These days, it lets fires burn when and where managers think it can be done safely.[38]

Controlled burning is at best an imperfect solution. Nature is full of surprises. Despite our most careful precautions, there can be unintended consequences, as was the case in the May 2000 Cerro Grande Fire in northern New Mexico, near Los Alamos National Laboratory, a center of secret atomic research. The Forest Service set off a controlled burn, but unexpected high winds made it uncontrolled. The resulting inferno consumed a seventy-five-square-mile area. The blaze ultimately threatened the multibillion-dollar laboratory and spread to the town of Los Alamos, where it destroyed 235 buildings, and to the Santa Fe National Forest, resulting in hundreds of millions of dollars in damage. Environmentalists and residents of wildland-urban interface areas often resist controlled burning, even where nearby forests are overgrown due to past efforts at fire suppression. And no politician wants to explain the casualties or property losses resulting from a controlled burn gone awry.[39]

Above all, we must recognize that wildfires are natural hazards, like earthquakes, volcanic eruptions, tsunamis, tornadoes, and hurricanes. As they are forces of nature, humans cannot master them, cannot wish them away, cannot turn them off like light switches. Be that as it may, we *can* manage the risks they pose by taking sensible precautions. We do this all the time. For instance, auto accidents are inevitable, and there is no telling who will be involved, or when, or under what circumstances. Thus, always wearing a seatbelt reduces the chance of serious injury and saves lives. Similarly, if one lives in an area with a history of earthquakes, it is best to play it safe. The Japanese do. Because their islands lie in one of the world's most active earthquake zones, they reinforce their homes and vital infrastructure such as bridges, dams, and power plants.

Prudence applies to wildfires as well. For as surely as night follows day, they will happen; it is just a matter of timing, location, and severity. Global warming increases their likelihood. And firefighters' best efforts, methods, and equipment cannot prevent every outbreak. Former Forest Service chief Vicki Christiansen says it best: "We don't ask the National Weather Service to prevent and stop all hurricanes. We ask communities and others to be prepared to receive a hurricane." Nevertheless, she warns that while we can stop some fires, there are some that are "hurricane fires," firestorms that will do their worst no matter how we feel or what we do.[40]

Acting defensively is the next best approach. Be sensible in the woods; douse campfires. Do not discard cigarettes or matches from vehicles. Homeowners in sensitive areas can use fire-resistant building materials, particularly on roofs. They can also create defensive perimeters by trimming branches and hedges and clearing brush on and around their property; experts recommend a 150-foot radius. Zoning laws can require wider streets to make it easier for emergency vehicles to enter and turn.[41]

At no time in history has it been possible to alert so many people to danger so easily and so quickly. Personal computers, the internet, and social media let both the authorities and everyday citizens deliver warnings about a wildfire's outbreak, speed, and direction. Should the worst happen, be ready; have an escape plan. Prepare in advance a few days' supply of necessities: food, water, clothing, medications, and essential documents. Know the best exit routes, and practice using them. If caught in a wildfire, look for a body of water, as the Peshtigo and Hinckley survivors did, and get into it. If there is no water nearby, find a depressed area, such as a dip in the ground, lie face-down, and protect your lungs by breathing the air closest to the ground, preferably through a moistened towel or handkerchief. Then hope for the best.

One last point: We must recognize that history is about the past; it is not destiny. Unlike the laws of nature, which govern how the world works, no human action must happen. People have minds; they choose what to do. Nor does history repeat itself. Though wildfires are bound to happen, humans need not be helpless before them. As fire ecologist Christopher Dicus reminds us, "The devastation we've seen doesn't have to be the 'new normal,' because it is largely a product of our own making. We have the potential to stop this cycle of repetitive loss, but only if we have the political will to do so."[42]

This is hardly a new insight. President Theodore Roosevelt was exercising political will when he created the Pelican Island federal bird reservation by executive order. TR and those like him—George Perkins Marsh, John Muir, Gifford Pinchot—taught Americans that one can do marvelous things through education, persuasion, and politics and, yes, by taking risks. Risking life in defense of our natural heritage is what wildland firefighters do every day.

NOTES

I. ICE, FIRE, AND FOREST

1. Rutherford Platt, *The Great American Forest* (Englewood Cliffs, NJ: Prentice Hall, 1965), 48, 51.

2. E. C. Pielou, *After the Ice Age: The Return of Life to Glaciated North America* (Chicago: University of Chicago Press, 1991), 147–148.

3. "Fire: A Myth from the Alabama Tribe," retold by S. E. Schlosser, *American Folklore*, americanfolklore.net /folklore/2011/07/fire.html.

4. Riley Black, "The History of Air," *Smithsonian Magazine*, April 28, 2010, smithsonianmag.com /science-nature/the-history-of-air-21082166.

5. Michael Marshall, "The Event That Transformed Earth," *BBC Earth*, July 2, 2015, bbc.com/earth /story/20150701-the-origin-of-the-air-we-breathe.

6. Stephen J. Pyne, "How Plants Use Fire (and Are Used by It)," *Nova Online*, pbs.org/wgbh/nova/fire/plants .html.

7. Jerry Adler, "Why Fire Makes Us Human," *Smithsonian Magazine*, June 2013, smithsonianmag.com/science -nature/why-fire-makes-us-human-72989884. Richard Wrangham's *Catching Fire: How Cooking Made Us Human* (New York: Basic Books, 2009) is the last word on this fascinating subject.

8. A fine survey of how humans arrived in the Americas is Brian Fagan's *The Great Journey: The Peopling of Ancient America* (London: Thames and Hudson, 1987).

9. Platt, *The Great American Forest*, 53, 55; Pielou, *After the Ice Age*, 1–2.

10. Pielou, *After the Ice Age*, 83, 89, 90; Platt, *The Great American Forest*, 53. See also Thomas M. Bonnicksen, *America's Ancient Forests: From the Ice Age to the Age of Discovery* (New York: Wiley, 2000).

11. "Importance and Value of Trees," savatree.com/why trees.html; Han de Groot, "A Low-Tech Climate Fix," *Scientific American*, April 2019, 7.

12. Abdul Sahim Ansari, "Influence of Forests on Environment," fao.org/3/xii/1018-b2.htm; Stelian Radu, "The Ecological Role of Deadwood in Natural Forests," in *Nature Conservation: Concepts and Practice*, ed. Dan Gafta and John Akeroyd (Berlin: Springer, 2006), doi:10.1007/978-3-540-47229-2_16.

13. Stephen J. Pyne, *Fire in America: A Cultural History of Wildland and Rural Fire* (Seattle: University of Washington Press, 1982), 35.

14. Ibid., 3, 9, 11, 12; Samantha Mathewson, "Ancient Wildfires: Researchers Examine Evolution of Forest Fires," *Nature World News*, October 25, 2015, natureworldnews.com/articles/17739/20151025 /ancient-wildfires-researchers-examine-evolution -forest-fires.htm.

15. T. J. Blackman, "The Ecological Benefits of Forest Fires," *Eartheasy*, September 3, 2015, learn.eartheasy .com/articles/the-ecological-benefits-of-forest-fires.

16. Luba Mullen, "How Trees Survive and Thrive After a Fire," *Your National Forests Magazine*, Summer/Fall 2017, nationalforests.org/our-forests/your-national -forests-magazine/how-trees-survive-and-thrive-after -a-fire.

17. "Fire in Nature," smokeybear.com/en/about-wildland
-fire/benefits-of-fire/fire-in-nature; Kevin Bonsor,
"How Wildfires Work," science.howstuffworks.com
/nature/natural-disasters/wildfire.htm.

18. Robert W. Wells, *Embers of October* (New York:
Prentice Hall, 1968), 201; Pyne, *Fire in America*, 26.

19. Chad Hanson, *The Myth of "Catastrophic" Wildfire:
A New Ecological Paradigm of Forest Health*, John
Muir Technical Report 1 (Cedar Ridge, CA: John
Muir Project of Earth Island Institute, 2010),
johnmuirproject.org/wp-content/uploads/2014/12
/TheMythOfTheCatastrophicWildfireReport.pdf.

II. ONCE UPON A TIME IN AMERICA

1. John Bakeless, *The Eyes of Discovery: The Pageant
of North America as Seen by the First Explorers*
(Philadelphia: J. B. Lippincott, 1950), 200–201.

2. David Peterson de Vries, *Voyages from Holland to
America, A.D. 1632 to 1644*, trans. Henry C. Murphy
(New York, 1853), 31.

3. Henry Tudor, *Narrative of a Tour in North America*
(London: James Duncan, 1834), 218.

4. E. N. Anderson, review of *Tending the Wild: Native
American Knowledge and the Management of California's
Natural Resources*, by M. Kat Anderson, *Journal of
California and Great Basin Anthropology* 25, no. 2
(2005), 256.

5. Michael Williams, *Americans and Their Forests:
A Historical Geography* (Cambridge: Cambridge
University Press, 1989), 27; Shepard Krech III, *The
Ecological Indian: Myth and History* (New York: Norton,
1999), 3, 110; Daniel Q. Thompson and Ralph H.
Smith, "The Forest Primeval in the Northeast—
a Great Myth?," *Proceedings: 10th Tall Timbers
Fire Ecology Conference* (1970), 259; Pyne, *Fire in
America*, 48.

6. Krech, *The Ecological Indian*, 106; Gerald W. Williams,
"References on the American Indian Use of Fire in
Ecosystems," 2005, nrcs.usda.gov/Internet/FSE_
DOCUMENTS/nrcs144p2_051334.pdf; Ted Steinberg,
Down to Earth: Nature's Role in American History
(New York: Oxford University Press, 2002), 18.

7. Pyne, *Fire in America*, 75.

8. Hu Maxwell, "The Use and Abuse of Forests by the
Virginia Indians," *William and Mary Quarterly* 19, no. 2
(October 1910), 81; Eric Rutkow, *American Canopy:
Trees, Forests, and the Making of a Nation* (New York:
Scribner, 2012), 20.

9. A first-rate study of European diseases in the New
World is Alfred W. Crosby Jr., *The Columbian Exchange:
Biological and Cultural Consequences of 1492* (Westport,
CT: Greenwood Press, 1972). The same subject is
thoroughly dealt with in a later work by David E.
Stannard, *American Holocaust: The Conquest of the New
World* (New York: Oxford University Press, 1992).

10. Krech, *The Ecological Indian*, 81; Williams, *Americans
and Their Forests*, 26; Thomas Hariot, *A Briefe and
True Report of the New Found Land of Virginia* (London,
1588), 28.

11. Hariot, *A Briefe and True Report*, 28.

12. Roy Harvey Pearce, "The 'Ruines of Mankind': The
Indian and the Puritan Mind," *Journal of the History
of Ideas* 13, no. 2 (April 1952), 201; Charles C. Mann,
1491: New Revelations of the Americas Before Columbus

(New York: Knopf, 2005), 55, 110; Crosby, *The Columbian Exchange*, 241.

13. Robert Beverley, *The History of Virginia, in Four Parts* (Richmond, VA: J. W. Randolph, 1855), 98; Pyne, *Fire in America*, 51.

14. George Perkins Marsh, *Man and Nature; or, Physical Geography as Modified by Human Action* (London: Sampson Low, Son and Marston, 1864), 281, 242; Jean R. Birrell, "The Medieval English Forest," *Journal of Forest History* 24, no. 2 (April 1980), 78–85.

15. Steinberg, *Down to Earth*, 35; Rutkow, *American Canopy*, 14.

16. George Wilson Pierson, *Tocqueville in America* (Baltimore: Johns Hopkins University Press, 1996), 263, 264.

17. Bakeless, *The Eyes of Discovery*, 371, 272; Richard G. Lillard, *The Great Forest* (New York: Knopf, 1948), 4; William Barillas, "Michigan's Pioneers and the Destruction of the Hardwood Forest," *Michigan Historical Review* 15, no. 2 (Fall 1989), 10–11.

18. Bakeless, *The Eyes of Discovery*, 373; Pierson, *Tocqueville in America*, 142, 269–270.

19. Krech, *The Ecological Indian*, 73; Franklin Everett, *Memorials of the Grand River Valley* (Chicago: Chicago Legal News, 1878), 48; Bakeless, *The Eyes of Discovery*, 371, 374.

20. William Bartram, *Travels Through North and South Carolina, Georgia, East and West Florida* [. . .] (London: J. Johnson, 1794), 81–82.

21. Joel Greenberg, *A Feathered River Across the Sky: The Passenger Pigeon's Flight to Extinction* (New York: Bloomsbury, 2014), 1, 5–6, 47.

22. Alexander Wilson, "Passenger Pigeon," in *American Ornithology* (Philadelphia: Bradford and Inskeep, 1812), 5:102–112, biodiversitylibrary.org/item/175520; W. B. Mershon, *The Passenger Pigeon* (New York: Outing Publishing, 1907), 43–44, 45.

23. Frank Graham Jr., *Man's Dominion: The Story of Conservation in America* (Philadelphia: J. B. Lippincott, 1971), 26; Greenberg, *A Feathered River*, 1; John James Audubon, "Passenger Pigeon," in *The Birds of America*, audubon.org/birds-of-america/passenger-pigeon.

24. Greenberg, *A Feathered River*, 54.

25. Roderick Nash, *Wilderness and the American Mind* (New Haven, CT: Yale University Press, 1967), 10–11.

26. Philip McCouat, "Fashion, Feathers and Animal Rights," *Journal of Art in Society* (2016), artinsociety.com/feathers-fashion-and-animal-rights; Ben Isacat, "Thomas Aquinas, the Church and Animals," chap. 7.1 in *How to Do Animal Rights* (2015), animalethics.org.uk/aquinas.html.

27. William Bradford, *History of Plymouth Plantation* (Boston: Massachusetts Historical Society, 1856), 78–79; Nash, *Wilderness and the American Mind*, 28–29.

28. Nash, *Wilderness and the American Mind*, 27; Benjamin Franklin, "Observations Concerning the Increase of Mankind, 1751," founders.archives.gov/documents/Franklin/01-04-02-0080.

29. Isaac Weld Jr., *Travels Through the States of North America, and the Provinces of Upper and Lower Canada, During the Years 1795, 1796, and 1797* (London: John Stockdale, 1799), 23, 24.

30. Alexis de Tocqueville, *Journey to America*, trans. George Lawrence (New Haven, CT: Yale University Press,

1959), 335; Alexis de Tocqueville, *Democracy in America* (New York: Knopf, 1956), 2:74; Basil Hall, *Travels in North America in the Years 1827 and 1828* (Philadelphia: Carey, Lea and Carey, 1829), 1:83.

31. François Jean, marquis de Chastellux, *Travels in North-America in the Years 1780–81–82* (New York, 1828), 35; Hall, *Travels in North America*, 1:71, 2:124.

32. Lillard, *The Great Forest*, 21, 22; David Hackett Fischer, *Albion's Seed: Four British Folkways in America* (New York: Oxford University Press, 1989), 689.

33. Anthony Trollope, *North America* (New York: Harper & Brothers, 1862), 128–129, italics added; Stewart Winger, "Lincoln's Economics and the American Dream: A Reappraisal," *Journal of the Abraham Lincoln Association* 22, no. 1 (Winter 2001), 50–80, hdl.handle.net/2027/spo.2629860.0022.106.

34. "The New England Dark Day, May 19, 1780," newenglandhistoricalsociety.com/new-england-dark-day-may-19-1780.

35. Thomas J. Campanella, " 'Mark Well the Gloom': Shedding Light on the Great Dark Day of 1780," *Environmental History* 12, no. 1 (January 2007), 37, 38.

36. Evan Andrews, "Remembering New England's 'Dark Day,' " history.com/news/remembering-new-englands-dark-day.

37. Randy Alfred, "May 19, 1780: Darkness at Noon Enshrouds New England," *Wired*, May 19, 2010, wired.com/2010/05/0519new-england-dark-day; Tom de Castella, "What Caused the Mystery of the Dark Day?," *BBC News Magazine*, May 18, 2012, bbc.com/news/magazine-18097177; William Gordon, *The History of the Rise, Progress, and Establishment of the Independence of the United States of America* (New York: Samuel Campbell, 1788), 3:57.

38. Stephen Bonsal, *When the French Were Here: A Narrative of the Sojourn of the French Forces in America, and Their Contribution to the Yorktown Campaign* (Garden City, NY: Doubleday, Doran, 1945), 92–99; Chastellux, *Travels in North-America*, 251, translator's note.

39. Frances Trollope, *Domestic Manners of the Americans* (London: Whittaker, Treacher, 1832), 1:29.

40. Charles Richard Weld, *A Vacation Tour in the United States and Canada* (London: Longman, Brown, Green, and Longmans, 1855), 85–87, 99; Pyne, *Fire in America*, 163.

III. HARVESTING THE NORTHWOODS

1. Williams, *Americans and Their Forests*, 295, 301; Platt, *The Great American Forest*, 71–72; Charles van Ravenswaay, "America's Age of Wood," *Proceedings of the American Antiquarian Society* 80, no. 1 (April 1970), 49–66, americanantiquarian.org/proceedings/44497992.pdf; John McCollough and Henry F. Check Jr., "The Baleen Whales' Saving Grace: The Introduction of Petroleum Based Products in the Market and Its Impact on the Whaling Industry," *Sustainability* 2, no. 10 (2010), 3142–3157, doi:10.3390/su2103142.

2. A useful summary of paper and printing is Lucien Febvre and Henri-Jean Martin, *The Coming of the Book: The Impact of Printing, 1450–1800* (New York: Verso Books, 1997).

3. Rutkow, *American Canopy*, 121.

4. See Peter Burger, *Charles Fenerty and His Paper Invention* (Toronto: PB Publishing, 2007).

5. Donald J. Pisani, "Forests and Conservation, 1865–1890," *Journal of American History* 72, no. 2 (September 1985), 342; Williams, *Americans and Their Forests*, 295.

6. Thomas Hamilton, *Men and Manners in America* (Edinburgh: William Blackwood, 1833), 2:187–188; David E. Schob, "Woodhawks & Cordwood: Steamboat Fuel on the Ohio and Mississippi Rivers, 1820–1860," *Forest and Conservation History* 21, no. 3 (July 1977), 125.

7. For the background of Cooper's achievement, see Craig Miner, *A Most Magnificent Machine: America Adopts the Railroad, 1825–1862* (Lawrence: University Press of Kansas, 2010), 19–32.

8. "Maps Showing the Progressive Development of U.S. Railroads—1830 to 1950," cprr.org/Museum /RR_Development.html; Crandall Shifflett, *Victorian America, 1876 to 1900* (New York: Facts on File, 1996), 65–66.

9. Williams, *Americans and Their Forests*, 299; Robert V. Bruce, *Lincoln and the Tools of War* (Champaign: University of Illinois Press, 1989), 215; Rutkow, *American Canopy*, 103.

10. Rutkow, *American Canopy*, 105; Pisani, "Forests and Conservation," 344; Williams, *Americans and Their Forests*, 298.

11. Charles Dickens, *American Notes for General Circulation* (London: Chapman and Hall, 1850), 48.

12. John Ise, *The United States Forest Policy* (New Haven, CT: Yale University Press, 1920), 26.

13. Rutkow, *American Canopy*, 109.

14. Barillas, "Michigan's Pioneers and the Destruction of the Hardwood Forest," 4.

15. "German American Corner: Weyerhaeuser, Frederick (1834–1914)," germanheritage.com /biographies/mtoz/weyerhaeuser.html; Luke Ritter, "Frederick Weyerhaeuser (1834–1914)," *Immigrant Entrepreneurship: German-American Business Biographies, 1720 to the Present*, immigrantentrepreneurship.org /entries/frederick-weyerhaeuser.

16. Robert F. Fries, *Empire in Pine: The Story of Lumbering in Wisconsin, 1830–1900* (Ellison Bay, WI: William Caxton, 1989), 26.

17. Norman S. Hayner, "Taming the Lumberjack," *American Sociological Review* 10, no. 2 (April 1945), 217, doi:10.2307/2085640.

18. Joseph Schafer, "John E. Nelligan's Story," *Wisconsin Magazine of History* 13, no. 1 (September 1929), 33; Wells, *Embers of October*, 21.

19. Schafer, "John E. Nelligan's Story," 19.

20. Ibid.; Robert W. Wells, *"Daylight in the Swamp!": Lumberjacking in the Late 19th Century* (Madison, WI: NorthWord Press, 1978), 12.

21. Lillard, *The Great Forest*, 213, 214.

22. Ibid., 215; Wells, *Daylight*, 21.

23. Estimated Log Weight Calculator, woodweb.com/cgi -bin/calculators/calc.pl?calculator=log_weight.

24. Williams, *Americans and Their Forests*, 245; Clifford Allen, ed., *Michigan Log Marks, Their Function and Use During the Great Michigan Pine Harvest* (East Lansing: Michigan Agricultural Experiment Station, 1942).

25. Fries, *Empire in Pine*, 45–47.

26. Rutkow, *American Canopy*, 108.

IV. PESHTIGO: THE NIGHT HELL YAWNED

1. Alasdair Wilkins, "October 8, 1871: The Night America Burned," *Gizmodo*, March 29, 2012, gizmodo.com/october-8-1871-the-night-america-burned-5897629.

2. John R. Chapin, "Chicago in Flames," *Harper's Weekly*, October 28, 1871.

3. Frank Luzerne, *The Lost City! Drama of the Fire Fiend! or, Chicago, as It Was, and as It Is!* (New York: Wells, 1872), 67.

4. Laura Ingalls Wilder, *Little House in the Big Woods* (New York: Harper & Row, 1932), 1–2, gutenberg.ca /ebooks/wilder-woods/wilder-woods-01-h.html.

5. "Mayor William B. Ogden Biography," chipublib.org /mayor-william-b-ogden-biography.

6. Elias Colbert and Everett Chamberlin, *Chicago and the Great Conflagration* (Chicago: J. S. Goodman, 1872), 479; Wells, *Embers of October*, 36.

7. Wells, *Embers of October*, 4, 7–8.

8. Ibid., 2; John Steele Gordon, "Forgotten Fury: A Long-Ago Calamity May Shed Light on a Current Impasse," *American Heritage*, April/May 2003, americanheritage .com/content/forgotten-fury.

9. Peter Pernin, "The Great Peshtigo Fire: An Eyewitness Account," *Wisconsin Magazine of History* 54, no. 4 (Summer 1971), 246–272.

10. Ibid., 248.

11. Ibid.

12. Ibid., 249.

13. Denise Gess and William Lutz, *Firestorm at Peshtigo: A Town, Its People, and the Deadliest Fire in American History* (New York: Henry Holt, 2002), 60.

14. Pernin, "The Great Peshtigo Fire," 250; Wells, *Embers of October*, 322.

15. Isaac Stephenson, *Recollections of a Long Life: 1829–1915* (Chicago: privately printed, 1915), 100; Wells, *Embers of October*, 45.

16. Wells, *Embers of October*, 109–110; Pernin, "The Great Peshtigo Fire," 252, 255.

17. Pernin, "The Great Peshtigo Fire," 254.

18. Robinson Meyer, "The Simple Reason That Humans Can't Control Wildfires," *Atlantic*, November 13, 2018, theatlantic.com/science/archive/2018/11/california -wildfire-why-humans-cant-control-them/575740.

19. Colbert and Chamberlin, *Chicago and the Great Conflagration*, 474; Wells, *Embers of October*, 119; Pyne, *Fire in America*, 206; Gess and Lutz, *Firestorm at Peshtigo*, 116.

20. Pernin, "The Great Peshtigo Fire," 256.

21. Ibid., 257.

22. *Journal of Proceedings of the Twenty-Sixth Annual Session of the Wisconsin Legislature* (Madison: Atwood & Culver, 1873), 223; Wells, *Embers of October*, 116, 117.

23. Wells, *Embers of October*, 115.

24. Pernin, "The Great Peshtigo Fire," 257.

25. Ibid., 258.

26. Colbert and Chamberlin, *Chicago and the Great Conflagration*, 483–484; Joseph M. Moran and E. Lee Somerville, "Tornadoes of Wildfire at Williamsonville, Wisconsin, October 8, 1871," *Transactions of the Wisconsin Academy of Sciences, Arts and Letters 78* (1990), 21–32, images.library.wisc.edu/WI/Efacs /transactions/WT1990/reference/wi.wt1990.jmmoran .pdf.

27. Gess and Lutz, *Firestorm at Peshtigo*, 118, 123–125.

28. Stewart H. Holbrook, *Burning an Empire: The Story of American Forest Fires* (New York: Macmillan, 1943), 206; Gess and Lutz, *Firestorm at Peshtigo*, 119.

29. Wells, *Embers of October*, 145; Rutkow, *American Canopy*, 118.

30. Wells, *Embers of October*, 174.

31. Pernin, "The Great Peshtigo Fire," 259; Wells, *Embers of October*, 132.

32. Colbert and Chamberlin, *Chicago and the Great Conflagration*, 479, 482; Gess and Lutz, *Firestorm at Peshtigo*, 165.

33. Stephenson, *Recollections of a Long Life*, 180, 181; Daniel James Brown, *Under a Flaming Sky: The Great Hinckley Firestorm of 1894* (Guilford, CT: Lyons Press, 2006), 85.

34. *Journal of Proceedings*, 224; Pernin, "The Great Peshtigo Fire," 263, 265, 269; Stephenson, *Recollections of a Long Life*, 182; Colbert and Chamberlin, *Chicago and the Great Conflagration*, 479; Wells, *Embers of October*, 173.

35. Rutkow, *American Canopy*, 119; Scott Knickelbine, *The Great Peshtigo Fire: Stories and Science from America's Deadliest Firestorm* (Madison: Wisconsin Historical Society Press, 2012), 9; Gess and Lutz, *Firestorm at Peshtigo*, 225.

36. Gess and Lutz, *Firestorm at Peshtigo*, 159, 181, 182.

V. THE HINCKLEY HORROR OF 1894

1. Martin Middlebrook, *The Battle of Hamburg: Allied Bomber Forces Against a German City in 1943* (New York: Charles Scribner's Sons, 1981), 224–225, 230–231.

2. Gess and Lutz, *Firestorm at Peshtigo*, 208.

3. Holbrook, *Burning an Empire*, 91.

4. Brown, *Under a Flaming Sky*, 16.

5. Ibid., 11, 16–17, 19.

6. Holbrook, *Burning an Empire*, 29.

7. Ibid.

8. Brown, *Under a Flaming Sky*, 55; [Gudmund Emanuel Akermark?], *The Cyclone of Fire; or, The Hinckley Fire*, trans. Charles John LaVine (Minneapolis: Companion Publishing, 1894), 17, 19, mnhs.org/library/findaids /lb00018/lb00018-000001.pdf.

9. [Akermark?], *The Cyclone of Fire*, 24; Elton T. Brown, *A History of the Great Minnesota Forest Fires: Sandstone, Mission Creek, Hinckley, Pokegama, Skunk Lake* (St. Paul, MN: Brown Bros., 1894), 27.

10. William Wilkinson, *Memorials of the Minnesota Forest Fires in the Year 1894* (Minneapolis: Norman E. Wilkinson, 1895), 169.

11. Ibid., 169–170.

12. Ibid., 129, 153.

13. Ibid., 162.

14. Brown, *Under a Flaming Sky,* 98.

15. [Akermark?], *The Cyclone of Fire,* 3–4.

16. Ibid., 39–40.

17. Brown, *Under a Flaming Sky,* 181.

18. Ibid., 185–186.

19. "Hinckley, MN," *Data USA,* datausa.io/profile/geo /hinckley-mn.

VI. AMERICA'S WAR ON WILDLIFE

1. Krech, *The Ecological Indian,* 125; Wayne Gard, *The Great Buffalo Hunt: Its History and Drama, and Its Role in the Opening of the West* (New York: Knopf, 1960), 6; Andrew C. Isenberg, *The Destruction of the Bison: An Environmental History, 1750–1920* (Cambridge: Cambridge University Press, 2000), 24.

2. "Express Train Crosses the Nation in 83 Hours," history.com/this-day-in-history/express-train-crosses -the-nation-in-83-hours; David D. Smits, "The Frontier Army and the Destruction of the Buffalo: 1865–1883," *Western Historical Quarterly* 25, no. 3 (Autumn 1994), 338.

3. Smits, "The Frontier Army," 315.

4. Theodore Roosevelt, *Hunting Trips of a Ranchman: Sketches of Sport on the Northern Cattle Plains* (New York: G. P. Putnam's Sons, 1885), 242–243, bartleby.com/52/8.html.

5. Levi Rickert, "US Presidents in Their Own Words Concerning American Indians," *Native News Online,* February 16, 2020, nativenewsonline.net/currents /us-presidents-in-their-own-words-concerning -american-indians.

6. Graham, *Man's Dominion,* 20, 51; Sears, Roebuck and Company, *1897 Sears Roebuck Catalogue* (New York: Chelsea House Publishers, 1968), 564–565.

7. Graham, *Man's Dominion,* 24.

8. William T. Hornaday, *Our Vanishing Wildlife: Its Extermination and Preservation* (New York: Charles Scribner's Sons, 1913), 107–108; Graham, *Man's Dominion,* 20.

9. Hornaday, *Our Vanishing Wildlife,* 106; Graham, *Man's Dominion,* 20; Kimberly Chrisman-Campbell, "Fowl Intentions: Fashion, Activism, Conservation," *Ornament* 40, no. 4 (2018).

10. Gary G. Gray, *Wildlife and People: The Human Dimensions of Wildlife Ecology* (Urbana: University of Illinois Press, 1993), 36; Chrisman-Campbell, "Fowl Intentions"; Graham, *Man's Dominion,* 47; "Historical Gold Prices—1833 to Present," piketty .pse.ens.fr/files/capital21c/xls/RawDataFiles/Gold Prices17922012.pdf.

11. Graham, *Man's Dominion,* 46; Frank M. Chapman, *Autobiography of a Bird-Lover* (New York: D. Appleton–Century, 1933), 39; Willoughby Dewar, "The Plumage Trade and the Destruction of Birds," *Journal of the Royal Society of Arts* 69, no. 3569 (April 15, 1921), 336.

12. Jeanmarie Tucker, "The Bird Hat: 'Murderous Millinery,'" mdhistory.org/the-bird-hat-murderous -millinery.

13. William Souder, "How Two Women Ended the Deadly Feather Trade," *Smithsonian Magazine,* March 2013, smithsonianmag.com/science-nature/how-two -women-ended-the-deadly-feather-trade-23187277.

14. Greenberg, *A Feathered River,* 91; Hornaday, *Our Vanishing Wildlife,* 12; Barry Yeoman, "Why the Passenger Pigeon Went Extinct," *Audubon,* May–June 2014, audubon.org/magazine/may-june-2014 /why-passenger-pigeon-went-extinct.

15. Kyle Bagnall, "Passenger Pigeons in Your State, Province or Territory: Wisconsin," *Project Passenger Pigeon,* passengerpigeon.org/states/Wisconsin .html; Stephen J. Bodio, "A Feathered Tempest: The Improbable Life and Sudden Death of the Passenger Pigeon," *All About Birds,* April 15, 2010, allaboutbirds .org/a-feathered-tempest-the-improbable-life-and -sudden-death-of-the-passenger-pigeon; Peter Matthiessen, *Wildlife in America* (New York: Viking, 1987), 160–161.

16. Jeff Elder, "This Species Became Extinct Through the Avarice and Thoughtlessness of Man," *Medium,* March 15, 2016, jeffelder.medium.com/this -species-became-extinct-through-the-avarice-and -thoughtlessness-of-man-b9609b2c3c8f.

17. James Fenimore Cooper, *The Pioneers* (New York: Charles Wiley, 1823), 124, archive.org/stream /pioneersorsource01cooprich.

VII. CHANGING MINDS

1. Rutkow, *American Canopy,* 94. See also David Lowenthal, *George Perkins Marsh: Prophet of Conservation* (Seattle: University of Washington Press, 2000).

2. Marsh, *Man and Nature,* 5.

3. Ibid., 109, 549.

4. Ibid., 36, 44.

5. Ibid., 42–43.

6. Ibid., 228.

7. Tony Perrottet, "John Muir's Yosemite," *Smithsonian Magazine,* July 2008, smithsonianmag.com/history /john-muirs-yosemite-10737, italics added.

8. Carolyn Merchant, "Shades of Darkness: Race and Environmental History," *Environmental History* 8, no. 3 (July 2002), 386.

9. John Muir, "By-Ways of Yosemite Travel: Bloody Cañon," *Overland Monthly,* September 1874, 267; John Muir, "The American Forests," *Atlantic Monthly,* August 1897, 154–155, scholarlycommons.pacific.edu /cgi/viewcontent.cgi?article=1233&context=jmb.

10. Edwin Way Teale, ed., *The Wilderness World of John Muir* (New York: Houghton Mifflin, 1954), 313; J. Baird Callicott and Priscilla Solis Ybarra, "The Puritan Origins of the American Wilderness Movement," nationalhumanitiescenter.org/tserve/nattrans /ntwilderness/essays/puritan.htm.

11. Merchant, "Shades of Darkness," 382.

12. Muir, "The American Forests."

13. Callicott and Ybarra, "The Puritan Origins."

14. John Muir, *Our National Parks* (Boston: Houghton Mifflin, 1901), 1–2; Rutkow, *American Canopy,* 149; Michael B. Smith, "The Value of a Tree: Public Debates

of John Muir and Gifford Pinchot," *Historian* 60, no. 4 (June 1998), 776; John Muir, *John of the Mountains: The Unpublished Journals of John Muir,* ed. Linnie Marsh Wolfe (Boston: Houghton Mifflin, 1938), 317.

15. Hiram Martin Chittenden, *The Yellowstone National Park: Historical and Descriptive* (Cincinnati: Stewart and Kidd, 1915), 77–78.

16. Muir, "The American Forests," 157.

17. Stephen Fox, *The American Conservation Movement: John Muir and His Legacy* (Madison: University of Wisconsin Press, 1985), 109.

18. Robert Hudson Westover, "Conservation Versus Preservation?," *USDA Blogs,* March 22, 2106, fs.usda .gov/features/conservation-versus-preservation.

19. Char Miller, "The Greening of Gifford Pinchot," *Environmental History Review* 16, no. 3 (Autumn 1992), 5, 6.

20. Rutkow, *American Canopy,* 153.

21. William Manners, *TR and Will: A Friendship That Split the Republican Party* (New York: Harcourt, Brace & World, 1969), 104; Forest History Society, "Gifford Pinchot (1865–1946)," foresthistory.org/research -explore/us-forest-service-history/people/chiefs /gifford-pinchot-1865-1946.

22. Miller, "The Greening of Gifford Pinchot," 7; Rutkow, *American Canopy,* 155.

23. Garland E. Allen, " 'Culling the Herd': Eugenics and the Conservation Movement in the United States, 1900–1940," *Journal of the History of Biology* 46 (Spring 2012), 42, doi:10.1007/s10739-011-9317-1; Gifford Pinchot, *Breaking New Ground* (New York: Harcourt, Brace, 1947), 31.

24. Gifford Pinchot, *The Fight for Conservation* (New York: Doubleday, Page, 1910), 79–81.

25. Ibid., 16, 17.

26. Pyne, *Fire in America,* 185.

27. Nathan Miller, *Theodore Roosevelt: A Life* (New York: William Morrow, 1992), 168. See also John F. Rieger, *American Sportsmen and the Origins of Conservation* (New York: Winchester Press, 1975).

28. Rutkow, *American Canopy,* 161; M. Nelson McGeary, *Gifford Pinchot: Forester-Politician* (Princeton: Princeton University Press, 1960), 66.

29. "Four Letters: Theodore Roosevelt and the Final Reported Sighting of the Now-Extinct Passenger Pigeon," raabcollection.com/presidential-autographs /roosevelt-pigeons.

30. Paul Russell Cutright, *Theodore Roosevelt the Naturalist* (New York: Harper & Brothers, 1956), 116; Theodore Roosevelt, *An Autobiography* (New York: Charles Scribner's Sons, 1922), 322; Constance Carter, "Roosevelt, Muir, and the Camping Trip," *Inside Adams* (blog), August 11, 2016, blogs.loc.gov/inside _adams/2016/08/roosevelt-muir-and-the-camping -trip; "The Camping Trip That Changed the Nation," nationalparksadventure.com/the-camping-trip-that -changed-the-nation.

31. The history of these expulsions is best described in Mark David Spence, *Dispossessing the Wilderness: Indian Removal and the Making of the National Parks* (New York: Oxford University Press, 1999), and in Isaac Kantor, "Ethnic Cleansing and America's Creation of National Parks," *Public Land and Resources Law Review* 28 (2007), 41–65, scholarship.law.umt.edu/cgi/viewcontent.cgi ?article=1267&context=plrlr.

32. Steven Erdmann, "The Feather Wars and Theodore Roosevelt," *Tustenegee,* October 2010, 11; "The Antiquities Act, 1900–06," nps.gov/articles/lee-story -antiquities.htm.

33. Smith, "The Value of a Tree," 766.

34. Roosevelt, *An Autobiography,* 394; Jeff Frantz, "Pinchot Was Teddy Roosevelt's 'Conscience' on Conservation," *York (PA) Daily Record.*

VIII. THE WORST FOREST FIRE EVER: THE BIG BLOWUP OF 1910

1. Frantz, "Pinchot Was Teddy Roosevelt's 'Conscience.'"

2. Betty Goodwin Spencer, *The Big Blowup* (Caldwell, ID: Caxton Printers, 1958), 41; "Life in 1910," orangepower.com/threads/life-in-1910-100-years -ago.96681.

3. Spencer, *The Big Blowup,* 41; Timothy Egan, *The Big Burn: Teddy Roosevelt and the Fire That Saved America* (Boston: Houghton Mifflin Harcourt, 2009), 109.

4. Pinchot, *Breaking New Ground,* 240, italics added.

5. Manners, *TR and Will,* 113. After leaving his post as head of the Forest Service, Pinchot wrote extensively on conservation, and he organized the National Conservation Association to continue the fight for his ideas. Pinchot was governor of Pennsylvania from 1923 to 1927 and from 1931 to 1935. During his time in office, he pressed for legislation on issues such as equal pay for women and men, child labor, working conditions in factories, and trade union rights. He died October 4, 1946, at the age of eighty-one.

Theodore Roosevelt died January 6, 1919, at the age of sixty.

6. Gifford Pinchot, *A Primer of Forestry* (Washington, DC: Government Printing Office, 1899), 77; Pinchot, *The Fight for Conservation,* 44–46.

7. Stephen J. Pyne, "The Source," foresthistory.org /wp-content/uploads/2016/12/The-Source-Stephen -Pyne-Lecture.pdf; H. H. Biswell, "Forest Fire in Perspective," *Proceedings: 7th Tall Timbers Fire Ecology Conference* (1967), talltimbers.org/wp-content /uploads/2018/09/43-Biswell1967_op.pdf.

8. Gifford Bryce Pinchot, "Could the 1910 Fire Happen Again?," *Evergreen Magazine,* Winter 1994–1995, toyfj40.freeshell.org/Stories/Fire1910p6.html.

9. Stephen J. Pyne, *Year of the Fires: The Story of the Great Fires of 1910* (New York: Viking, 2001), 61, 62.

10. Jim Petersen, "The 1910 Fire," *Evergreen Magazine,* Winter 1994–1995, toyfj40.freeshell.org/Stories /Fire1910p1.html.

11. Thomas A. Krainz, "Conflict and Fire: Community Tensions Surrounding the Big Blowup," *Pacific Northwest Quarterly* 103 (Winter 2011/2012), 14, 16.

12. Pyne, *Year of the Fires,* 109; Pyne, *Fire in America,* 244.

13. Spencer, *The Big Blowup,* 40; Krainz, "Conflict and Fire," 17, 19; Elers Koch, *Forty Years a Forester* (Lincoln: University of Nebraska Press, 2019), 101, 103.

14. Egan, *The Big Burn,* 4.

15. *Seattle Daily Times,* August 12, 1910; Spencer, *The Big Blowup,* 68, 78.

16. Forest Service, U.S. Department of Agriculture, *When the Mountains Roared: Stories of the 1910*

Fire (Washington, DC: Forest Service, 1978), 3, foresthistory.org/wp-content/uploads/2017/01 /When-the-Mountains-Roared.pdf; Pyne, *Year of the Fires*, 128; Timothy Egan, "Why Foresters Prefer to Fight Fire with Fire," *New York Times*, August 20, 2000, nytimes.com/2000/08/20/weekinreview /ideas-trends-why-foresters-prefer-to-fight-fire-with -fire.html; John Galvin, "The Big Burn: Idaho and Montana, August 1910," *Popular Mechanics*, July 30, 2007, popularmechanics.com/science/environment /a1961/4219853; Jim Kershner, "Forest Fire, the Largest in U.S. History, Left Stories of Awe, Tragedy," *Spokesman-Review* (Spokane, WA), August 15, 2010, spokesman.com/stories/2010/aug/15/1910-fire -region-consumed.

17. Spencer, *The Big Blowup*, 79–82; Pyne, *Fire in America*, 247.

18. Joe B. Halm, "The Big Fire," in Forest Service, *When the Mountains Roared*, 29, 30.

19. Ibid., 30; Egan, *The Big Burn*, 218–219.

20. Halm, "The Big Fire," 30.

21. Spencer, *The Big Blowup*, 72–73.

22. E. C. Pulaski, "Surrounded by Forest Fires: My Most Exciting Experience as a Forest Ranger," *American Forestry* 29 (August 1923), 485, 486, foresthistory.org /wp-content/uploads/2017/02/Surrounded-by-Forest -Firest-By-E.C.-Pulaski.pdf.

23. Pulaski, "Surrounded by Forest Fires," 486; Pyne, *Year of the Fires*, 169; Egan, *The Big Burn*, 167; Michael Kodas, "Bigger, Hotter, Faster," *BioGraphic*, August 15, 2017, biographic.com/posts/sto/bigger-hotter-faster.

24. Pulaski, "Surrounded by Forest Fires," 486.

25. Ibid.

26. Pyne, *Year of the Fires*, 146, 162.

27. Egan, *The Big Burn*, 3, 4; Spencer, *The Big Blowup*, 119; Krainz, "Conflict and Fire," 19.

28. Pyne, *Year of the Fires*, 199.

29. Forest Service, *When the Mountains Roared*, 4; Spencer, *The Big Blowup*, 185; "The 1910 Fires," foresthistory.org /research-explore/us-forest-service-history/policy -and-law/fire-u-s-forest-service/famous-fires/the -1910-fires; Pyne, *Year of the Fires*, 201; Petersen, "The 1910 Fire," 11.

30. Arthur Chapman, "The Forest Fire Fighters," *Ames Forester* 10 (1922), 99, lib.dr.iastate.edu/amesforester /vol10/iss1/18.

31. Petersen, "The 1910 Fire"; Egan, *The Big Burn*, 241– 242, 272.

32. Pyne, *Year of the Fires*, 196.

33. Steve Nelson and Jack Rollins, "Smokey the Bear" (New York: Hill and Range Songs, 1952), wvforestry .com/pdf/Smokey%20Song.pdf.

IX. BIGGER, HOTTER, FASTER

1. Katie Hoover and Laura A. Hanson, "Wildfire Statistics," Congressional Research Service, October 1, 2020, crsreports.congress.gov/product /pdf/if/if10244; National Interagency Fire Center, "Federal Firefighting Costs (Suppression Only)," nifc .gov/fire-information/statistics/suppression-costs.

2. Chris Kornelis, "Chief U.S. Forester Vicki Christiansen Thinks Some Fires Should Be Left to Burn," *Wall Street Journal*, October 5, 2019.

3. "Hotshots," fs.usda.gov/science-technology/fire/people/hotshots.

4. "Components of Wildland Fire P.P.E.," fs.fed.us/eng/pubs/htmlpubs/htm93512851/com.htm.

5. Brian Mockenhaupt, "Fire on the Mountain," *Atlantic*, June 2014, theatlantic.com/magazine/archive/2014/06/fire-on-the-mountain/361613.

6. Pyne, "The Source"; "Edward Pulaski," 4, 6–7, fs.usda.gov/Internet/FSE_DOCUMENTS/stelprdb5444775.pdf.

7. Pyne, *Fire in America*, 489.

8. Ibid., 372–373.

9. Kathy Aney, "Breaking Barriers from 1,500 Feet," *East Oregonian*, June 24, 2015, eastoregonian.com/news/local/breaking-barriers-from201-500-feet20/article_44776d4a-4bd9-5df5-9d2d-2d693e541db2.html.

10. Norman Maclean, *Young Men and Fire* (Chicago: University of Chicago Press, 1992). *Smokejumper: A Memoir by One of America's Most Select Airborne Firefighters* (New York: William Morrow Paperbacks, 2016), by Jason Ramos and Julian Smith, is a marvelous description of these heroic people in action.

11. National Interagency Fire Center, "RT-273: Retardant Review, 2018 Season," PowerPoint slides, 50 frames, nifc.gov/sites/default/files/blm/aviation/BLMseat/RT:273RetardantReview.pptx.

12. Renee Lewis, "Blanketing California in Fire Retardant Is Potentially Very Harmful," *Gizmodo*, December 11, 2017, gizmodo.com/blanketing-california-in-fire-retardant-is-potentially-1821181258.

13. "The Warming Effects of the Industrial Revolution," climate-policy-watcher.org/global-temperatures/the-warming-effects-of-the-industrial-revolution.html.

14. Brian Fagan, *The Little Ice Age: How Climate Change Made History, 1300–1850* (New York: Basic Books, 2000), 14, 38–44, 86–90.

15. Jonathan Strickland and Ed Grabianowski, "How Global Warming Works," science.howstuffworks.com/environmental/green-science/global-warming.

16. Ibid.

17. Matthew Mason, "History of the Study of Climate Change in Field of Environmental Science," environmentalscience.org/history-climate-change; Amanda MacMillan, "Global Warming 101," March 11, 2016, nrdc.org/stories/global-warming-101.

18. A link to the original report is in Chris D'Angelo, "New Documents Show Oil Industry Even More Evil Than We Thought," *HuffPost*, April 14, 2016, huffpost.com/entry/oil-cover-up-climate_n_570e98bbe4b0ffa5937df6ce; Justin Worland, "This Island Is Sinking," *Time*, June 24, 2019.

19. Debora Mackenzie, "America's Hidden Epidemic of Tropical Diseases," *New Scientist*, December 11, 2013, newscientist.com/article/mg22029473-200-americas-hidden-epidemic-of-tropical-diseases.

20. "To Stop Pandemics, Stop Deforestation," editorial, *Scientific American*, June 2020, 8, doi:10.1038/scientificamerican0620-8.

21. Dana Nuccitelli, "The Many Ways Climate Change Worsens California Wildfires," *Yale Climate Connections*, November 13, 2018, yaleclimateconnections.org/2018/11/the-many-ways-climate-change-worsens-california-wildfires; Timothy Puko,

"2018 Was Fourth-Hottest Year in Modern Records, U.S. Government Scientists Say," *Wall Street Journal,* February 6, 2019 wsj.com/articles/2018-was-fourth -hottest-year-in-modern-records-u-s-government -scientists-say-11549471691; Kevin Trenberth, "Is There a Link Between Climate Change and Wildfires?," *Newsweek,* August 10, 2018, newsweek .com/there-link-between-climate-change-and -wildfires-1068201.

22. Krystina Skurk, "How Misguided Environmentalism Is to Blame for California's Wildfires," *Federalist,* November 16, 2018, thefederalist.com/2018/11/16 /misguided-environmentalism-blame-californias -wildfires; Trenberth, "Is There a Link?"

23. Nathan Masters, "Why Did a 1542 Spanish Voyage Refer to San Pedro Bay as the 'Bay of the Smoke'?," March 28, 2013, kcet.org/shows/lost-la/why-did-a -1542-spanish-voyage-refer-to-san-pedro-bay-as-the -bay-of-the-smoke.

24. Insurance Information Institute, "Facts and Statistics: Wildfires," iii.org/fact-statistic/facts-statistics -wildfires.

25. Nicola Twilley, "A Trailblazing Plan to Fight California Wildfires," *New Yorker,* August 26, 2019, 46; Ash Ngu and Sahil Chinoy, "The Benefits of Letting the Forest Burn," *Wall Street Journal,* December 2, 2018.

26. Holman W. Jenkins Jr., "California Burns for Better Leaders," *Wall Street Journal,* January 15, 2019.

27. Joel Achenbach and Angela Fritz, "Hot Summers, Wildfires: Scientists Say It's Climate Change, and They Told You So," *Chicago Tribune,* July 27, 2018, chicagotribune.com/news/nationworld/ct-summer -climate-change-20180727-story.html; Christina

Anderson and Alan Cowell, "Heat Wave Scorches Sweden as Wildfires Rage in the Arctic Circle," *New York Times,* July 19, 2018; Jamie Tarabay, "Australia Is So Hot the Pits Are Burning the Peaches," *New York Times,* January 26, 2019.

28. Damien Cave, "The End of Australia as We Know It," *New York Times,* February 15, 2020, nytimes. com/2020/02/15/world/australia/fires-climate -change.html.

29. Hoover and Hanson, "Wildfire Statistics"; Robinson Meyer, "Why the Wildfires of 2018 Have Been So Ferocious," *Atlantic,* August 10, 2018.

30. Umair Irfan, "Why the Carr Fire in Northern California Is So Severe," *Vox,* August 14, 2018, vox .com/energy-and-environment/2018/8/1/17637026 /carr-fire-california-heat-wildfire-deaths.

31. Russell Gold, Katherine Blunt, and Rebecca Smith, "Utility Sparked 1,500 Wildfires, Now Faces Collapse," *Wall Street Journal,* January 14, 2019.

32. Jon Mooallem, "'We Have Fire Everywhere,'" *New York Times Magazine,* July 31, 2019; Don Sweeney, "'It Got Darker and Darker': Wildfire Survivors Detail Harrowing Escapes," *Sacramento Bee,* November 15, 2018; Sarah Almukhtar et al., "'Hell on Earth': The First 12 Hours of California's Deadliest Wildfire," *New York Times,* November 20, 2018; Insurance Information Institute, "Facts and Statistics: Wildfires"; Talal Ansari and Alejandro Lazo, "Fire Crews Work to Get Ahead of Wind," *Wall Street Journal,* October 29, 2019.

33. Damien Cave, "Climate Change Puts Strain on World's Ability to Douse the Flames," *New York Times,* November 23, 2019.

34. "2020 Incident Archive," fire.ca.gov/incidents/2020/.

35. Dave Eggers, "All That Could Burn: Life as a Californian During the 2020 Fire Season," *New Yorker,* October 11, 2020, newyorker.com/news/dispatch/all -that-could-burn; James Temple, "Yes, Climate Change Is Almost Certainly Fueling California's Massive Fires," technologyreview.com/2020/08/20/1007478 /california-wildfires-climate-change-heatwaves/.

36. Eggers, "All That Could Burn."

37. Michael Kodas, *Megafire: The Race to Extinguish a Deadly Epidemic of Flame* (Boston: Houghton Mifflin Harcourt, 2017), 62; Twilley, "A Trailblazing Plan," 45.

38. Skurk, "How Misguided Environmentalism Is to Blame"; Geoffrey H. Donovan and Thomas C. Brown, "Fire Management in the U.S. Forest Service: A Brief History," *Natural Hazards Observer* 29, no. 6 (July 2005), fs.fed.us/pnw/pubs/journals/pnw _2005_donovan003.pdf; Forest History Society, "U.S. Forest Service Fire Suppression," foresthistory .org/research-explore/us-forest-service-history/policy -and-law/fire-u-s-forest-service/u-s-forest-service-fire -suppression.

39. *Cerro Grande Prescribed Fire: Board of Inquiry Final Report* (Washington, DC: National Park Service, 2001), 1; Kodas, *Megafire,* 65.

40. Kornelis, "Chief U.S. Forester Vicki Christiansen."

41. "Protecting Your Home from Wildfire," californiachaparral.org/fire/protecting-your-home; "How to Prepare for a Wildfire," fema.gov/media -library-data/1409003859391-0e8ad1ed42c129f 11fbc23d008d1ee85/how_to_prepare_wildfire _033014_508.pdf.

42. Christie Aschwanden et al., "Why California's Wildfires Are So Destructive, in 5 Charts," fivethirtyeight.com/features/why-californias -wildfires-are-so-destructive-in-5-charts.

SELECTED SOURCES

Achenbach, Joel, and Angela Fritz. "Hot Summers, Wildfires: Scientists Say It's Climate Change, and They Told You So." *Chicago Tribune*, July 27, 2018. chicagotribune.com/news/nationworld/ct-summer-climate-change-20180727-story.html.

Adler, Jerry. "Why Fire Makes Us Human." *Smithsonian Magazine*, June 2013. smithsonianmag.com/science-nature/why-fire-makes-us-human-72989884.

[Akermark, Gudmund Emanuel?]. *The Cyclone of Fire; or, The Hinckley Fire*. Translated by Charles John LaVine. Minneapolis: Companion Publishing, 1894. mnhs.org/library/findaids/lb00018/lb00018-000001.pdf.

Alfred, Randy. "May 19, 1780: Darkness at Noon Enshrouds New England." *Wired*, May 19, 2010. wired.com/2010/05/0519new-england-dark-day.

Allen, Clifford, ed. *Michigan Log Marks, Their Function and Use During the Great Michigan Pine Harvest*. East Lansing: Michigan Agricultural Experiment Station, 1942.

Allen, Garland E. "'Culling the Herd': Eugenics and the Conservation Movement in the United States, 1900–1940." *Journal of the History of Biology* 46 (Spring 2012): 31–72.

Almukhtar, Sarah, Troy Griggs, Kirk Johnson, Jugal K. Patel, Anjali Singhvi, and Derek Watkins. "'Hell on Earth': The First 12 Hours of California's Deadliest Wildfire." *New York Times*, November 20, 2018.

Anderson, Christina, and Alan Cowell. "Heat Wave Scorches Sweden as Wildfires Rage in the Arctic Circle." *New York Times*, July 19, 2018.

Anderson, E. N. Review of *Tending the Wild: Native American Knowledge and the Management of California's Natural Resources*, by M. Kat Anderson. *Journal of California and Great Basin Anthropology* 25, no. 2 (2005): 255–259.

Andrews, Evan. "Remembering New England's 'Dark Day.'" history.com/news/remembering-new-englands-dark-day.

Andrews, Richard N. L. *Managing the Environment, Managing Ourselves: A History of American Environmental Policy*. New Haven, CT: Yale University Press, 1999.

Aney, Kathy. "Breaking Barriers from 1,500 Feet." *East Oregonian*, June 24, 2015. eastoregonian.com/news/local/breaking-barriers-from201-500-feet20/article_44776d4a-4bd9-5df5-9d2d-2d693e541db2.html.

Ansari, Abdul Sahim. "Influence of Forests on Environment." fao.org/3/xii/1018-b2.htm.

Ansari, Talal, and Alejandro Lazo. "Fire Crews Work to Get Ahead of Wind." *Wall Street Journal*, October 29, 2019.

"The Antiquities Act, 1900–06." nps.gov/articles/lee-story-antiquities.htm.

Aschwanden, Christie, Anna Maria Barry-Jester, Ella Koeze, and Maggie Koerth. "Why California's Wildfires Are So Destructive, in 5 Charts." fivethirtyeight.com/features/why-californias-wildfires-are-so-destructive-in-5-charts.

Audubon, John James. "Passenger Pigeon." In *The Birds of America.* audubon.org/birds-of-america/passenger-pigeon.

Bagnall, Kyle. "Passenger Pigeons in Your State, Province or Territory: Wisconsin." *Project Passenger Pigeon.* passengerpigeon.org/states/Wisconsin.html.

Bakeless, John. *The Eyes of Discovery: The Pageant of North America as Seen by the First Explorers.* Philadelphia: J. B. Lippincott, 1950.

Barillas, William. "Michigan's Pioneers and the Destruction of the Hardwood Forest." *Michigan Historical Review* 15, no. 2 (Fall 1989): 1–22.

Bartram, William. *Travels Through North and South Carolina, Georgia, East and West Florida* [. . .]. London: J. Johnson, 1794.

Bates, J. Leonard. "Fulfilling American Democracy: The Conservation Movement, 1907 to 1921." *Mississippi Valley Historical Review* 44, no. 1 (June 1957): 29–57. doi:10.2307/1898667.

Berry, Alison. "Forest Policy Up in Smoke: Fire Suppression in the United States." perc.org/wp-content/uploads/2007/09/Forest_Policy_Up_in_Smoke.pdf.

Beverley, Robert. *The History of Virginia, in Four Parts.* Richmond, VA: J. W. Randolph, 1855.

Birrell, Jean R. "The Medieval English Forest." *Journal of Forest History* 24, no. 2 (April 1980): 78–85.

Biswell, H. H. "Forest Fire in Perspective." *Proceedings: 7th Tall Timbers Fire Ecology Conference* (1967). talltimbers.org/wp-content/uploads/2018/09/43-Biswell1967_op.pdf.

Black, Riley. "The History of Air." *Smithsonian Magazine,* April 18, 2010. smithsonianmag.com/science-nature/the-history-of-air-21082166.

Blackman, T. J. "The Ecological Benefits of Forest Fires." *Eartheasy,* September 3, 2015. learn.eartheasy.com/articles/the-ecological-benefits-of-forest-fires.

Blockstein, David E., and Harrison B. Tordoff. "A Contemporary Look at the Extinction of the Passenger Pigeon." *American Birds* 39, no. 5 (Winter 1985): 845–851.

Bodio, Stephen J. "A Feathered Tempest: The Improbable Life and Sudden Death of the Passenger Pigeon." *All About Birds,* April 15, 2010. allaboutbirds.org/a-feathered-tempest-the-improbable-life-and-sudden-death-of-the-passenger-pigeon.

Bonnicksen, Thomas M. *America's Ancient Forests: From the Ice Age to the Age of Discovery.* New York: Wiley, 2000.

Bonsal, Stephen. *When the French Were Here: A Narrative of the Sojourn of the French Forces in America, and Their Contribution to the Yorktown Campaign.* Garden City, NY: Doubleday, Doran, 1945.

Bonsor, Kevin. "How Wildfires Work." science.howstuffworks.com/nature/natural-disasters/wildfire.htm.

Bradford, William. *History of Plymouth Plantation.* Boston: Massachusetts Historical Society, 1856.

Brinkley, Douglas. *The Wilderness Warrior: Theodore Roosevelt and the Crusade for America.* New York: HarperCollins, 2009.

Bronaugh, Whit. "North American Forests in the Age of Nature." *American Forests,* Spring 2012. americanforests.org/magazine/article/north-american-forests-in-the-age-of-nature.

Brown, Daniel James. *Under a Flaming Sky: The Great Hinckley Firestorm of 1894.* Guilford, CT: Lyons Press, 2006.

Brown, Elton T. *A History of the Great Minnesota Forest Fires: Sandstone, Mission Creek, Hinckley, Pokegama, Skunk Lake.* St. Paul, MN: Brown Bros., 1894.

Brown, Hutch. "Wildland Burning by American Indians in Virginia." *Fire Management Today* 60 (Summer 2000): 29–37.

Bruce, Robert V. *Lincoln and the Tools of War.* Champaign: University of Illinois Press, 1989.

Burger, Peter. *Charles Fenerty and His Paper Invention.* Toronto: PB Publishing, 2007.

Busbey, L. White. *Uncle Joe Cannon: The Story of a Pioneer American.* New York: Henry Holt, 1927.

Callicott, J. Baird, and Priscilla Solis Ybarra. "The Puritan Origins of the American Wilderness Movement." nationalhumanitiescenter.org/tserve/nattrans /ntwilderness/essays/puritan.htm.

Campanella, Thomas J. " 'Mark Well the Gloom': Shedding Light on the Great Dark Day of 1780." *Environmental History* 12, no. 1 (January 2007): 35–58.

"The Camping Trip That Changed the Nation." nationalparksadventure.com/the-camping-trip-that -changed-the-nation.

Carter, Constance. "Roosevelt, Muir, and the Camping Trip." *Inside Adams* (blog), August 11, 2016. blogs.loc .gov/inside_adams/2016/08/roosevelt-muir-and-the -camping-trip.

Castella, Tom de. "What Caused the Mystery of the Dark Day?" *BBC News Magazine,* May 18, 2012. bbc.com /news/magazine-18097177.

Cave, Damien. "Climate Change Puts Strain on World's Ability to Douse the Flames." *New York Times,* November 23, 2019.

———. "The End of Australia as We Know It." *New York Times,* February 15, 2020. nytimes. com/2020/02/15/world/australia/fires-climate -change.html.

Cerro Grande Prescribed Fire: Board of Inquiry Final Report. Washington, DC: National Park Service, 2001.

Chapin, John R. "Chicago in Flames." *Harper's Weekly,* October 28, 1871.

Chapman, Arthur. "The Forest Fire Fighters." *Ames Forester* 10 (1922): 99. lib.dr.iastate.edu/amesforester/vol10 /iss1/18.

Chapman, Frank M. *Autobiography of a Bird-Lover.* New York: D. Appleton–Century, 1933.

Chastellux, François Jean, marquis de. *Travels in North-America in the Years 1780–81–82.* New York, 1828.

Chittenden, Hiram Martin. *The Yellowstone National Park: Historical and Descriptive.* Cincinnati: Stewart and Kidd, 1915.

Chrisman-Campbell, Kimberly. "Fowl Intentions: Fashion, Activism, Conservation." *Ornament* 40, no. 4 (2018).

Clayton, John. *Natural Rivals: John Muir, Gifford Pinchot, and the Creation of America's Public Lands.* New York: Pegasus, 2019.

Colbert, Elias, and Everett Chamberlin. *Chicago and the Great Conflagration.* Chicago: J. S. Goodman, 1872.

"Components of Wildland Fire P.P.E." fs.fed.us/eng/pubs /htmlpubs/htm93512851/com.htm.

Cooper, James Fenimore. *The Pioneers.* New York: Charles Wiley, 1823. archive.org/stream/pioneers orsource01cooprich.

Cox, Thomas, Robert S. Maxwell, Philip Drennon Thomas, and Joseph J. Malone. *This Well-Wooded Land: Americans and Their Forests from Colonial Times to the Present.* Lincoln: University of Nebraska Press, 1985.

Cronon, William. *Nature's Metropolis: Chicago and the Great West.* New York: Norton, 1991.

Crosby, Alfred W., Jr. *The Columbian Exchange: Biological and Cultural Consequences of 1492.* Westport, CT: Greenwood Press, 1972.

Cutright, Paul Russell. *Theodore Roosevelt the Naturalist.* New York: Harper & Brothers, 1956.

D'Angelo, Chris. "New Documents Show Oil Industry Even More Evil Than We Thought." *HuffPost,* April 14, 2016. huffpost.com/entry/oil-cover-up -climate_n_570e98bbe4b0ffa5937df6ce.

Day, Gordon M. "The Indian as an Ecological Factor in the Northeastern Forest." *Ecology* 34, no. 2 (April 1953): 329–346.

Defebaugh, James Elliott. *History of the Lumber Industry of America.* 2 vols. 2nd ed. Chicago: American Lumberman, 1906.

Deffenbaugh, Daniel G. "The Ecological Indian Revisited." *Soundings* 83, no. 2 (Summer 2000): 477–485.

DeLuca, Kevin, and Anne Demo. "Imagining Nature and Erasing Class and Race: Carleton Watkins, John Muir, and the Construction of Wilderness." *Environmental History* 6, no. 4 (October 2001): 541–560.

Denevan, William M. "The Pristine Myth: The Landscape of the Americas in 1492." *Annals of the Association of American Geographers* 82, no. 3 (September 1992): 369–385.

Dewar, Willoughby. "The Plumage Trade and the Destruction of Birds." *Journal of the Royal Society of Arts* 69, no. 3569 (April 15, 1921): 332–349.

Dickens, Charles. *American Notes for General Circulation.* London: Chapman and Hall, 1850.

Donovan, Geoffrey H., and Thomas C. Brown. "Fire Management in the U.S. Forest Service: A Brief History." *Natural Hazards Observer* 29, no. 6 (July 2005): 1–3. fs.fed.us/pnw/pubs/journals/pnw _2005_donovan003.pdf.

Eckert, Allan W. *The Silent Sky: The Incredible Extinction of the Passenger Pigeon.* Boston: Little, Brown, 1965.

Egan, Timothy. *The Big Burn: Teddy Roosevelt and the Fire That Saved America.* Boston: Houghton Mifflin Harcourt, 2009.

———. "Why Foresters Prefer to Fight Fire with Fire." *New York Times,* August 20, 2000. nytimes. com/2000/08/20/weekinreview/ideas-trends-why -foresters-prefer-to-fight-fire-with-fire.html.

Elder, Jeff. "This Species Became Extinct Through the Avarice and Thoughtlessness of Man." *Medium,* March 15, 2016. jeffelder.medium.com/this -species-became-extinct-through-the-avarice-and -thoughtlessness-of-man-b9609b2c3c8f.

Erdmann, Steven. "The Feather Wars and Theodore Roosevelt." *Tustenegee,* October 2010, 8–11.

Estimated Log Weight Calculator. woodweb.com/cgi-bin /calculators/calc.pl?calculator=log_weight.

Everett, Franklin. *Memorials of the Grand River Valley.* Chicago: Chicago Legal News, 1878.

"Express Train Crosses the Nation in 83 Hours." history.com/this-day-in-history/express-train-crosses-the-nation-in-83-hours.

Fagan, Brian. *The Great Journey: The Peopling of Ancient America.* London: Thames and Hudson, 1987.

———. *The Little Ice Age: How Climate Change Made History, 1300–1850.* New York: Basic Books, 2000.

Febvre, Lucien, and Henri-Jean Martin. *The Coming of the Book: The Impact of Printing, 1450–1800.* New York: Verso Books, 1997.

"Fire: A Myth from the Alabama Tribe." Retold by S. E. Schlosser. *American Folklore.* americanfolklore.net/folklore/2011/07/fire.html.

"Fire in Nature." smokeybear.com/en/about-wildland-fire/benefits-of-fire/fire-in-nature.

Fischer, David Hackett. *Albion's Seed: Four British Folkways in America.* New York: Oxford University Press, 1989.

Forest History Society. "Gifford Pinchot (1865–1946)." foresthistory.org/research-explore/us-forest-service-history/people/chiefs/gifford-pinchot-1865-1946.

———. "The 1910 Fires." foresthistory.org/research-explore/us-forest-service-history/policy-and-law/fire-u-s-forest-service/famous-fires/the-1910-fires.

———. "U.S. Forest Service Fire Suppression." foresthistory.org/research-explore/us-forest-service-history/policy-and-law/fire-u-s-forest-service/u-s-forest-service-fire-suppression.

Forest Service, U.S. Department of Agriculture. *When the Mountains Roared: Stories of the 1910 Fire.* Washington, DC: Forest Service, 1978. foresthistory.org/wp-content/uploads/2017/01/When-the-Mountains-Roared.pdf.

"Four Letters: Theodore Roosevelt and the Final Reported Sighting of the Now-Extinct Passenger Pigeon." raabcollection.com/presidential-autographs/roosevelt-pigeons.

Fox, Stephen. *The American Conservation Movement: John Muir and His Legacy.* Madison: University of Wisconsin Press, 1985.

Franklin, Benjamin. "Observations Concerning the Increase of Mankind, 1751." founders.archives.gov/documents/franklin/01-04-02-0080.

Frantz, Jeff. "Pinchot Was Teddy Roosevelt's 'Conscience' on Conservation." *York (PA) Daily Record.*

Freemuth, John. "The Progressive Movement and Conservation (1890s–Present)." In *Guide to U.S. Environmental Policy,* edited by Sally K. Fairfax and Edmund Russell, 129–140. Thousand Oaks, CA: CQ Press, 2014.

Fries, Robert F. *Empire in Pine: The Story of Lumbering in Wisconsin, 1830–1900.* Ellison Bay, WI: William Caxton, 1989.

Galvin, John. "The Big Burn: Idaho and Montana, August 1910." *Popular Mechanics,* July 30, 2007. popularmechanics.com/science/environment/a1961/4219853.

Gard, Wayne. *The Great Buffalo Hunt: Its History and Drama, and Its Role in the Opening of the West.* New York: Knopf, 1960.

Gaston, Bibi. *Gifford Pinchot and the First Foresters: The Untold Story of the Brave Men and Women Who*

Launched the American Conservation Movement. New Milford, CT: Baked Apple Club Productions, 2016.

Gess, Denise, and William Lutz. *Firestorm at Peshtigo: A Town, Its People, and the Deadliest Fire in American History.* New York: Henry Holt, 2002.

Gold, Russell, Katherine Blunt, and Rebecca Smith. "Utility Sparked 1,500 Wildfires, Now Faces Collapse." *Wall Street Journal,* January 14, 2019.

Goodspeed, E. J. *History of the Great Fires in Chicago and the West.* Chicago: J. W. Goodspeed, 1871.

Gordon, John Steele. "Forgotten Fury: A Long-Ago Calamity May Shed Light on a Current Impasse." *American Heritage,* April/May 2003. americanheritage.com/content/forgotten-fury.

Gordon, William. *The History of the Rise, Progress, and Establishment of the Independence of the United States of America,* vol. 3. New York: Samuel Campbell, 1788.

Graham, Frank, Jr. *Man's Dominion: The Story of Conservation in America.* Philadelphia: J. B. Lippincott, 1971.

Gray, Gary G. *Wildlife and People: The Human Dimensions of Wildlife Ecology.* Urbana: University of Illinois Press, 1993.

"The Great Fires of October 1871." glenallenweather .com/historylinks/1871/ChicagoFire.pdf.

Greenberg, Joel. *A Feathered River Across the Sky: The Passenger Pigeon's Flight to Extinction.* New York: Bloomsbury, 2014.

Groot, Han de. "A Low-Tech Climate Fix." *Scientific American,* April 2019.

Hall, Basil. *Travels in North America in the Years 1827 and 1828.* 2 vols. Philadelphia: Carey, Lea and Carey, 1829.

Halm, Joe B. "The Big Fire." In Forest Service, U.S. Department of Agriculture, *When the Mountains Roared: Stories of the 1910 Fire.* Washington, DC: Forest Service, 1978, 52–61. foresthistory.org/wp -content/uploads/2017/01/When-the-Mountains -Roared.pdf.

Hamilton, Thomas. *Men and Manners in America.* Edinburgh: William Blackwood, 1833.

Handlin, Oscar. *This Was America.* Cambridge, MA: Harvard University Press, 1969.

Hanson, Chad. *The Myth of "Catastrophic" Wildfire: A New Ecological Paradigm of Forest Health.* John Muir Technical Report 1. Cedar Ridge, CA: John Muir Project of Earth Island Institute, 2010. johnmuirproject.org/wp-content/uploads/2014/12 /TheMythOfTheCatastrophicWildfireReport.pdf.

Hariot, Thomas. *A Briefe and True Report of the New Found Land of Virginia.* London, 1588.

Hayner, Norman S. "Taming the Lumberjack." *American Sociological Review* 10, no. 2 (April 1945): 217–225. doi:10.2307/2085640.

Hidy, Ralph W., Frank Ernest Hill, and Allan Nevins. *Timber and Men: The Weyerhaeuser Story.* New York: Macmillan, 1963.

"Hinckley, MN." *Data USA.* datausa.io/profile/geo /hinckley-mn.

"Historical Gold Prices—1833 to Present." piketty.pse .ens.fr/files/capital21c/xls/RawDataFiles/Gold Prices17922012.pdf.

Holbrook, Stewart H. *Burning an Empire: The Story of American Forest Fires*. New York: Macmillan, 1943.

———. "The Peshtigo Fire." *American Scholar* 13, no. 2 (Spring 1944): 201–209.

Hoover, Katie, and Laura A. Hanson. "Wildfire Statistics." Congressional Research Service, October 1, 2020. crsreports.congress.gov/product/pdf/if/if10244.

Hornaday, William T. *The Extermination of the American Bison*. Washington, DC: Smithsonian Institution Press, 2002.

———. *Our Vanishing Wildlife: Its Extermination and Preservation*. New York: Charles Scribner's Sons, 1913.

"Hotshots." fs.usda.gov/science-technology/fire/people/hotshots.

"How to Prepare for a Wildfire." fema.gov/media-library-data/1409003859391-0e8ad1ed42c129f11fbc23d008d1ee85/how_to_prepare_wildfire_033014_508.pdf.

"Importance and Value of Trees." savatree.com/whytrees.html.

Insurance Information Institute. "Facts and Statistics: Wildfires." iii.org/fact-statistic/facts-statistics-wildfires.

Irfan, Umair. "Why the Carr Fire in Northern California Is So Severe." *Vox*, August 14, 2018. vox.com/energy-and-environment/2018/8/1/17637026/carr-fire-california-heat-wildfire-deaths.

Isacat, Ben. "Thomas Aquinas, the Church and Animals." Chap. 7.1 in *How to Do Animal Rights*. 2015. animalethics.org.uk/aquinas.html.

Ise, John. *The United States Forest Policy*. New Haven, CT: Yale University Press, 1920.

Isenberg, Andrew C. *The Destruction of the Bison: An Environmental History, 1750–1920*. Cambridge: Cambridge University Press, 2000.

Jenkins, Holman W., Jr. "California Burns for Better Leaders." *Wall Street Journal*, January 15, 2019.

Johnston, Jeremy. "Preserving the Beasts of Waste and Desolation: Theodore Roosevelt and Predator Control in Yellowstone." *Yellowstone Science* 10, no. 2 (Spring 2002): 14–21.

Journal of Proceedings of the Twenty-Sixth Annual Session of the Wisconsin Legislature. Appendix to the Assembly Journal. Madison: Atwood & Culver, 1873.

Kantor, Isaac. "Ethnic Cleansing and America's Creation of National Parks." *Public Land and Resources Law Review* 28 (2007): 41–65. scholarship.law.umt.edu/cgi/viewcontent.cgi?article=1267&context=plrlr.

Kershner, Jim. "Forest Fire, the Largest in U.S. History, Left Stories of Awe, Tragedy." *Spokesman-Review* (Spokane, WA), August 15, 2010. spokesman.com/stories/2010/aug/15/1910-fire-region-consumed.

Knickelbine, Scott. *The Great Peshtigo Fire: Stories and Science from America's Deadliest Firestorm*. Madison: Wisconsin Historical Society Press, 2012.

Kodas, Michael. "Bigger, Hotter, Faster." *BioGraphic*, August 15, 2017. biographic.com/posts/sto/bigger-hotter-faster.

———. *Megafire: The Race to Extinguish a Deadly Epidemic of Flame*. Boston: Houghton Mifflin Harcourt, 2017.

Kornelis, Chris. "Chief U.S. Forester Vicki Christiansen Thinks Some Fires Should Be Left to Burn." *Wall Street Journal,* October 5, 2019.

Krainz, Thomas A. "Conflict and Fire: Community Tensions Surrounding the Big Blowup." *Pacific Northwest Quarterly* 103 (Winter 2011/2012): 13–24.

Krajick, Kevin. "Fire in the Hole." *Smithsonian Magazine,* May 2005. smithsonianmag.com/science-nature /fire-in-the-hole-77895126.

Krech, Shepard, III. *The Ecological Indian: Myth and History.* New York: Norton, 1999.

Lapham, Increase A. "The Great Fires of 1871 in the Northwest." *Wisconsin Academy Review* 12, no. 1 (1965): 6–9. digicoll.library.wisc.edu/WIReader /WER0133.html.

———. *Report on the Disastrous Effects of the Destruction of Forest Trees, Now Going On So Rapidly in the State of Wisconsin.* Madison: Atwood and Rublee, 1867.

Lewis, Renee. "Blanketing California in Fire Retardant Is Potentially Very Harmful." *Gizmodo,* December 11, 2017. gizmodo.com/blanketing-california-in-fire -retardant-is-potentially-1821181258.

"Life in 1910." orangepower.com/threads/life-in-1910 -100-years-ago.96681.

Lillard, Richard G. *The Great Forest.* New York: Knopf, 1948.

Little, John James. "1910 Forest Fires in Montana and Idaho: Their Impact on Federal and State Legislation." Master's thesis, University of Montana, 1968. scholarworks.umt.edu/etd/1455.

Lowe, David, ed. *The Great Chicago Fire: In Eyewitness Accounts and 70 Contemporary Photographs and Illustrations.* New York: Dover Publications, 1979.

Lowenthal, David. *George Perkins Marsh: Prophet of Conservation.* Seattle: University of Washington Press, 2000.

Luzerne, Frank. *The Lost City! Drama of the Fire Fiend! or Chicago as It Was, and as It Is!* New York: Wells, 1872.

Mackenzie, Debora. "America's Hidden Epidemic of Tropical Diseases." *New Scientist,* December 11, 2013. newscientist.com/article/mg22029473-200 -americas-hidden-epidemic-of-tropical-diseases.

Maclean, Norman. *Young Men and Fire.* Chicago: University of Chicago Press, 1992.

MacMillan, Amanda. "Global Warming 101." March 11, 2016. nrdc.org/stories/global-warming-101.

Mann, Charles C. *1491: New Revelations of the Americas Before Columbus.* New York: Knopf, 2005.

———. *1493: Uncovering the New World Columbus Created.* New York: Knopf, 2011.

Manners, William. *TR and Will: A Friendship That Split the Republican Party.* New York: Harcourt, Brace & World, 1969.

"Maps Showing the Progressive Development of U.S. Railroads—1830 to 1950." cprr.org/Museum/RR _Development.html.

Marsh, George Perkins. *Man and Nature; or, Physical Geography as Modified by Human Action.* London: Sampson Low, Son and Marston, 1864.

Marshall, Michael. "The Event That Transformed Earth." *BBC Earth,* July 2, 2015. bbc.com/earth/story /20150701-the-origin-of-the-air-we-breathe.

Mason, Matthew. "History of the Study of Climate Change in Field of Environmental Science." environmentalscience.org/history-climate-change.

Masters, Nathan. "Why Did a 1542 Spanish Voyage Refer to San Pedro Bay as the 'Bay of the Smoke'?" March 28, 2013. kcet.org/shows/lost-la/why-did-a-1542-spanish-voyage-refer-to-san-pedro-bay-as-the-bay-of-the-smoke.

Mathewson, Samantha. "Ancient Wildfires: Researchers Examine Evolution of Forest Fires." *Nature World News*, October 25, 2015. natureworldnews.com/articles/17739/20151025/ancient-wildfires-researchers-examine-evolution-forest-fires.htm.

Matthiessen, Peter. *Wildlife in America.* New York: Viking, 1987.

Maxwell, Hu. "The Use and Abuse of Forests by the Virginia Indians." *William and Mary Quarterly* 19, no. 2 (October 1910): 73–103.

"Mayor William B. Ogden Biography." chipublib.org/mayor-william-b-ogden-biography.

McCollough, John, and Henry F. Check Jr. "The Baleen Whales' Saving Grace: The Introduction of Petroleum Based Products in the Market and Its Impact on the Whaling Industry." *Sustainability* 2, no. 10 (2010): 3142–3157. doi:10.3390/su2103142.

McCouat, Philip. "Fashion, Feathers and Animal Rights." *Journal of Art in Society* (2016). artinsociety.com/feathers-fashion-and-animal-rights.

McGeary, M. Nelson. *Gifford Pinchot: Forester-Politician.* Princeton: Princeton University Press, 1960.

Merchant, Carolyn, ed. *Major Problems in American Environmental History.* Lexington, MA: D. C. Heath, 1993.

Merchant, Carolyn. "Shades of Darkness: Race and Environmental History." *Environmental History* 8, no. 3 (July 2002): 380–394.

Mershon, W. B. *The Passenger Pigeon.* New York: Outing Publishing, 1907.

Meyer, John M. "Gifford Pinchot, John Muir, and the Boundaries of Politics in American Thought." *Polity* 30, no. 2 (Winter 1997): 267–284.

Meyer, Robinson. "The Simple Reason That Humans Can't Control Wildfires." *Atlantic*, November 13, 2018. theatlantic.com/science/archive/2018/11/california-wildfire-why-humans-cant-control-them/575740.

———. "Why the Wildfires of 2018 Have Been So Ferocious." *Atlantic*, August 10, 2018.

Miller, Char. "All in the Family: The Pinchots of Milford." *Pennsylvania History: A Journal of Mid-Atlantic Studies* (Spring 1999): 117–142.

———. "The Greening of Gifford Pinchot." *Environmental History Review* 16, no. 3 (Autumn 1992): 1–20.

Miller, Nathan. *Theodore Roosevelt: A Life.* New York: William Morrow, 1992.

Miner, Craig. *A Most Magnificent Machine: America Adopts the Railroad, 1825–1862.* Lawrence: University Press of Kansas, 2010.

Mockenhaupt, Brian. "Fire on the Mountain." *Atlantic*, June 2014. theatlantic.com/magazine/archive/2014/06/fire-on-the-mountain/361613.

Mooallem, Jon. " 'We Have Fire Everywhere.' " *New York Times Magazine*, July 31, 2019.

Moran, Joseph M., and E. Lee Somerville. "Tornadoes of Wildfire at Williamsonville, Wisconsin, October 8, 1871." *Transactions of the Wisconsin Academy of Sciences, Arts and Letters* 78 (1990): 21–32. images

.library.wisc.edu/WI/Efacs/transactions/WT1990
/reference/wi.wt1990.jmmoran.pdf.

Muir, John. "The American Forests." *Atlantic Monthly,*
April 1897, 145–157. scholarlycommons.pacific.edu
/cgi/viewcontent.cgi?article=1233&context=jmb.

———. "By-Ways of Yosemite Travel: Bloody Cañon."
Overland Monthly, September 1874, 267–273.

———. *John of the Mountains: The Unpublished Journals
of John Muir.* Edited by Linnie Marsh Wolfe. Boston:
Houghton Mifflin, 1938.

———. *Our National Parks.* Boston: Houghton Mifflin,
1901. vault.sierraclub.org/john_muir_exhibit
/writings/our_national_parks.

———. *The Story of My Boyhood and Youth.* Madison:
University of Wisconsin Press, 1965.

Mullen, Luba. "How Trees Survive and Thrive After a
Fire." *Your National Forests Magazine,* Summer/Fall
2017. nationalforests.org/our-forests/your-national
-forests-magazine/how-trees-survive-and-thrive-after
-a-fire.

Narendran, K. "Forest Fires: Origins and Ecological
Paradoxes." *Resonance* 6 (2001): 34–41. doi:10.1007
/BF02868242.

Nash, Roderick. "The American Wilderness in Historical
Perspective." *Forest and Conservation History* 6, no. 4
(Winter 1963): 2–13.

———. *Wilderness and the American Mind.* New Haven:
Yale University Press, 1967.

National Interagency Fire Center. "Federal Firefighting
Costs (Suppression Only)." nifc.gov/fire-information
/statistics/suppression-costs.

———. "RT-273: Retardant Review, 2018 Season."
PowerPoint slides, 50 frames. nifc.gov/sites/default
/files/blm/aviation/BLMseat/RT-273 Retardant
Review.pptx.

Nelligan, John E., and Charles M. Sheridan. "The Life of
a Lumberman, Part II." *Wisconsin Magazine of History*
13, no. 2 (December 1929): 131–185.

———. "The Life of a Lumberman, Part III." *Wisconsin
Magazine of History* 13, no. 3 (March 1930): 241–304.

Nelson, Steve, and Jack Rollins. "Smokey the Bear." New
York: Hill and Range Songs, 1952. wvforestry.com
/pdf/Smokey%20Song.pdf.

"The New England Dark Day, May 19, 1780."
newenglandhistoricalsociety.com/new-england-dark
-day-may-19-1780.

Ngu, Ash, and Sahil Chinoy. "The Benefits of Letting the
Forest Burn." *Wall Street Journal,* December 2, 2018.

Nuccitelli, Dana. "The Many Ways Climate
Change Worsens California Wildfires." *Yale
Climate Connections,* November 13, 2018.
yaleclimateconnections.org/2018/11/the-many-ways
-climate-change-worsens-california-wildfires.

Oberle, Mark. "Forest Fires: Suppression Policy Has
Its Ecological Drawbacks." *Science* 165, no. 3893
(August 8, 1969): 568–571. doi:10.1126/science
.165.3893.568.

Opie, John. *Nature's Nation: An Environmental History of
the United States.* New York: Harcourt Brace College
Publishers, 1998.

Pausas, Guli G., and Jon E. Keeley. "A Burning Story: The
Role of Fire in the History of Life." *BioScience* 59,
no. 7 (July/August 2009): 593–601.

Pearce, Roy Harvey. "The 'Ruines of Mankind': The Indian and the Puritan Mind." *Journal of the History of Ideas* 13, no. 2 (April 1952): 200–217. doi:10.2307/2707611.

Pernin, Peter. "The Great Peshtigo Fire: An Eyewitness Account." *Wisconsin Magazine of History* 54, no. 4 (Summer 1971): 246–272.

Perrottet, Tony. "John Muir's Yosemite." *Smithsonian Magazine,* July 2008. smithsonianmag.com/history /john-muirs-yosemite-10737.

Petersen, Jim. "The 1910 Fire." *Evergreen Magazine,* Winter 1994–1995. toyfj40.freeshell.org/Stories/Fire1910pl .html.

Pielou, E. C. *After the Ice Age: The Return of Life to Glaciated North America.* Chicago: University of Chicago Press, 1991.

Pierson, George Wilson. *Tocqueville in America.* Baltimore: Johns Hopkins University Press, 1996.

Pinchot, Gifford. *Breaking New Ground.* New York: Harcourt, Brace, 1947.

———. *The Fight for Conservation.* New York: Doubleday, Page, 1910.

———. *A Primer of Forestry.* Washington, DC: Government Printing Office, 1899.

Pinchot, Gifford Bryce. "Could the 1910 Fire Happen Again?" *Evergreen Magazine,* Winter 1994–1995. toyfj40.freeshell.org/Stories/Fire1910p6.html.

Pinkett, Harold T. *Gifford Pinchot: Private and Public Forester.* Urbana: University of Illinois Press, 1970.

———. "Gifford Pinchot, Consulting Forester, 1893– 1898." *New York History* 39, no. 1 (January 1958): 34–49.

Pisani, Donald J. "Forests and Conservation, 1865–1890." *Journal of American History* 72, no. 2 (September 1985): 340–359.

Platt, Rutherford. *The Great American Forest.* Englewood Cliffs, NJ: Prentice Hall, 1965.

Ponder, Stephen. "Gifford Pinchot: Press Agent for Forestry." *Forest and Conservation History* 31, no. 1 (January 1987): 26–35.

Ponting, Clive. *A Green History of the World: The Environment and the Collapse of Great Civilizations.* New York: St. Martin's Press, 1991.

"Protecting Your Home from Wildfire." california chaparral.org/fire/protecting-your-home.

Puko, Timothy. "2018 Was Fourth-Hottest Year in Modern Records, U.S. Government Scientists Say." *Wall Street Journal,* February 6, 2019.

Pulaski, E. C. "Surrounded by Forest Fires: My Most Exciting Experience as a Forest Ranger." *American Forestry* 29 (August 1923): 485–486. foresthistory .org/wp-content/uploads/2017/02/Surrounded-by -Forest-Firest-By-E.C.-Pulaski.pdf.

Purdy, Jedediah. "Environmentalism's Racist History." *New Yorker,* August 13, 2015. newyorker.com/news/news -desk/environmentalisms-racist-history.

Pyne, Stephen J. *Fire: A Brief History.* Seattle: University of Washington Press, 2001.

———. *Fire in America: A Cultural History of Wildland and Rural Fire.* Seattle: University of Washington Press, 1982.

———. "How Plants Use Fire (and Are Used by It)." *Nova Online.* pbs.org/wgbh/nova/fire/plants.html.

———. "The Source." foresthistory.org/wp-content /uploads/2016/12/The-Source-Stephen-Pyne -Lecture.pdf.

———. *Tending Fire: Coping with America's Wildland Fires.* Washington, DC: Island Press, 2004.

———. *Year of the Fires: The Story of the Great Fires of 1910.* New York: Viking, 2001.

Radu, Stelian. "The Ecological Role of Deadwood in Natural Forests." In *Nature Conservation: Concepts and Practice,* edited by Dan Gafta and John Akeroyd, 137–141. Berlin: Springer, 2006. doi:10.1007/978-3 -540-47229-2_16.

Ramos, Jason A., and Julian Smith. *Smokejumper: A Memoir by One of America's Most Select Airborne Firefighters.* New York: William Morrow, 2016.

Raney, William F. "Pine Lumbering in Wisconsin." *Wisconsin Magazine of History* 19, no. 1 (September 1935): 71–90.

Ravenswaay, Charles van. "America's Age of Wood." *Proceedings of the American Antiquarian Society* 80, no. 1 (April 1970): 49–66. americanantiquarian.org /proceedings/44497992.pdf.

Rickert, Levi. "US Presidents in Their Own Words Concerning American Indians." *Native News Online,* February 16, 2020. nativenewsonline.net/currents /us-presidents-in-their-own-words-concerning -american-indians.

Rieger, John F. *American Sportsmen and the Origins of Conservation.* New York: Winchester Press, 1975.

Ritter, Luke. "Frederick Weyerhaeuser (1834–1914)." *Immigrant Entrepreneurship: German-American Business Biographies, 1720 to the Present.* immigrantentrepreneurship.org/entries/frederick -weyerhaeuser.

Robinson, C. D. "The Great Peshtigo Fire of 1881 [*sic*]: Account as Published by C. D. Robinson." In *Report on Forestry Submitted to Congress by the Commissioner of Agriculture,* edited by Franklin B. Hough, 3:231–236. Washington, DC: Government Printing Office, 1882.

Roosevelt, Theodore. *An Autobiography.* New York: Charles Scribner's Sons, 1922.

———. *Hunting Trips of a Ranchman: Sketches of Sport on the Northern Cattle Plains.* New York: G. P. Putnam's Sons, 1885. bartleby.com/52/8.html.

Russell, Emily W. B. "Indian-Set Fires in the Forests of Northeastern America." *Ecology* 64, no. 1 (February 1983): 78–88.

Rutkow, Eric. *American Canopy: Trees, Forests, and the Making of a Nation.* New York: Scribner, 2012.

Schafer, Joseph. "Great Fires of Seventy-One." *Wisconsin Magazine of History* 11, no. 1 (September 1927): 96– 106.

———. "John E. Nelligan's Story." *Wisconsin Magazine of History* 13, no. 1 (September 1929): 4–65. For the rest of Nelligan's story, see Nelligan and Sheridan entries on p. 220.

Schob, David E. "Woodhawks & Cordwood: Steamboat Fuel on the Ohio and Mississippi Rivers, 1820–1860." *Forest and Conservation History* 21, no. 3 (July 1977): 124–132.

Sears, Roebuck and Company. *1897 Sears Roebuck Catalogue.* New York: Chelsea House Publishers, 1968.

Serratore, Angela. "Keeping Feathers off Hats—and on Birds." *Smithsonian Magazine*, May 15, 2018. smithsonianmag.com/history/migratory-bird-act -anniversary-keeping-feathers-off-hats-180969077.

Shifflett, Crandall. *Victorian America, 1876 to 1900*. New York: Facts on File, 1996.

Skurk, Krystina. "How Misguided Environmentalism Is to Blame for California's Wildfires." *Federalist*, November 16, 2018. thefederalist.com/2018/11/16 /misguided-environmentalism-blame-californias -wildfires.

Smith, Michael B. "The Value of a Tree: Public Debates of John Muir and Gifford Pinchot." *Historian* 60, no. 4 (June 1998): 757–778.

Smits, David D. "The Frontier Army and the Destruction of the Buffalo: 1865–1883." *Western Historical Quarterly* 25, no. 3 (Autumn 1994): 312–338.

Snow, Richard F. "The Hinckley Fire." *American Heritage*, August 1977.

Souder, William. "How Two Women Ended the Deadly Feather Trade." *Smithsonian Magazine*, March 2013. smithsonianmag.com/science-nature/how-two -women-ended-the-deadly-feather-trade-23187277.

Spence, Mark David. *Dispossessing the Wilderness: Indian Removal and the Making of the National Parks*. New York: Oxford University Press, 1999.

Spencer, Betty Goodwin. *The Big Blowup*. Caldwell, ID: Caxton Printers, 1958.

Sprengel, Merton E. "The Dark Day Plus 200 Years." angusmcphee.wordpress.com/appendix-4-the-dark -day-of-may-19-1780.

Stankey, George F. "Beyond the Campfire's Light: Historical Roots of the Wilderness Concept." *Natural Resources Journal* 29, no. 1 (Winter 1999): 9–24.

Stannard, David E. *American Holocaust: The Conquest of the New World*. New York: Oxford University Press, 1992.

Steinberg, Ted. *Down to Earth: Nature's Role in American History*. New York: Oxford University Press, 2002.

Stephenson, Isaac. *Recollections of a Long Life: 1829–1915*. Chicago: privately printed, 1915.

Strickland, Jonathan, and Ed Grabianowski. "How Global Warming Works." science.howstuffworks.com /environmental/green-science/global-warming.

Sweeney, Don. " 'It Got Darker and Darker': Wildfire Survivors Detail Harrowing Escapes." *Sacramento Bee*, November 15, 2018.

Tarabay, Jamie. "Australia Is So Hot the Pits Are Burning the Peaches." *New York Times*, January 26, 2019.

Teale, Edwin Way, ed. *The Wilderness World of John Muir*. New York: Houghton Mifflin, 1954.

Thompson, Daniel Q., and Ralph H. Smith. "The Forest Primeval in the Northeast—a Great Myth?" *Proceedings: 10th Tall Timbers Fire Ecology Conference* (1970): 255–265.

Tocqueville, Alexis de. *Democracy in America*. New York: Knopf, 1956.

———. *Journey to America*. Translated by George Lawrence. New Haven, CT: Yale University Press, 1959.

"To Stop Pandemics, Stop Deforestation." Editorial. *Scientific American*, June 2020, 8. doi:10.1038 /scientificamerican0620-8.

Trefethen, James B. *An American Crusade for Wildlife.* New York: Winchester Press, 1975.

Trenberth, Kevin. "Is There a Link Between Climate Change and Wildfires?" *Newsweek,* August 10, 2018. newsweek.com/there-link-between-climate-change-and-wildfires-1068201.

Trollope, Anthony. *North America.* New York: Harper & Brothers, 1862.

Trollope, Frances. *Domestic Manners of the Americans.* London: Whittaker, Treacher, 1832.

Tucker, Jeanmarie. "The Bird Hat: 'Murderous Millinery.'" mdhistory.org/the-bird-hat-murderous-millinery.

Tudor, Henry. *Narrative of a Tour in North America.* London: James Duncan, 1834.

Twilley, Nicola. "A Trailblazing Plan to Fight California Wildfires." *New Yorker,* August 26, 2019.

Twining, Charles E. "Plunder and Progress: The Lumbering Industry in Perspective." *Wisconsin Magazine of History* 47, no. 2 (Winter 1963–1964): 116–124.

Vries, David Peterson de. *Voyages from Holland to America, A.D. 1632 to 1644.* Translated by Henry C. Murphy. New York, 1853.

"The Warming Effects of the Industrial Revolution." climate-policy-watcher.org/global-temperatures/the-warming-effects-of-the-industrial-revolution.html.

Weld, Charles Richard. *A Vacation Tour in the United States and Canada.* London: Longman, Brown, Green, and Longmans, 1855.

Weld, Isaac, Jr. *Travels Through the States of North America, and the Provinces of Upper and Lower Canada,* During the Years 1795, 1796, and 1797. London: John Stockdale, 1799.

Wells, Robert W. *"Daylight in the Swamp!": Lumberjacking in the Late 19th Century.* Madison, WI: NorthWord Press, 1978.

———. *Embers of October.* New York: Prentice Hall, 1968.

Westover, Robert Hudson. "Conservation Versus Preservation?" *USDA Blogs,* March 22, 2106. fs.usda.gov/features/conservation-versus-preservation.

Whelan, Robert J. *The Ecology of Fire.* Cambridge: Cambridge University Press, 1995.

White, Lynn, Jr. "The Historical Roots of Our Ecological Crisis." *Science* 155 (March 10, 1967): 1203–1207.

Wilder, Laura Ingalls. *Little House in the Big Woods.* New York: Harper & Row, 1932. gutenberg.ca/ebooks/wilder-woods/wilder-woods-01-h.html.

Wilkins, Alasdair. "October 8, 1871: The Night America Burned." *Gizmodo,* March 29, 2012. gizmodo.com/october-8-1871-the-night-america-burned-5897629.

Wilkinson, William. *Memorials of the Minnesota Forest Fires in the Year 1894.* Minneapolis: Norman E. Wilkinson, 1895.

Wildfire Today. News and opinion about wildland fire. wildfiretoday.com.

Williams, Gerald W. "References on the American Indian Use of Fire in Ecosystems." 2005. nrcs.usda.gov/Internet/FSE_DOCUMENTS/nrcs144p2_051334.pdf.

Williams, Michael. *Americans and Their Forests: A Historical Geography.* Cambridge: Cambridge University Press, 1989.

———. *Deforesting the Earth: From Prehistory to Global Crisis.* Chicago: University of Chicago Press, 2006.

Wilson, Alexander. "Passenger Pigeon." In *American Ornithology,* 5:102–112. Philadelphia: Bradford and Inskeep, 1812. biodiversitylibrary.org/item/175520.

Winger, Stewart. "Lincoln's Economics and the American Dream: A Reappraisal." *Journal of the Abraham Lincoln Association* 22, no. 1 (Winter 2001): 50–80. hdl .handle.net/2027/spo.2629860.0022.106.

Wolfe, Linnie Marsh. *Son of the Wilderness: The Life of John Muir.* NewYork: Knopf, 1945.

Worland, Justin. "This Island Is Sinking." *Time,* June 24, 2019.

Wrangham, Richard. *Catching Fire: How Cooking Made Us Human.* New York: Basic Books, 2009.

Wuerthner, George, ed. *The Wildfire Reader: A Century of Failed Forest Policy.* Washington, DC: Island Press, 2006.

Wyman, Walker D. *The Lumberjack Frontier: Life of a Logger in the Early Days on the Chippeway.* Lincoln: University of Nebraska Press, 1969.

Yeoman, Barry. "Why the Passenger Pigeon Went Extinct." *Audubon,* May–June 2014. audubon.org/magazine /may-june-2014/why-passenger-pigeon-went-extinct.

PICTURE CREDITS

INDEX

Note: *Italic* page numbers refer to illustrations.